girl talk

52 WEEKLY DEVOTIONS

Other fantastic books in the growing Faithgirlz™ library

BIBLES

The NIV Faithgirlz Bibles

The NKJV Faithgirlz Bible

NIV Faithgirlz Backpack Bibles

FICTION

Natalie Grant's Glimmer Girls Series

London Art Chase (Book One)

A Dolphin Wish (Book Two)

Miracle in Music City (Book Three)

Light Up New York (Book Four)

Samantha Sanderson Series

At the Movies (Book One)

On the Scene (Book Two)

Off the Record (Book Three)

Without a Trace (Book Four)

Good News Shoes Series

Riley Mae and the Rock Shocker Trek (Book One)

Riley Mae and the Ready Eddy Rapids (Book Two)

Riley Mae and the Sole Fire Safari (Book Three)

The Girls of Harbor View

Girl Power (Book One)

Take Charge (Book Two)

Raising Faith (Book Three)

Secret Admirer (Book Four)

Sophie's World Series (2 books in 1)

Meet Sophie

Sophie Steps Up

Sophie and Friends

Sophie's Friendship Fiasco

Sophie Flakes Out

Sophie's Drama

The Lucy Series

Lucy Doesn't Wear Pink (Book One)

Lucy Out of Bounds (Book Two)

Lucy's "Perfect" Summer (Book Three)

Lucy Finds Her Way (Book Four)

From Sadie's Sketchbook

Shades of Truth (Book One)

Flickering Hope (Book Two)

Waves of Light (Book Three)

Brilliant Hues (Book Four)

NONFICTION

Devotionals

No Boys Allowed

What's a Girl to Do?

Whatever Is Lovely

Shine on, Girl!

That Is So Me

Finding God in Tough Times

Girl Talk

Girlz Rock

Faithgirlz Bible Studies

The Secret Power of Love

The Secret Power of Joy

The Secret Power of Goodness

The Secret Power of Grace

Lifestyle and Fun

Faithgirlz Journal

Faithgirlz Cookbook

True You

Best Party Book Ever!

101 Ways to Have Fun

101 Things Every Girl Should Know

Best Hair Book Ever

Redo Your Room

God's Beautiful Daughter

Everybody Tells Me to Be Myself but I Don't Know Who I Am

faithgirlz

girl talk

52 WEEKLY DEVOTIONS

lois walfrid johnson

ZONDERKIDZ

Girl Talk

With the exception of *A Look in the Mirror, The Hidden Puzzle Piece*, and *Are You a Quitter?* the characters in these stories are fictitious and spring with gratitude for life from the author's imagination. Any resemblance to persons living or dead is coincidental.

In the story, "It's Not Fair!," thank you to Steve Lampi, president, Bridgeman's Ice Cream, for the use of their La La Palooza, its description and advertising slogans—"Eat it all and you get a medal!" and "Try it...You only live once!"

Requests for information should be addressed to:
Zondervan, 3900 *Sparks Dr. SE, Grand Rapids, Michigan 49546*

This edition: ISBN 978-0-310-75500-5 (softcover)

Library of Congress Cataloging-in-Publication Data
Johnson, Lois Walfrid.
Girl talk : 52 weekly devotions / Lois Walfrid Johnson.
p. cm. – (Faithgirlz!)
Includes bibliographical references and index.
ISBN 978-0-310-71449-1 (softcover)
1. Girls—Prayers and devotions. 2. Christian children—Prayers and devotions. I. Title.
BV4860.J625 2009
242'.62—dc22 2009015209

Published in association with the literary agency of Alive Communications, Inc., 7680 Goddard Street, Suite 200, Colorado Springs, Colorado 80920. www.alivecommunications.com.

Editor: Kathleen Kerr
Cover design and art direction: Sarah Molegraaf
Interior design: Denise Froehlich

Printed in the United States of America

16 17 18 19 20 21 22 /DCI/ 20 19 18 17 16 15 14 13 12 11 10 9 8 7 6 5 4 3 2 1

To every girl
who chooses
to run close to Jesus
and
become a faithgirl
with
special love to
Jessica Lee
Karin Lyn
Jennifer Christine
and
Elise Grace

Contents

To the Girls Who Read this Book

Dear Girls,

This book is about making choices.

Choices that begin small, but grow big. Choices that require you to get up, start over again, and go beyond failure. Choices in which you need to face your fear of what others think and choose your friends with wisdom.

Choices that ask you to act with courage, learn to care, find integrity, and walk with honor. Choices that encourage you to reach out to shape your destiny.

Choices that give you the opportunity to dream. To want the best, not only for yourself, but also for those who need your caring heart, your helping hand, your gift of reaching back and bringing others along with you.

This book will ask you to face obstacles. To read about those who did and those who didn't. To know as friends those people who say, "I cannot do this by myself. But I know Who can help me."

Most of all, this book will ask you to reach up, to put your hand within the hand of Jesus and become a Faithgirl.

The 52 stories in this devotional are about girls who have fun times but also know the kinds of choices you face. There's a story for each week, and you can begin reading any time of the year that you'd like. As you read, ask yourself, "What would I do if this happened to me or one of my friends?" Talk about it with that special person who understands how you feel.

It might be your mom or dad, a grandma or grandpa, aunt or uncle. It might be an older sister or brother, a friend, neighbor, or teacher. When you find that person start talking.

You'll make an important discovery. Not every problem is suddenly solved, but the right person can help you see what's happening from a different viewpoint. Instead of feeling alone, you know there's someone who wants the best for you.

With each story there are questions to help you think about the choices you make. You can use those questions as jumping-off places for talking with someone. Or, you can make this book your own special journal. Often it helps to sort out your feelings by writing about what happened. Other times you may want to put down questions you have or ideas you'd like to think through. You can also write about special things people tell you and good times you'd like to remember. Elise did that in *The Hidden Puzzle Piece*.

When you read the verse at the beginning of each week, be honest with Jesus. Ask him, "What do you want me to know?" Tell him why you need his help. If you repeat the verse to yourself, you'll receive the hope it offers. You'll also catch on to something big. It's important to use the Bible in making choices. It's important to memorize verses that will help you at any time of the day or night. And if you memorize the verse at the beginning of each story you'll know 52 more verses by the time you finish reading this book.

Have you noticed that some girls and women have an inner beauty and an outward faith? When you choose to follow Jesus, he will help you become that kind of Faithgirl. In spite of the difficulties you may face, you'll learn to recognize the choices he wants you to make. You'll have the opportunity to do the kinds of things God wants to bless.

Learning to make wise choices will help you the rest of your life. A long time ago, a runner named Eric Liddell made a hard choice because he loved and respected Jesus. It was only a few months before the Eighth Olympics, and Eric was Great Britain's biggest hope for the 100 meters. When he learned the date of the competition for the qualifying races, Eric said he wouldn't run on Sunday. He wanted to honor the Lord by respecting his day.

Some people were horrified. They felt Eric was throwing away a gold medal for Scotland and Britain. They even called him a traitor to his country. For a time it looked as if Eric would lose out in every way. The 100 meters was where he excelled. But then, because he said no to running on Sunday, he qualified for a different event.

Later Eric said that because he stood for what he believed, he discovered that the 400 meters was the race that fit him best. He would not have known that otherwise. Nor would he have dreamed of trying the 400 at the Olympics. Yet because of his choice to honor the Lord, Eric ran the race he was created to win.

In spite of all the years that have passed, people still remember Eric Liddell because of what happened. First, for the difficult choice he made, and then for winning the 400 meters. That win was the Olympic gold in a world record time of 47.6 seconds. At that moment in history Eric's time was beyond all expectations.

Right now, whoever you are, in whatever you do, you're in the race of your life. In that race you may face obstacles that make you feel you will lose. Yet you can overcome those obstacles because you ask Jesus for his help. When you choose to follow him, Jesus will not only go ahead of you. He will be with you all the way.

Be a girl—become a young woman—who has an inner beauty and an outward faith. Live the adventure of running close to Jesus. In every choice you make he wants to help you become a Faithgirl.

Are You a Quitter?

WEEK 1

God didn't give us a spirit that makes us weak and fearful. He gave us a spirit that gives us power and love. It helps us control ourselves.
2 Tim. 1:7 (NIrV)

For three days Jessica had looked forward to this moment. Standing on the corral fence, she watched as Sarah slipped a bridle over her pony's head.

"Reggie's a good pony," she said. "I've been riding him for three years."

Jessica glanced at two larger horses drinking water at a trough. They seemed so tall that she was glad to start out on a pony. Yet she felt sure she could handle any horse well.

"Let me give you a lift," Sarah offered. Jessica put one foot in Sarah's clasped hands and swung up over Reggie's bare back.

"Lay your rein on the right side of his neck, and he'll turn left," Sarah told her. "Lay your rein on the left side, and he'll go right."

Moments later Jessica was off. As she and Reggie started

down the drive, she felt excited, then sure of herself. *I knew I could handle it!*

Soon they reached a place where the road ran close to the pasture. As Jessica passed by, the other horses ran straight for the fence. Without warning, Reggie plunged away from them. As he went right, Jessica went left. With a jolt she landed in the middle of the road.

"Ouch!" she groaned. Too stunned to move, she felt shaken in every bone of her body.

"Are you okay?" Sarah called as she ran to help.

"Stupid horse!" answered Jessica. "I won't try that again."

But Sarah had a different idea. "You need to get back on."

"Are you kidding?" Jessica asked.

"You don't have to be afraid," Sarah said. "Reggie has never thrown me. He was frightened by the horses coming at him."

"But he's your pony. Reggie likes you."

"So, are you a quitter? If you don't get back on now, you'll be too afraid to try again. Besides, Reggie has to know you're boss, or he'll think he can get by with throwing people."

"Well—" Slowly Jessica stood up. "Maybe you're right. The longer I think about it, the more scared I get."

Sarah led Reggie to a stump. "This time I'll ride with you. You first. I'll hold him."

A moment later they were off. Soon Jessica's fear disappeared. She even started to feel excited. After a while Sarah slid off.

By the end of the afternoon, Jessica felt like a seasoned rider. She even knew how to make Reggie mind. *What if I had missed this?* she asked herself. *What if I hadn't tried again?*

Let's Talk ... or Journal

DAY 1

Think about something you especially like to do. How did you feel when you faced something new? Were you good at it the first time you tried? Or did you have to make a choice the way Jessica did? Tell what happened to you.

DAY 2

In real life Jessica got her own horse, took lessons, and became such a good rider that she won many awards. She even won a zone championship—a six-state competition in the Hunter/Jumper class. Now Jessica gives lessons to others and rides world-class horses to have them ready both at home and for shows. How can knowing that Jessica got up and tried again give you courage in what you're trying to learn?

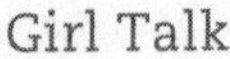

DAY 3

If you're afraid to try something, should you always try it anyway? Give reasons for your yes or no answers. Do you believe God might use fear or uneasiness to protect you from doing some things? Tell why you think the way you do.

DAY 4

Have there been other times when you felt that God wanted you to keep trying, even though it was hard? Give examples.

DAY 5

Make a list of some ways in which you feel you've failed. Now take a look at that list. Put a star by the example that you thought was the scariest or the most difficult. Tell why you felt that way.

What happened when you faced what made you afraid? When you look back on that time, do you feel good or bad about how you faced the problem? Why?

DAY 6

Make another list of some ways in which you have succeeded. Did you need to "get up" and try again? Tell what happened. How did you feel about succeeding? Did you do it by yourself or did you ask for help?

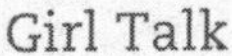

DAY 7

At the beginning of this week we read a verse from 2 Timothy. Timothy was young and Paul encouraged him by saying, "God didn't give us a spirit that makes us weak and fearful. He gave us a spirit that gives us power and love. It helps us control ourselves." In other words, if we feel weak and fearful it's not God who makes us feel that way. Instead, he promises to give us a spirit of love and power that helps us act in strong, good ways.

But the choice is up to each of us. Do you want to be weak and afraid? Or do you want to ask Jesus to help you act in strong, good ways? What are some ways you'd like to receive his help?

Memorize 2 Timothy 1:7 and hug it to yourself when you need it. Pray in the name of Jesus and ask for his help.

Let's Pray About It

Jesus, you know how scared I get about doing something new. Show me if I'm uneasy because you want to protect me. If, instead, you want me to learn something, help me start over if needed and keep trying. I need your help, Jesus, your Holy Spirit power. Thank you!

Captain for the Js, Jordan crouched, ready for the jump. If there was anyone in the world she wanted to beat, it was Carla, captain of the Cs. They had played against each other often, and Carla always won. By now Jordan's feelings about winning went far beyond a game in gym class.

Once in a while, she wished she could be Carla's friend. But most of the time, Jordan just wanted to prove she could do something better. Now as she faced Carla, their gym teacher, Miss Mackey, held up the basketball.

"How you play is more important than winning," she often said. "People are more important than points."

But Jordan just wanted to win. As the whistle blew, she leaped high in the air, tipping the ball to her teammate Amy. Amy dribbled her way out of a tight spot and moved down the court. Jordan slipped under the basket and waited for the ball. When it came she managed a jump shot.

Swish! It went in!

Jordan's team, the Js, cheered, but Carla's team, the Cs, looked ready to fight every step of the way. It was their ball.

Standing at the end of the court, Carla looked around. When she spotted a break in the Js' defense, she threw the ball in. Her teammate caught it and headed toward the basket. Then the ball returned to Carla. Her long shot bounced on the board but dropped in.

Back and forth the score jumped with one side leading, then the other. At the half the score was tied, 24 to 24. Jordan knew the game would be hard fought to the end. Facing Carla was always tough.

I'm just as good a player, Jordan told herself. *But I always seem to lose.*

With only a few minutes left in the final quarter, the score was 40 to 38, the Js ahead. *If only we can keep it!* Jordan ached with the desire to win.

Muscles tense, she guarded Carla closely. Swinging her arms up and down, Jordan tried to block a pass to the Cs. Then, as Carla started in for a basket, Jordan grabbed the ball.

The whistle blew. "Foul!"

Jordan groaned. Carla moved to the free-throw line. Her first try fell short. Jordan breathed deeply. But the second one dropped in. 40 to 39. Her team led by one point.

As the ball went into play, Jordan's team caught it and started moving toward their basket. Amy passed the ball to Jordan. Carla leaped high and intercepted. In the same moment, she lost her footing and landed on the floor. The ball spun out of her hands.

Jordan grabbed for it. Just before the ball rolled out of bounds, she touched it.

Miss Mackey's whistle shrilled. "Js' ball!"

Jordan looked back, surprised at the call. Had Carla's body blocked Miss Mackey's view? Jordan knew she didn't have the right to take the ball, but the teacher hadn't seen her touch it.

In that split second, Jordan's thoughts jumped ahead. Having the ball now could make the difference between winning and losing. *Carla was on her back. She didn't see*, Jordan told herself. *No one will ever know.*

As she picked up the basketball, Jordan saw Carla look at her. For an instant Jordan wondered if Carla knew. *If she did, she'd say something*, Jordan told herself. *I can get by with it.*

She walked to the sideline, and Miss Mackey joined her there. Jordan waited for the whistle that would send the ball into play. *If my team can keep it one minute, we'll win*, she thought.

But as Jordan stood there, she remembered her teacher's favorite saying: "*People are more important than points.*"

Unsure what to do, Jordan debated with herself again. A knot formed in the pit of her stomach. *We're almost there*, she thought. *We can win. But what if we beat Carla, and I know it wasn't fair?*

Though her feelings weren't in it, Jordan turned to the coach. "I don't think I should have the ball. I touched it just before it went out."

Miss Mackey looked surprised, but signaled for Carla to take Jordan's place. When Carla threw the ball out, everyone snapped into action. Jordan kept close, but suddenly Carla broke loose. One of the Cs passed her the ball.

Instantly Carla took a long shot. Just as it went in, the final whistle blew. Final score was 40 to 41! The Cs had won the game.

Jordan groaned. Her shoulders slumped. "By *one* point! By one point we *lost!*"

As soon as she could, Jordan headed for the locker room and a bench in an out-of-the way corner. She didn't want to talk with anyone.

But her friend Amy found her there. "How come you told Miss Mackey? We would have won."

Jordan couldn't answer. She felt mad at herself. Mad for being honest. Mad for letting the game go. She had almost tasted victory, then she'd let it slip out of her hands.

"No one would have known," said Amy.

Feeling even more discouraged, Jordan looked up at her. "I guess you're right. I hate to say it, but I guess you're right."

"I would have known." Carla said from behind Jordan. "As I

rolled over, I saw you touch the ball. I would have said something. I was waiting to see what you'd do."

As Jordan turned, she looked straight into Carla's eyes and felt glad that she could.

"You played a good game, Jordan." Carla offered her hand.

Jordan grasped it. "Thanks, Carla. You did too." Jordan felt surprised that she meant it.

Carla grinned. "When we start playing other schools, we'll be on the same team. I'll like that."

In that moment Jordan saw something new in Carla's eyes. Jordan felt warm all the way through. *Maybe we'll even be friends.*

Let's Talk . . . or Journal

DAY 1

It was hard for Jordan to be honest. Then she lost the game besides. Why is it important to be honest, even when things don't seem to turn out right?

b/c then pll will trust u + also u will show Integrity!

DAY 2

Sometimes it's easy to think *win, no matter what you have to do.* What are some of the thoughts and feelings Jordan might have had if she had beaten Carla by cheating?

Why do you think this story is called "The Real Winner"? Who really won in the end?

- Gulit
- doubt
- emptyness

Jordan

b/c the actually winner is the person who had a heart.

DAY 3

Jordan and Carla were playing against each other in gym class. For some people that kind of game doesn't seem very important, but Jordan really cared about winning. In what ways do you want to win in your own life?

being

Right

DAY 4

Think about whether you've ever had a friend who didn't tell the truth. Were you able to trust that friend? Why or why not? What happened to your friendship? Explain.

No I was not able to trust her b/c she lied & ur Freindship broke apart!

DAY 5

How has someone helped you by being fair and honest? In what ways have you helped someone else by being honest?

Yes my Mom by teaching me not to Sin & be nice! xoxo ♡ by teaching all not to sin.

DAY 6

What is your favorite sport? How can you be a good sport when you take part in that game? What character qualities do you especially like to see in an athlete?

Gymnastics Say Good Job, etc.,.,.,

- nice
- competeive
- good sportsmanship

DAY 7

In 1 Corinthians 9:24 – 25 Paul compares being a Christian to running a race. What does it mean to run in such a way that you will get the prize? What does it mean to get a crown that will last forever? How can you make those ideas count in your life?

Let's Pray About It

Jesus, I want to be someone people can count on. Help me to be honest and play fair in every game of life. Help me to run close to you and do what's right, even when you're the only one who knows. Thank you!

The Big Choice

WEEK 3

[Jesus said,] "Well done, good and faithful servant! You have been faithful with a few things; I will put you in charge of many things."
Matthew 25:21

"Trish-ah-a-a-a-a-a!" came a little voice from the bedroom.

"Just a minute," Trisha said into her cell. She was babysitting at the Robinson's again. Whenever Trisha was having the most fun talking with a friend, Emmy wanted her attention.

"I'll be there soon," Trisha shouted to Emmy.

"You said that last time," answered the little voice.

A minute later the Robinson's phone rang. Trisha sighed. *It's not important*, she decided, and let it go. After the seventh or eighth ring the phone stopped. Trisha felt relieved.

For a few moments everything was quiet. Trisha slid into a more comfortable position and started texting. Soon she forgot about the little girl she was babysitting.

Trisha was just about to check on her when the Robinson's phone rang again. By now Trisha was texting back and forth between two friends. How could she ever leave such important conversations?

For an instant Trisha looked at the Robinson's phone. *It's just someone wanting to sell something,* she decided. Pushing the ringing phone out of her mind, she went back to texting.

A loud crash broke into her conversation. Filled with panic, Trisha jumped up. *What happened?* Closing her cell, she ran for Emmy's bedroom.

No one there.

"Where are you, Emmy?" Trisha called out. "Em-m-m-m-y!"

In that instant Trisha heard a small sound. Heading down the hallway, she saw the door to the master bedroom partly open. As she tried to push it the rest of the way, the door wouldn't move.

Looking down, Trisha discovered the reason. A large piece from a glass lamp had spun across the hardwood floor. Other pieces lay all around one side of the bed.

Emmy sat on that bed, only a few feet above most of the broken glass.

"Emmy, shame on you!" Trisha snapped. "You're supposed to be in bed. What are you doing in here?"

Looking scared, Emmy pushed back into a pillow and huddled there. "You didn't come when I called." Tears welled up in Emmy's eyes and slid down her cheeks. "I want my mommy."

Trisha looked at Emmy, then at the floor. *I'm in big trouble*, she thought. *What am I going to tell her mom and dad?*

An instant later an even worse thought struck Trisha. *Emmy must have pushed the lamp off the bedside table. What if she'd been on the floor and* pulled *it off?* It wasn't hard to imagine the little girl all cut up from flying glass.

Though Trisha didn't want to face the truth, it hit her hard. *It was really my fault, wasn't it, God?* In that moment Trisha didn't like herself very much.

Ashamed now, she walked around to the side that was free of glass. Crawling onto the bed, she picked up Emmy. With the little girl in her arms, Trisha carried her to the living room.

There she sat down in a big rocker and tried to comfort Emmy. But the little girl's sobs increased.

Just then the phone jangled again. This time Trisha picked it up.

"We've been trying to reach you for over an hour," Mrs. Robinson said. "We couldn't get through. Is there some reason you didn't answer? Is something wrong?"

I'll lie, thought Trisha. *I'll pretend nothing happened.* She wanted to act as if it were all Emmy's fault. But as she opened her mouth to make excuses, something made her stop.

In that instant Trisha knew she had to make a choice. *Am I going to be honest about what happened or not?*

Trisha took a deep breath. "We've had a problem here," she said. "But I'm taking care of it. I'll tell you about it when you get home."

"You're sure?" asked Emmy's mother.

"I'm sure," Trisha said. "We're doing fine now."

As she hung up the phone, Trisha made another choice—a promise to herself and to God. *I'm going to be different.*

Let's Talk . . . or Journal

DAY 1

What do you think Trisha should tell Mr. and Mrs. Robinson when they come home?

Emmy was calling but I didn't listen b/c I was texting so she push the lamp & it broke so she can my attention.

DAY 2

It would be easy for Trisha to make up excuses or lie about what happened. Why is it important for her own sake that she doesn't?

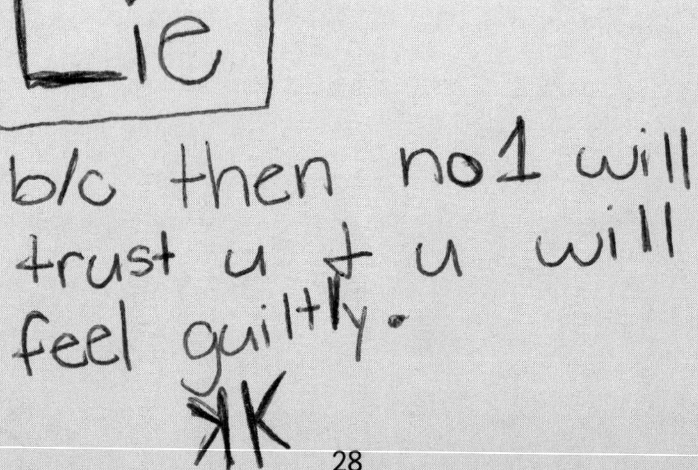

DAY 3

Trisha wants to be someone others can count on and trust. What habits will she need to break in order to keep her promise to herself and to God?

DAY 4

Do you babysit, either at home or in someone else's house? What are some ideas you can give Trisha to help her become a better babysitter?

No I don't.
- Listen
- Watch more
- more Attention

DAY 5

Sometimes babysitting seems like a boring job that can be done any way you want. In what ways can your relationships with the children you babysit be some of the most important relationships you have?

DAY 6

If you get in a hard place and ask for God's help, do you still need to make your own choices? Why or why not? Give examples.

DAY 7

People who hire grown-ups for a job often say, "I want to hire a person with integrity." There's a test for whether a person has integrity: Integrity is doing the right thing when no one except you and God know. Can you think of a time when you did not have integrity? How do you feel about it now?

Describe a time when you *did* have integrity, even though it was very difficult. In what ways do you feel good about what you did? Who or what helped you have integrity? In what ways do you feel an honest respect for yourself now?

I feel guitily

Let's Pray About It

Lord, I want to be faithful to you. I want to be a person other people can count on. When I baby-sit, help me keep the children safe. Help me love them the way you do. Thanks, Lord! I need you, and I need your help.

It's Not Fair!

WEEK 4

"None of you should look out just for your own good. You should also look out for the good of others."
Phil. 2:4 NIrV

Lexee was angry when she came to the supper table. What made it even worse was that she was angry about being angry. Recently Dad had come home from his tour of duty with the military, and Lexee didn't like the way she felt.

I should be happy, she thought. *I should be glad Dad is home.*

Then, deep inside, there was something Lexee knew. *I am glad that he's home safe.* But she also had mixed-up feelings about all that was going on.

Mom was no longer making every decision about what she, Lexee, could do. And Lexee had to admit that Mom had been easier to twist around her little finger — most of the time, that is. Now Dad and Mom were agreeing on the decisions they made, and Lexee didn't like it.

Partway through the meal, she started in. "You always let Brianna do what she wants. Why does she get to go to the volleyball tournament, and I don't?"

"She's older than you," Dad said. "When you're Brianna's age, you'll get to do the things she's doing now."

But Lexee wasn't satisfied. "You and Mom treat her different than you treat me. And you treat Ethan different, too. No matter what he does, you think it's cute."

Dad sighed. "Lexee, you know that Brianna is four years older than you, and Ethan is five years younger. We can't possibly treat you all the same."

"It's not fair!" said Lexee. "I think you *should* treat us all the same."

"Do you really?" asked Dad. "Do you want a baby-sitter like Ethan has when we go out?"

"Well, no," Lexee said. "But he always gets the prize in the cereal box."

Dad laughed. "Are you sure you want those prizes? A lot of them are for four- or five-year-olds. Or do you want the prizes because Ethan wants them?"

"Just the same, it's not fair!"

"Some things aren't fair," Dad said. "Sometimes we need to treat each of you differently. It's not because we love one of you more than another. We try to do what's best for each of you."

For a moment Lexee was quiet. *Is that really true? Do Mom and Dad* really *try to do what's best for each of us?*

Mom broke into her thoughts. "How many for apple pie? There's a bit left over from last night."

Except for Brianna and Lexee, everyone was too full, "I'll cut it," Lexee said. "Brianna always takes more than her share."

"Go ahead," said Mom. "You cut it, but then Brianna gets first choice."

Lexee groaned, making sure everyone heard. Ever since Lexee was a little kid, she had hated that rule. If she didn't cut something even, she never got a chance to have the biggest piece. But that was a family rule to head off arguments.

While eating her pie, Lexee started thinking again. *Do Mom and Dad* really *love me as much as Brianna and Ethan? They always seem to get more attention.* They always *get the best!*

Just then the phone rang. Brianna jumped up. When she returned to the table, her face glowed. "Dave said he'd give me and some other kids a ride to the game. Okay?"

Mom looked at Dad. "Okay," they said, almost together.

A moment later the phone rang again. This time the call was for Ethan. The neighbor boy wanted him to come over to his house to play.

"Okay, Mom?" Ethan asked.

"Okay," she answered. "But come home at eight o'clock and be sure to tell them thank you."

When Brianna and Ethan left, the kitchen suddenly grew quiet. Lexee sat with elbows on the table, hunched over and thinking hard.

I could call Janie.

No, she's gone.

Brooke.

On vacation.

Courtney.

Shopping.

Vanessa—

Most of the time Lexee had friends that surrounded her. Where were they when she needed them? Full of despair, Lexee stood up.

"I've been thinking." Dad broke into her thoughts.

Lexee picked up her dishes and started toward the sink.

"When I was away, I kept thinking about what I'd like to do with each of you when I got home."

Lexee kept walking. *Sure. Take Ethan to the circus. Take Brianna to—* But that was as far as Lexee got.

"When it was really hot—it felt like 300 degrees at least—I remembered how you love ice cream. You and I are the only ones that can eat a whole La La Palooza. Eight scoops of Bridgeman's ice cream smothered in a double serving of butterscotch, pineapple and strawberry toppings, nuts, cherries, and a sliced banana!"

Lexee turned back to look at Dad. He was right. Scoop after

scoop of ice cream. Yes. It had to be eight. "All in one big dish!" she exclaimed.

Usually only a grown man could eat a whole La La Palooza. But she could too! It was absolutely the only thing she could do better than both Brianna and Ethan.

Lexee giggled. "Eat it all and you get a medal!"

"Try it . . . You only live once!" Dad answered.

Lexee thought back. And last time she and Dad went—

As though hearing her thoughts, Dad broke in. "Last time you and I went to Bridgeman's—the very last time was just before I shipped out. You and I sat and ate and talked. We talked about all the ways you were going to grow up when I was gone."

Tears welled up in Lexee's eyes. It had been one of the most special times of her life.

"Want to go now?" Dad asked.

Lexee glanced toward Mom.

"Your mom needs to be here when Ethan comes back. Just you and me?"

Lexee nodded.

"And you can tell me all the good things that have happened to you this year. No Ethan to interrupt. No Brianna with a phone growing out of her ear. How about it?"

Lexee smiled. *Neither Brianna nor Ethan could eat a whole La La Palooza. And neither of them would just sit and talk for an hour, telling their dreams to Dad.*

"Give me five," Lexee said, as she headed to her room to change. In that moment she knew. *Dad really does think about what's best for each of us.*

Then she remembered the look that had passed between her parents. The nod that meant her mother guessed what Dad was thinking.

Feeling loved right down to her toes, Lexee knew something else. *Mom understands too.*

Let's Talk . . . or Journal

DAY 1

In a happy family do people talk about what upsets them? Or are there never any disagreements? Explain why you think the way you do.

Yes

DAY 2

What feelings did Lexee have that made her want to compete with her older sister and younger brother?

DAY 3

Which kind of family is stronger—the one where everyone competes with each other or the one where family members cooperate? Explain why you think the way you do.

the 2nd fam. b/c if u cooperate ur fam. get stronger.

DAY 4

Lexee is a middle child. Sometimes a middle child such as Lexee wants to keep up with an older brother or sister, such as Brianna. At the same time that middle child might think a younger sibling is "too cute," always getting away with something. Or maybe a middle child feels pushed because the younger brother or sister can do something better. What is your birth order? How does that make a difference in your life?

DAY 5

If you have siblings, what special qualities do you have in your life because of the order in which you were born? If you are an only child, what special advantages do you have?

DAY 6

In what ways does your family work together to do something fun or reach a goal? Give examples of things you like to do to help your family.

DAY 7

When Jesus walked here on earth, he showed us how he loves every person as an individual. You, too, can help each person in your family feel there is something you especially like about them. List the name of each person in your immediate family. After the name write down one or more special qualities that you like about that person. In what practical ways can you show a sister, brother, or parent that you love and value them the way they are?

Let's Pray About It

Jesus, you know that sometimes it's fun to compete—in a game, for instance. But other times it means I'm trying to grab what is best for me and might not be good for us as a family. Will you help me remember the difference? Help me work together with the rest of my family? Help me care about them? And Jesus, give me a special way to show love to each one of them.

French Fries and Love

WEEK 5

"Do not be joined to unbelievers. What do right and wrong have in common? Can light and darkness be friends?"
2 Corinthians 6:14 NIrV

Book in hand, Brittany flopped down on her bed and rolled onto her stomach.

Kim slouched deeper in a comfy chair nearby. Mom had told Brittany she could invite Kim over today. It was fun being together again.

When they were younger, they had gone to the same school and had been close friends. Then, two years ago, the boundary lines changed, putting them in different schools even though they still lived near each other.

Now Kim leaned forward. "Is that your sister's book about dating?"

Brittany flipped pages. "Yup. Here's where we left off." She began reading aloud. "*Love isn't something that just happens. You choose whom you love or don't love.*"

Kim stopped her. "Just a minute. What does that mean?"

"Let me finish," Brittany kept reading. "*Some people say, 'I fell in love. I just couldn't help myself. But—'* "

Again Kim interrupted. "That's true. I *do* fall in love. If I like a boy, I like him. And right now I like Todd. What's so bad about that?"

"What's *good* about it?" Brittany's blue eyes met Kim's brown ones. Brittany had never liked Todd because of the way he acted. More than once the two girls had talked about how he treated others.

Brittany went back to the book. "*Some people say, 'I fell in love. I just couldn't help myself.' But early in every relationship there's a moment of choice, whether we think about it or not. We decide, 'I'm not interested in that boy as more than just a friend.' Or we tell ourselves, 'I like that boy. I hope he becomes my boyfriend.'* "

"That's true," Kim said. "I decide, all right. When I meet a boy, I know real soon if he's the one for me. I don't know why my mom won't let me start dating."

Brittany sighed. "Kim, we're too young. It's better to just be in families or groups of kids."

As Kim made a face, Brittany went on. "But you're missing the whole point of the book. We can know a lot of people and be nice to them. But the book says there are times when we should choose *not* to date someone—especially someone we feel romantic about. We can wind up getting hurt. Some guys will try to take advantage of us."

"Oh, phooey!" Kim said. "You choose your friends, and I'll choose mine." Then she grinned. "Of course, you can keep choosing *me*!"

Brittany rolled off the bed and stood up. "C'mon. It's Mom's night to work. She left money and said we can walk to McDonald's."

A short time later, the girls slid into a booth. As Kim picked up her first French fry, she glanced out the window. "Look! Todd and Chris!"

Brittany felt glad to see Chris. As she and Kim watched, the two boys bought burgers and headed over to the girls.

The minute he sat down, Todd tugged a strand of Kim's long brown hair. "Hey, kid, how're you doing?"

Pushing his baseball cap to a cocky angle, he smiled lazily. "Saw you at the game Friday, sitting with your school. Were you watching me play? Got the best hit of my whole team."

Kim nodded, her eyes shining. "You were a hero!"

"Well, next game I'll do even better. Just keep those pretty brown eyes of yours on me."

Chris coughed and winked at Brittany, as though guessing how she felt about Todd's bragging.

Brittany smiled back at Chris. "You got a hit that brought in two runs." But instead of bragging about it, Chris just nodded and grinned.

As the four of them ate, Brittany started thinking. *That's what the book was talking about! Usually I'm with families or a group of kids, like at church or school. That's where I get to know what other kids are like.*

While she and Kim ate burgers and shared French fries, Brittany remembered more. *I can choose to like the kind of person Chris is. I can choose to like the way he acts. Or I can choose to like Todd. And I like more things about Chris than about Todd. A whole lot more!*

Soon the boys finished eating. As they started to leave, Chris turned back to Brittany. "See you at the church car wash."

Brittany waved, then watched them go. The minute the boys went out the door, Kim started talking again.

"Isn't he the very best?"

"Who?" Through the window Brittany was still watching Chris.

"Todd, of course! Who else?"

Brittany groaned. "Kim, does Todd ever think about anyone besides himself?"

As though the question had never occurred to her, Kim stared at Brittany.

"Would he ever care about what happens to someone else—someone like you?"

"Sure." Kim smiled. "Didn't you hear him? He likes my brown eyes."

"Does Todd ever go to church?"

Kim thought for a moment. "No, I guess not. What does that have to do with it?"

"You know that book we were reading? It talked about choosing Christians for our best friends."

"What's the big deal? I'm not going to *marry* Todd. I just *like* him. When I get old enough, maybe he'll ask me out."

"If you start going out with a guy like Todd, you'll keep going with guys just like him. And Todd thinks of only one person—himself."

"But church kids do too," Kim said. "Remember what it was like when I went to your youth group? All the kids from your school were one big clique. They ignored me—treated me like dirt because I go to another school."

You're right, Brittany thought. The worst of it was that at first she hadn't even noticed what the kids were doing. She had hoped that if Kim went to something fun she'd start going to church. But the whole evening had gone wrong.

"So why go to church?" Kim asked.

Brittany stared at her. Putting it that way—

"I'm sorry." Brittany said for the tenth time since it happened. "I wanted you to have fun—to feel like it's an awesome group of kids."

"It's not," Kim said simply. "You're great, but not all your friends. In fact, some of your friends stink."

"Okay. I admit it. But there are other reasons for going to church. Other reasons besides finding a bunch of kids, I mean."

"Not for me. Not right now. You want a group? So do I. I won't find it at your church."

Brittany fell silent. The knot she felt in her stomach was growing. There was nothing more she could say. Kim's hurt had gone deep.

"But look at Todd," Kim went on. "He's fun. He likes me." Kim sighed. "And he's really romantic!"

"Kim—"

"But if you think it's so important, maybe when I'm ready to get married, I'll find someone who goes to church."

Brittany didn't believe her, but knew that right now she wouldn't change Kim's mind.

Will I ever be able to change her thinking? As Brittany gathered up her food wrappers and tray, she thought about it. A group that had been so special for her had fallen apart for someone else. Why did that happen?

Kim knew the reason. Brittany had better remember it too.

When they left McDonald's, Kim turned one way and Brittany the opposite direction. As she started home, she couldn't get Kim out of her mind. Brittany couldn't push aside the way she felt about what had happened.

The kids from church aren't perfect, just like I'm not perfect. Yet more than once they had shut out someone from a different school. Someone of a different color. Or someone who didn't dress the way they did.

Brittany *liked* her church friends. Nearly every time she was with them, she saw some good quality she wanted in a special friend. Yet she also had to be honest.

I'm not perfect, and neither are they. I can't change my whole church group. But I can change how I *act toward others.*

In that moment Brittany started praying. "Jesus, will you give me another chance with Kim? Will you change me and the way I act so she gets to know you?"

Brittany was nearly home when she remembered the church car wash. Though she wasn't perfect and the other kids weren't perfect, she looked forward to being with them. And maybe someday . . .

Brittany smiled.

Let's Talk . . . or Journal

DAY 1

From what you've learned about Chris and Todd, which boy do you respect most? Which boy do you think would be most thoughtful of the girl he someday marries? Why?

DAY 2

Why is it important to get to know others through family, church, and other small groups instead of getting involved with one person? What kinds of things do you want to learn in a small group?

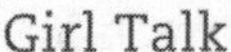

DAY 3

If you choose Christians as your special friends, does it always mean you won't have any problems? Why or why not? What are some things you should look for, even when you're with Christian kids?

When you feel hurt about something that happened to you how can you use that feeling to help you grow up strong?

DAY 4

Jesus can use our friendships as an opportunity for us to tell others about him. Yet some girls think, "I'll go out with that boy, and I'll witness to him so he becomes a Christian." Do you think it really works that way? Why or why not?

DAY 5

Kim described Todd as being "really romantic." What is your idea of "romantic"? Does the word "romantic" describe someone who is faithful and true to his friends? Why or why not? Give reasons for your answer.

DAY 6

When you choose Christians for your best friends, you meet other kids through them. Soon you know a whole group of Christian kids who are fun to be with. Why is that important?

DAY 7

A person who is really a friend won't ask you to do something that hurts you. What does it mean to have friends who choose the best for you? Think of an example. How can you help other kids be strong?

Let's Pray About It

Jesus, for my closest friends I want to choose Christians who will help me make good choices. And I want to do the same thing for them. I want to live in a way that helps them know you and be strong in how you want us to live.

And Jesus, one more thing. It seems a long way off. But if you want me to get married someday, I want to marry a Christian who loves you the way I do. In your name, Jesus, I ask you for exactly the right person at the right time. Thank you!

Mia's Special Book

WEEK 6

Jesus said, "I will not leave you as orphans.
I will come to you."
John 14:18

All afternoon the sand had been warm. Bright sunlight touched the Wisconsin lake with a thousand sparkles. It had been fun meeting new friends at Bible camp, but tomorrow it would all end.

Now a haze covered the sun. Ashley shivered. Her swimsuit was wet and her fingernails blue from the cold. She stood up to go change her clothes, then heard Ryan's shout. "Hey, Ashley, wanna come for a boat ride?"

"Just a minute," she called. "I'll change into jeans and be right back."

Inside her cabin, Ashley shed her swimsuit and slipped into jeans. As she pulled on a sweatshirt, she heard a muffled sound from the back room.

Ashley paused. Listened. Heard the sound again. Was someone crying?

Moving quietly, Ashley followed the sobs to the bedroom. There she found Mia lying face down, weeping into her pillow.

Ashley stopped, edged away, and then stepped back. *What should I do? Pretend I don't see her? Sneak away?*

Though they were in the same cabin, Mia came from another church. Ashley had just met her this week. With all her heart Ashley wanted to go back to the fun. Yet Mia's sobs shook the bed.

For a moment Ashley stood there, thinking about what to do. She hated scenes. She had been part of too many of them at home. Besides, her friends were waiting. Ashley felt torn in two directions.

Just then Mia blew her nose, and Ashley made up her mind. "Hey, what's wrong?" she asked, stepping forward. "Can I help?"

As Mia looked up, her shoulders stopped shaking. Her red, swollen eyes forced Ashley to think back. As though seeing herself in a DVD, she remembered the times she had fallen asleep crying.

Still feeling torn, yet knowing she'd hate herself if she didn't stay, Ashley sat down on the edge of the bed. From somewhere came the courage to ask, "Did you get bad news about your dad?"

Mia shook her head.

"Then what's wrong?"

"I am so scared." Mia spoke between sniffs. "This week has been perfect. I don't want to go home. It's awful watching Daddy get sicker every day."

Her words ended in a sob, and she stopped, drew a deep breath. "I'm scared he's going to die."

"Oh, Mia, I'm so sorry!" Reaching forward, Ashley gave her a hug.

When Mia finally spoke, her words were muffled. "Before I came, Mom said—"

Mia began sobbing again.

Ashley's hug tightened. For a time she just hugged Mia as she cried it out. At last Mia reached for a box of Kleenex.

As she finished blowing her nose, Mia drew another long, shaky breath. "Before I came, Mom said she wanted me to go and have a good time. Daddy said the same thing. He said, "Mia, my little one, you need time with friends. You need time to know that whatever happens to me, God will be with you."

Mia's voice broke. "But I can't see God. What will I do if I can't see my Daddy? What will I do if I can't talk to him? What will I do if he's not there when I go to bed at night? When I wake up in the morning?"

Tears welled up in Ashley's eyes. As they ran down her cheeks she brushed them aside. But the tears kept coming.

Suddenly Mia looked at Ashley. "How did you know?" she asked. "How did you know how it feels?" Reaching out, she gave Ashley the Kleenex. "Did your daddy die too?"

Ashley shook her head. "My parents are divorced. My dad lives way out in Oregon. I see him only three weeks a year. And sometimes at Christmas. Not always."

Ashley stopped. Made herself uncurl her tense fingers. "What happened to me is different from what's happening to you. But when my dad left— "

Ashley swallowed, then went on. "When it was really hard— "

When she couldn't speak, Mia waited, finally said, "When it was really hard, you— "

"Sometimes it helped me to look at pictures. At first that made it worse. Made me feel even more lonesome. But then, after awhile it helped."

"Mom's been taking lots of pictures," Mia said. "That must be why. She knows."

"And I try to remember the good times. Times when my mom and dad weren't fighting."

"Like what?"

"When I was a little kid they got along better. We'd go swimming, like now, at a lake. We went camping, even though my mom didn't like it. When we sat around a campfire, we'd sing songs. Funny songs that made us laugh. Real songs, like the ones we sing here."

Ashley stopped. "Mia, if your daddy dies, what will you remember about him?"

Mia jumped up, pulled a book out of her backpack. When she sat down on the bed again, Ashley saw it was a hardcover book with blank pages. The kind of book in which Mia could write her own special thoughts.

Then Ashley saw the words on the cover. *My Daddy Thoughts.*

"He gave me this book," Mia said. "He asked me to write whatever memories mean the most to me. Sometimes at night before I go to bed, we read them together. When we get too serious, Daddy helps me write something about him that makes me laugh."

Mia smiled. "He says I have the best giggle ever invented. That someday he's going to capture my giggle in a bottle and release it to the whole world."

Mia giggled just thinking about it. But then she grew serious. "Before I left for camp, Daddy told me I should write down the verses that mean the most to me. He said, "Write down the verses that jump out at you. Write down the verses that seem to be lit by a holy flashlight. And when someone says something that means a lot to you, write that down, so you remember."

Ashley blinked, tried to smile, and couldn't. Finally she said, "I think I better start my own book."

When Mia spoke again, she looked Ashley straight in the eye. "Why don't you start your book with something you tell me?"

Ashley stared at her. "Oh, no, I can't—"

"Yes, you can. You can say, 'I hugged this girl who was crying, and she was glad."

Ashley laughed.

"Or you can say, 'Instead of bringing a garter snake into the cabin—instead of waking up Mia by swinging the snake in her face—I cheered her up.'"

Ashley stared again. "How did you find out that last year a crazy girl woke me up that way?"

"Or you could say—"

"I know." Ashley lifted her right hand. "I could say something serious. Something that would help both you and me."

For a moment she thought about it. "You can put this in your book, wherever you're writing now. But I'll put it at the beginning of *my* book."

Mia grabbed a pencil, ready to write.

Ashley spoke the words slowly, so Mia could get them down. "If something happens to your daddy, you will still have a Heavenly Father. He will take care of both you and me."

When Mia finished writing, she looked up. Tears streamed down her face again. "Another hug," she said. "It's what Daddy has been trying to tell me—that God will be with me."

In that moment Ashley knew without doubt that her words had not been her own. Reaching out, she hugged Mia again.

Oh, Lord, how did you manage to do that? Ashley thought. *What if I had sneaked out instead of talking to Mia? And how did you manage to help me too?*

Let's Talk ... or Journal

DAY 1

What made the conversation between Mia and Ashley very special?

DAY 2

Have you ever noticed some unusual timing in your own life? Maybe you suddenly met someone who helped you. Or someone you already knew told you something both important and surprising. Perhaps that person said just the right thing at the right time. What happened?

DAY 3

Who do you think arranged that help with such good timing? Why?

DAY 4

When someone dies, do you ever wish you had gotten to know him or her better? What questions would you like to ask that person?

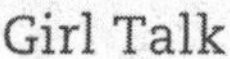

DAY 5

Even if Mia's father dies, something very special will happen. Someday Mia and her father will see each other again in heaven. How do you know that's true? Look up the words of Jesus in John 14:1 – 6. What does he promise about preparing a place for those who believe in him?

DAY 6

If someone you love has died, it helps to write down or tell someone your special memories about that person. What do you remember about ...

The fun times?
Something special that person did for you?
What he or she believed?

DAY 7

What thought from the Bible means especially much to you right now? Write the words and where they are found. If you haven't memorized those words, take time to do it now.

Let's Pray About It

Jesus, you know I find it hard to talk with someone who's facing something really difficult. Thank you that when you expect me to help someone you've often taught me about something similar. Thanks for helping me with the questions to ask, the words to say, and the hugs to give. Thanks even more for being the biggest Hugger there is because of the way you love every one of us.

First Day for Abby

WEEK 7

*"I can do everything by the power of Christ.
He gives me strength."*
Phil. 4:13 NIrV

Ready to leave the bedroom she knew so well, Abby looked around. On her bulletin board were reminders of special times—a dried flower from a wedding, a ticket stub from the San Diego Zoo, a photo of her friends on the last day of school.

In that school she had known everyone and everything. Looking at the picture, Abby felt sad for what was past and afraid of what was ahead. During the summer her family had moved, and this was Abby's first day in her new school.

Though the day was bright with sunshine, Abby's heart felt cold. Here she would know only one person—a girl named Taylor who had also moved into the city that summer. As Abby left home, she wondered, *What if I can't remember where my classes are? What if I get lost?*

Sure, there had been a special day for new students. She and Taylor and other kids in their class went through their schedules.

But now the school would be full of kids who knew each other and had no doubt about where to go.

Butterflies fluttered in Abby's stomach. *What if*—She could imagine all kinds of things. But one question seemed the worst of all. *What if I can't find my classrooms? What if kids laugh at me?*

When Abby reached school, she pulled open the heavy door. The sunshine disappeared in the long halls and endless classrooms.

I can't do it, Abby thought. The words set up a chant in her brain. *I'll never find my way.* Like a spinning bike wheel, the words went round and round in her mind. Then she spotted Taylor.

"Hi, Abby!" Taylor called. Her warm smile chased away the scared feelings squirming inside Abby's stomach. *Taylor will remember where to go. She'll find her way around. All I have to do is follow her. What a big relief!*

As they set out for their first class, Taylor chattered nonstop. "Good thing we have the same schedule."

Soon Taylor took a right, and a left, then started down another long hall. Confused by all the turns, Abby followed step by step.

I don't remember going this way. She felt glad that her new friend was there to take the lead.

"Here it is," Taylor said. "Room 111."

The girls slid into seats across from each other. Soon the teacher asked them to open their math books. As Abby looked at the problems, her brain felt fuzzy.

"They're so hard," she whispered to Taylor. "I'm dumb in math."

When the class ended, they started out once more. Again Taylor took the lead. Turning one way, then another, she climbed a flight of stairs and rounded a corner.

I can't remember this, either. Abby didn't want to admit that she had no idea where they were. *How does Taylor manage to do it?*

"Room 238," Taylor said as though she had discovered the New World. As far as Abby was concerned, she had.

It was English class. "Just wait," Abby told her new friend. "We'll have to write about what we did this summer."

Sure enough. "Do one page," the teacher told them.

"That's easy," Abby said in a low voice. "I did lots of fun things." Besides, she liked to write.

But as Abby bent over her desk, she remembered another class and another time. As though it were yesterday, she saw herself in third grade, trying to write about her summer. She could still remember every wall of the classroom.

That time she couldn't come up with one sentence. Abby still remembered how she felt when the teacher collected her blank paper. Since then she had formed a habit of putting herself down.

Now, like words spinning around in Abby's head, a DVD started to play, images and all. *You're going to tell about the time on the beach? That doesn't sound like fun.*

Abby wrote one sentence, then sat back to look at it. *Now if that doesn't sound stupid!*

Crumpling up her paper, Abby tried again, then again. Suddenly Taylor leaned into the aisle between them. "Just do it!" she whispered.

Abby grinned. *Just do it!* she told herself. It was the thought she needed.

Leaning over her desk, she started to write as fast as she could. If the teacher didn't think it was good enough she could always rewrite. Revise. Change. Right now she just needed to get something down.

When the teacher told them to stop, Abby had filled a whole page. And it was good. It was a beginning. Having the words in front of her, Abby knew she could make them better on another day.

When the bell rang, Abby followed her new friend out of class. By now Abby wanted to be like Taylor—to just move ahead, doing her best when that was needed.

Together they walked down a flight of stairs, around a corner, then into a long hall.

Suddenly Taylor stopped in her tracks. "Where are we? You'll have to help me on this one, Abby."

"You really don't know?"

Taylor shook her head.

"But all day long you've led us to every class."

Taylor giggled. "You think so? You didn't notice I was just going around in circles? I forgot to bring the floor plan they gave us."

Abby giggled too. "I thought you knew what you were doing." Believing she could depend on Taylor, Abby hadn't taken out her floor plan.

"If I couldn't find the rooms, I just kept trying." Taylor grinned. "I figured if I got lost, I could always ask someone—someone like you. Like right now."

"And all day long I thought—"

In that moment Abby remembered Taylor's words. "Just do it!" How often did Taylor think "Just do it!" to the best of her ability? And it was enough?

Looking around, Abby recognized a display window. This time she didn't listen to the voice that told her she couldn't do anything.

"C'mon!" Abby wanted to make a new start that fit her new discovery.

When she found the room they needed, Taylor grinned at her. "You know something? You're worth more than you think!"

Taylor's words were a happy sound in Abby's ears.

Let's Talk . . . or Journal

DAY 1

Abby and Taylor faced the same problems, but Abby was afraid of the "what ifs." What did Abby tell herself when she used "what ifs" to put herself down?

DAY 2

How did Abby's habit of putting herself down keep her from doing new things? Abby liked to write. Yet how did her memories of failure and her habit of putting herself down keep her from doing even the things she liked?

DAY 3

The way you look at yourself can become a mountain that keeps you from trying. You start to believe the negative thoughts you tell yourself. In what ways do you put yourself down?

DAY 4

Are you really a failure in what you've tried to do, or is that something you tell yourself? Give reasons for your answer.

DAY 5

Abby could tell herself, "If I fail, I can start over again." Why is it better to try and fail than to never try at all?

DAY 6

Your enemy, Satan, wants you to feel that you're no good. It's a trick he uses to keep you from becoming all that Jesus wants you to be. Instead of letting enemy thoughts go round and round in your head, let the Holy Spirit help you. Make a choice. The minute an enemy thought enters your mind, choose to focus on Jesus instead of what you can't do. Pray in his name, something like "Thank you, Jesus, that you can help me in whatever way I need. In your name I ask you for that help." Then think about a Bible verse you know. What is a verse you can repeat when the enemy tells you that you're no good? Write it down. Here are some verses that might be especially helpful to you.

Look up the verses and write the words. Then turn those verses into a prayer.

Here are some examples:

- James 1:5

- Isaiah 41:10

- Jeremiah 1:5 – 7

Now choose a verse and repeat it until the words become real to you. Memorize that verse so you can say it back to yourself at any time of the day or night. Repeat the words to yourself whenever needed.

DAY 7

Go back to the verse you memorized yesterday. Notice how the words come alive as you repeat them to yourself. Keep building up a storehouse of verses that help you when you have a difficult time. Copy them on a 3 x 5 index card. Keep a small box (a recipe box works great!) that holds the cards you are memorizing. Use the cards to review what you have memorized.

A Faithgirl does things in spite of the way her enemy, Satan, tries to defeat her. The next two pages have space for you to write. On the first page make a list of the ways you feel defeated right now. On the second page put a Bible verse that will help you win over the plans of the enemy to defeat you. Draw a line from the problem on the left to the answer on the right.

Ways I Feel Defeated

Bible Verses

Free writing clue #1 from someone who finds it easy to put herself down: When you need to write something, think about what you want to say until you have some ideas. If needed, organize your thoughts in a brief outline or story plan. Then write down your thoughts as fast as they come to you. Don't stop to think whether what you're saying is good or bad. Then, when you have a first draft, go back and start revising. If you have words in front of you it's easy to change them. Keep revising until what you want to say is in the best form that you can make it. You'll be amazed to discover that you can write even a book this long if you don't let your enemy convince you that you can't.

Let's Pray About It

Forgive me, Jesus, for telling myself I can't do things even before I try. Help me to stop putting myself down. Help me to find my confidence and strength in you. In your name, Jesus, I ask for your wisdom, power, and strength. Thank you for your gifts of wisdom to everyone who asks. Thank you for not finding fault. Thank you that when I trust in you, you help me do my best.

Popcorn Plus

WEEK 8

If any of you need wisdom, ask God for it. He will give it to you. God gives freely to everyone. He doesn't find fault.
James 1:5 NIrV

All week Bobbi had looked forward to this sleepover. Ever since Amanda invited her, she'd thought, *How can I be so lucky? They're the in-group at school. And they asked me!*

For a long time, Bobbi had wanted to be friends with Amanda, Tara, and Carina. Now was her chance!

Standing on the front step of Amanda's house, sleeping bag in one hand and overnight bag in the other, Bobbi felt the first twinge of uneasiness. Her friend Lizbeth and three other girls were also having a sleepover that night. Bobbi had helped plan it.

Then came Amanda's invitation, and Bobbi decided she would tell Lizbeth that she'd rather be with the other girls. That had been a bad moment.

"Oh," Lizbeth said. A cloud seemed to enter her clear blue eyes. Then she tried to cover up how she felt. "Well, have a good time."

As Bobbi punched the doorbell, she tried to push the memory aside.

Amanda swung the door wide open. "C'mon in, Bobbi."

With clothes and sleeping bags spread out on the floor of the family room, the girls soon gathered in a circle. *This is great!* Bobbi thought as she munched chips and popcorn and listened to Tara tell a story.

Suddenly everyone laughed. *What for?* Bobbi didn't understand, but she pasted a smile on her lips and pretended that she did.

When it was Carina's turn, she told something she'd seen in an R-rated movie. This time Bobbi did understand. She felt dirty all over.

Then Amanda spoke up, telling what she thought another girl and her boyfriend did when they were alone together.

Listening to Amanda, Bobbi felt the hotness of embarrassment start deep inside and creep up into her neck and cheeks. It was hard to pretend she was laughing.

"It's your turn, Bobbi." Amanda gave her a poke.

Bobbi looked at the floor. "I ... I don't know your kind of stories."

"You don't? Where have you been? In church all your life?"

Bobbi swallowed around the lump in her throat. "Yes, that's right. I've been in church." Too embarrassed to meet their gaze, she looked down and began twisting the bottom of her sweat shirt.

"Hey, leave her alone," Carina said. "Let the little baby stay a baby."

The others laughed, but Bobbi felt sick inside. Jumping up, she escaped to an upstairs bedroom. Combing her hair at least a hundred times, she stayed as long as she could. Finally she went back to the family room. As she entered the room, the conversation stopped.

Must have been saying something about me, Bobbi thought. The hollow feeling in her stomach made her feel sick all over.

Then just as suddenly everyone began talking again. Around Bobbi the conversation flowed like a stream swollen by a spring rain. It seemed that no one could say anything good about her teachers.

Well, I guess teachers are fair game, Bobbi told herself. *But do they have to go that far?* She reached for the popcorn, hoping to hide her uncomfortable feelings by eating.

Then the conversation shifted again. For some reason everyone kept talking about the girls Bobbi usually did things with.

They're my friends, Bobbi thought. Until that moment she had never realized how much she liked them. *But what should I do? Defend them? I'm afraid to.*

A moment later the meanness centered on her friend Lizbeth. "Did you know she got caught shoplifting?" Amanda asked.

Bobbi could stand it no longer. Anger filling every part of her being, she jumped up. "That's not true!" she cried out. "Lizbeth is my best friend. She would never do that!"

Amanda pulled Bobbi back down. "Hey, kid," she said. "What are you getting so excited about?"

Too miserable to answer, Bobbi crawled into her sleeping bag. *This is a whole lot more than I bargained for. How could something I thought would be so nice be so awful?* Even worse, she was missing out on a party with her *real* friends. Would this miserable night ever end?

Let's Talk . . . or Journal

DAY 1

Sometimes when we're outside a group, the kids that are "in" seem really cool. But is an "in" group always the best one to be in? Give reasons for your answer. When you aren't in an "in" group can it sometimes be a way that God protects you? Explain why you feel the way you do.

DAY 2

When the party became too much for Bobbi, she escaped upstairs. Then she returned downstairs and eventually crawled into her sleeping bag. What are some other choices that Bobbi could have made? What can you do when kids tell dirty stories or watch TV shows or DVDs that fill your mind with the wrong things?

DAY 3

What do you think Bobbi should tell her friend Lizbeth? What qualities do you value in your best friends? What do you like to see in girls with whom you'd like to be forever friends?

DAY 4

Make a list of practical ideas for how you and your family can work together if you face something difficult or even dangerous. Here are starters that would have helped Bobbi at the sleepover:

- At any time of the day or night, it's okay to call Mom or Dad and ask for a ride home.
- I don't have to feel at home with every crowd. If I feel uncomfortable it's probably time to find a way to leave.

DAY 5

Bobbi needed God's help, and the Bible tells us about people who felt the same way. When God told Solomon to ask for whatever he wanted, King Solomon prayed, "So give me a heart that understands. Then I can rule over your people. I can tell the difference between what is right and what is wrong" (1 Kings 3:9 NIrV). In what ways would it help you to ask for a heart that understands?

DAY 6

Describe some ways in which Jesus knew what people were like. For clues see:

- John 1:45 – 51
- Mark 2:6 – 12
- John 2:23 – 25
- John 4:28 – 29

DAY 7

How do you think Jesus would feel about your being in a group with friends who love him too? Give reasons for your answers. You may want to include your ideas about what Jesus saw in people in the verses you read for Day 6.

Let's Pray About It

Forgive me, Jesus, for wanting something that seems better just because I don't have it. Give me your wisdom and understanding to know what is good, or not so good, or even wrong. In your name I ask for friends who help and support me in the way you want me to live. Thank you!

No Longer Dark

WEEK 9

I will lie down and sleep in peace.
Lord, you alone keep me safe.
Psalm 4:8 NIrV

Mei Ling flicked off the light and took a running leap into bed. Outside, the November wind blew around the corner of the house. A wavering light filled the room. Eerie sounds sent shivers through her whole body.

Shadows danced on the walls, growing long in corners and melting down into the stairway outside her door. Feeling scared and alone, Mei Ling huddled under the blankets.

Minutes later her adoptive father came into her room to say good-night. He gently pulled the blankets off her head. "Something wrong, Mei Ling? Can I help?"

Afraid to admit her fear of the dark, she shook her head. But Dad guessed. "Are you afraid of the wind and the dark?"

This time Mei Ling nodded.

"All of us have times when we're afraid," Dad told her. "What counts is what we do about it—like choosing to face the reason, for instance."

Going over to the door, he flicked the light switch. The bright light reached into the corners, and every shadow melted. As Mei Ling looked around the room, her fear vanished.

"Now watch." Dad turned off the light and went to the window. "I can close the blinds if you want." When he did, the room became dark with no dancing shadows. "But there's something we're missing."

When Mei Ling joined him at the window, Dad pulled the blinds back up. Bare branches, stripped of leaves, moved back and forth—first blocking the streetlight, then letting the light shine through. As Mei Ling watched, the light kept changing. Now she understood the sound she heard—branches tapping against the side of the house.

"What happened when I opened the blinds again?" Dad asked.

"I saw what made me afraid. The branches moving back and forth. Touching the side of the house."

"Are you afraid now?"

Mei Ling shook her head. "I know what the shadows are. I don't have any reason to be afraid."

Dad smiled. "And what do you see instead?"

"The wildness of the November wind."

It was a game they had played before when Dad showed her how to enjoy the moods of weather.

"And what is the wind doing?" Dad asked.

This time it was Mei Ling who smiled. "Sending the dry, fallen leaves around to find new friends."

When Dad hugged her, Mei Ling knew he was delighted that she remembered.

Dad picked up the Bible next to her bed. "Let's read Psalm 121 tonight." Once more he turned on the light.

Mei Ling began reading. Her voice grew stronger when she reached the third and fourth verses. "He who watches over you won't get tired. In fact, he who watches over Israel won't get tired or go to sleep."

When Dad turned off the light and left, Mei Ling snuggled

down under the blankets. This time she pulled them only as high as her shoulders. *It's not so bad when I face things*, she thought.

Drowsiness settled around her as she repeated the verses from Psalm 121 that meant the most to her. Then she turned the words into a prayer. *He who watches over me won't get tired. He won't get tired or go to sleep.*

Moments later, Mei Ling fell asleep.

Let's Talk . . . or Journal

DAY 1

Sometimes we have a good reason to be afraid. Other times we're afraid about something we imagine. Which was it for Mei Ling?

DAY 2

Many people are afraid of the dark. What happened when Mei Ling chose to face her fear and talk about it?

DAY 3

Are there other things that make you afraid? Are they real or something you imagine? When you talk about them, try to remember when these things started making you afraid and why. Ask Jesus to heal that memory.

DAY 4

Have you ever been afraid of taking a test? Why can that fear sometimes be good?

DAY 5

Is it fair to ask for God's protection if we are foolish and purposely do things that aren't safe?

DAY 6

Often we're afraid of things that never happen, but now and then there can be good reasons to be afraid of the weather. If a storm damages or destroys your belongings, those are things that can often be replaced. What's most important is what happens to people. If you know that severe weather is coming, how do people in your area take shelter?

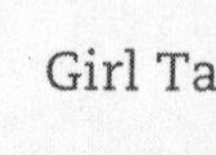

DAY 7

People who have courage are not people who are never afraid. People with courage have learned to act wisely in spite of their fear. It may be important to think about a way in which you're afraid long enough to face it. Then ask God, "Do I need to get over that fear? Or is that something you want me to know so I act wisely?"

Talk with a parent or other grownup who can help you know the difference. Then call upon Jesus by praying in his name and repeating Bible verses you've memorized.

Let's Pray About It

Thank you, Jesus, that when I repeat Bible verses and think about you, my fears go away. Thank you that when I'm afraid, it helps me to talk with you or my mom or dad—not someone who scares me more. Thanks for promising to be with me always.

I Dare You!

WEEK 10

"Don't be afraid! Stand firm. You will see how the Lord will save you today. Do you see those Egyptians? You will never see them again. The Lord will fight for you. Just be still."

Exodus 14:13 – 14 NIrV

Kelsey yawned and looked up at the hands of the clock. With a new boy in school, it had been an exciting day. Yet now time seemed to have stopped.

Finally the hands moved on, minute by minute. Kelsey couldn't wait to be out for the day, free as a breeze.

Annette, the most popular girl in the room, had chosen her, Kelsey. Nina, the second most popular girl, was coming along. Sure, it was longer to walk home the way they chose, but it would be worth it.

At last the moment came. Surrounded by a hundred other kids, they pushed their way out the school door and started down the street. Soon they left the others behind.

Annette giggled. "Don't you like the new boy? I just love Rob's brown eyes. And his muscles—*wow!*" She tossed her head, and her blond hair swung around her shoulders. "Did you see the way Rob watches me? I'm sure he likes me."

Sure that clouds had moved across the sun, Kelsey glanced up. But nothing had changed. Twice Rob had spoken to her that morning. When they traded test papers, he grinned at the funny mark Kelsey used for corrections. He liked the cartoon she drew at the bottom. She had wondered, *Could he really like me?* But now Annette said—

Kelsey ached inside. *How can I make Rob like me? What can I do to be as popular as Annette?*

Just then Annette opened her book bag. "Look! I've got half a pack of cigarettes my mom left out. Let's cut down this street, and no one will see us."

Kelsey stopped in her tracks. "No, I don't think so."

"Oh, come on," Annette said. "I've smoked before, and it's really cool."

"I've tried it, too," Nina joined in. "It won't hurt you any."

"Then why do they put a warning on cigarettes?" Kelsey asked.

"That's just for people who aren't strong," answered Annette. "Nothing will happen to you."

"Sorry," Kelsey said. "I know people who can't stop smoking. I don't want to start."

"Are you kidding?" Annette asked. "You'll never be popular that way!"

"You're just a chicken," Nina said. "I dare you to give it a try."

Kelsey cringed. Her mixed-up feelings seemed like a waterfall tumbling over rocks. "I *like* you!" she wanted to cry out. "I don't want you dying of lung cancer the way my uncle did!" But the words stuck in her throat.

She wondered if Annette and Nina could see that her face felt hot with embarrassment. *Is this what it means to be popular? If I say no, does it mean I can't be their friend?*

Let's Talk ... or Journal

DAY 1

What do you think Kelsey will do? If she keeps saying no to cigarettes, what do you think Annette and Nina will do?

DAY 2

Is it important to be popular with everyone? Why or why not? Do you think God sometimes wants us to be *unpopular*? Give some reasons for your answer.

DAY 3

The nicotine used in cigarettes is a poisonous substance that is used to kill insects. Nicotine can also cause smokers to become addicted. What happens when a person becomes addicted to something?

DAY 4

If someone asks you to do something that will hurt you, do you believe that person is really your friend? Why or why not? Give your reasons.

DAY 5

It can be your protection that you don't feel at home with every group. What might be a consequence of choosing to be in the wrong group? Why is it important to understand that?

What does it mean to stand firm in what you believe? Think about a time when you needed to stand firm. Be honest about how you felt and tell what happened.

DAY 6

The Bible shows us how God wants us to live. If you're tempted to do something wrong, how can the Bible verses you've memorized help you make the right choice? In what ways are you getting help from the verses you memorized?

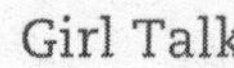

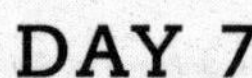

DAY 7

How did Jesus use Bible verses when he was tempted? Big clue: See Luke 4:1 – 13.

Let's Pray About It

When I'm tempted to do wrong, help me to say no, Jesus, even if I'm scared. Help me remember the tricks of the enemy and stand my ground. Help me to answer in such a way that kids know I mean NO! Thank you that I don't have to choose wrong things in order to be popular. Thank you that though you often weren't popular when you lived on earth, you have become the most important Person who ever lived.

Wedding in the Family

WEEK 11

Pleasant words are like honey. They are sweet to the spirit and bring healing to the body.
Proverbs 16:24 NIrV

With a final look in the mirror, Kallie pushed aside a strand of her blond hair. Then she lined up at the back of the church with her sisters Melissa and Morgan.

As the shortest bridesmaid, Kallie would lead the others down the aisle. The youngest of four girls in their family, she often felt like a tagalong. Too old to be a flower girl, but much younger than her sisters, Kallie had wondered if she'd be in the wedding. But when her sister Caryn became engaged, she settled the problem.

"When I marry Adam, I want you with us," she said. "You're my junior bridesmaid! Okay?"

From that moment on, Kallie felt excited just thinking about the wedding. At the same time, she wished she were as grown-up and attractive as her older sisters.

Nervously Kallie touched the soft folds of her saffron dress. When she shifted her bouquet from one hand to the other, she saw that every church pew was filled. Suddenly the aisle seemed to stretch out forever.

Just then Melissa leaned forward to tell Kallie that she looked great. But Kallie felt sure she was kidding. "Hey, don't make fun of me!" she whispered. "I wish I looked as awesome as you."

Melissa shook her head, but before she could answer, the signal came.

Remembering to walk slowly, Kallie started down the aisle. When she reached the steps, she managed to get up them without tripping on her long dress. Then she turned and looked toward the back of the church.

Next came Melissa and Morgan. Then Caryn started forward. With her long white dress, her dark hair and eyes looked especially beautiful. Caryn seemed to shimmer all the way down the aisle. *I've never seen her so beautiful!* thought Kallie.

Caryn's face shone. When she and Adam turned toward the altar, he looked just as happy and excited.

No one will ever love me like that, Kallie thought.

During the pastor's message Kallie wondered if everyone was looking at her. She did all she could not to fidget. But soon Caryn and Adam exchanged rings, and it was time for Kallie to follow them and Melissa and Morgan back down the aisle.

At the wedding reception, Gran found her. "Kallie, your hair is lovely that way!"

"Oh, Gran, I just couldn't get it the way I wanted!"

"You couldn't possibly improve on how it is," answered Gran. "And you held your long skirt just right as you went up the steps."

"Didn't I look clumsy? I was sure I did."

"Best of all, the way you stood at the altar, quietly listening, was respectful and nice."

Kallie sighed. "I wanted to itch every minute. I felt like scratching my back. Melissa and Morgan look so much nicer than I do."

Gran's smile faded. Her voice was gentle, yet firm. "Kallie, I gave you three compliments. What do you want to do about it?"

Gran moved away, and Kallie felt uneasy. *What was she telling me?*

As Kallie watched, Gran walked over to Melissa and her boyfriend, Steve. Looking at Melissa, then at Gran, Steve grinned. Kallie heard the low rumble of his voice.

"How about this awesome girl? I found a really good one, don't you think, Gran?"

Melissa blushed but smiled up at him. "Thanks, Steve. I'm glad you like the way I am."

Steve's slow smile reached his eyes. In that moment something clicked in Kallie's mind. *So that's what Gran meant!*

As Melissa and Steve turned toward Kallie, he let out a low whistle. "Whew! You look beautiful, Kallie! I thought you were your sister Morgan coming over here!"

Out of long habit Kallie almost answered, "Oh no, I don't look as nice as Morgan."

But then she remembered Gran. In the next instant Kallie found some other words. "Thanks, Steve, I feel great! Isn't this wedding fun?"

When Melissa and Gran smiled, Kallie knew she'd given the right answer.

Let's Talk ... or Journal

DAY 1

What is a compliment?

DAY 2

When Melissa and Gran complimented Kallie, what did she do? How do you suppose Kallie's answers made Melissa and Gran feel?

DAY 3

When someone answers the way Kallie did at first, we say they're fishing for more compliments. What does that mean?

DAY 4

If you respond to a compliment in the right way, you not only say thank you. You also make the other person feel good about giving the compliment. Think of a time when someone complimented you. How did you feel about what that person said? What would be a good way to answer that compliment?

DAY 5

If you continually put yourself down, it's the same as saying you don't like the way God made you. How do you think God feels about the way he created you? What has Jesus done that helps you know how much he cares about you?

DAY 6

When we give a compliment, it's important to pick out something that we really like about someone so it sounds honest and real. It also helps to tell a person that she has a special skill. Or that she has a helpful personality trait, such as kindness. Think about the people around you. Is there someone you'd like to encourage by giving a compliment? Write down what you'd like to say.

DAY 7

In the Bible God the Father gave Jesus the biggest compliment anyone could ever receive. Speaking from a cloud, God said, "This is my Son, whom I love; with him I am well pleased. Listen to him!" (Matthew 17:5) Why do you think God was so pleased with Jesus?

Let's Pray About It

Thank you, Jesus, that compliments are special gifts. Thanks for the good way they make me feel. Help me know what to say when people compliment me. And help me encourage others with honest compliments that make them feel special because I've noticed their abilities and special traits.

Never Good Enough

WEEK 12

The Lord your God is with you, he is mighty to save. He will take great delight in you, he will quiet you with his love, he will rejoice over you with singing.

Zephaniah 3:17

I'm afraid to see my report card, Molly thought. *I've never worked so hard in my life. If my grades aren't better, I'll feel like giving up.*

When her teacher stopped at Molly's desk, her warm smile offered hope. The moment Molly saw her grades, she wanted to shout. She could barely keep the good news inside.

As she walked home, Molly hugged her best friend. "Can you believe it? I got three *B*s and one *A*. I've never done so well!"

Alycia hugged her back. "You studied hard, Molly. You earned those grades. I'm proud of you!"

A warm feeling of satisfaction filled Molly till she felt like a soda ready to fizz over.

"Do you know what?" Alycia asked. "I think God is proud of you too."

The warm feeling of satisfaction stayed with Molly as she reached her house. She found her mom home early from work. But when she walked into the kitchen, Molly discovered the day was not going well for her mother.

"Hi, Molly," she said. "Put away your things, okay? The Fischers will be here in an hour."

"Sure, Mom, but I want to show you my grades."

"Not right now. I have to get this meat in the oven, and the veggies ready, and the table set."

"But, Mom, it just takes a minute. I want you to see what I got—three *B*s and one *A*!"

"That's nice, Molly. Now go clean the bathroom for me. When you're done with that, vacuum the hall."

Molly walked slowly to her bedroom. Some of the fizz had gone out of her day. All that work and Mom hadn't even heard what she said. Well, maybe Dad would be interested.

As Molly finished vacuuming, her dad came in. "Hi, pumpkin," he said with a quick hug.

As he headed down the hall, Molly stopped him. "I got my grades today, Dad. I think you'll like them. I worked as hard as I could, just like you said."

Dad waited while Molly got her report card. "See? Isn't that great?"

"Hmm," Dad said.

Molly anxiously watched his face. *I just want to know that he cares. If he likes what I did, all the work will be worth it.*

"Hmm," Dad said again. Then he looked up. "I bet if you had really tried you could have gotten all *A*s."

The sparkling can of soda inside Molly fizzed out. Taking the report card, she walked to her bedroom without another word. Though she blinked away tears, Dad didn't seem to notice.

Once she was alone, the torrent came. "Oh, God!" Molly cried out. "I wanted them to be proud of me! I tried so hard. But I studied and studied, and it wasn't enough! Whatever I do, it's never good enough!"

Molly's shoulders shook as she cried into her pillow so Mom and Dad wouldn't hear. Like a bike wheel spinning very fast, the words went round and round in her head. "Not good enough. Not good enough. Not good enough."

Finally Molly blew her nose. *Should I stop trying? Should I give up? What's the use?*

Then from deep inside came a memory. Her friend Alycia had said, "*I'm proud of you!*" Then she said something more. "*I think God is proud of you, too!*"

A new thought came to Molly. *Jesus, you know I really tried, don't you? What do you think about my three B's and one A? Are they good enough for you?*

Molly felt sure she knew the answer.

Let's Talk ... or Journal

DAY 1

If you could talk to Molly about her three Bs and one A, what would you say?

DAY 2

Can everyone be a straight A student? Why or why not? Why does it mean so much to have the approval of a parent or others close to us? Do you think it would help Molly to show her report card again later when her mom isn't so busy? Explain.

DAY 3

Molly knows she has done her best. What is more important — the sense of satisfaction she feels about her grades or how someone else reacts? Give reasons for your answer.

DAY 4

Think about some times when you did your best, but it wasn't good enough. You may not have gotten a part in a play or a place on a team. What did you learn from those times?

DAY 5

In a letter Paul told Timothy, "Do your best to please God. Be a worker who doesn't need to be ashamed." (2 Timothy 2:15 NIrV) What is the difference between doing your best and doing something perfectly? Who gives us the ability to please God?

When we choose to please God we don't have to continually push ourselves to do something we honestly can't do. Instead, he gives us the desire to do something we can do and then he helps us do it. Have you ever asked God for help and been surprised by being able to do something you really didn't know how to do? What happened? Who helped you?

DAY 6

Even if you don't receive praise or an outward reward, it's important for you to know that you did your best. Without putting yourself down, describe some things that you've learned to do well. Include everyday things like knowing how to dust your room. Or sew on a button. Clean up dishes when it's not your turn, but Mom is tired. Or take a younger sister's hand to help her across a street. Then include things like studying or doing a project where you have to keep working over a period of time. Try to make your list as long as you can.

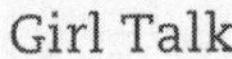

DAY 7

Alycia was a truly special friend. Go back to the story and see what she told Molly about her good grades. Molly gave an honest compliment, didn't she? Now go back to Week 11 and see if that's a way you'd like to encourage others. Out of the encouragement you've received from God, how can you reach out and find other ways to encourage others?

Let's Pray About It

Jesus, it means so much to me when the people I love tell me I'm doing great. If they don't encourage me, help me to do my best and then be glad that I did. Thank you for being with me, for being mighty to save. For taking great delight in me, quieting me with you love, and rejoicing over me with singing. Thank you for being glad for who I am!

How Can I Like Me?

WEEK 13

But the fruit of the Spirit is love, joy, peace, patience, kindness, goodness, faithfulness, gentleness and self-control.
Galatians 5:23 – 24a

Jamie slid onto a chair in the school lunch room. Propping her elbows on the table, she leaned forward to close her mouth around a straw. For several moments she thought only about how hungry she felt.

When she picked up her burger, Jamie glanced across the table at Lisa. There she sat, nice and thin. *Just the perfect weight*, thought Jamie. *Why do I always look so fat?*

"Watch it!" whispered Lisa. "Big trouble! Those guys are coming."

Looking down at her 600-calorie cookie, Jamie pretended that she didn't see the two boys. As they headed her direction, Jamie's heart fell to the floor and rolled over.

Passing too close, the larger boy bumped into her chair. "Sorry, Chubs," he said in a loud voice.

Still staring at her plate, Jamie tried to not let the hurt show in her face. But the boys circled the table. When the second boy bumped her chair, he exclaimed, "Uh-oh, so-o-o sorry!"

Without looking at either boy, Jamie stood up and started for the door.

The boys followed. "Running away? Scared of us?"

Her eyes flashing anger, Jamie faced them. "I'm not scared of you. I can't *stand* you!"

As she headed out the door, she wanted only one thing—a place to hide. A place away from the boys, away from staring eyes, away from her own self.

The minute she reached home that afternoon, Jamie went to the kitchen. *I can't stand those awful boys!* she told herself. Most of all she couldn't stand their mean words.

She looked down at her faded jeans—big across the legs, big across the hips. *No matter how big my clothes are, they don't hide how much I weigh.*

Pulling out her baggy sweat shirt, Jamie sighed. *I want to be the right weight. I want to look good.*

One by one, she opened the cupboard doors, then slammed them shut. After a search, she found the cookie can her mom had hidden. As Jamie dropped into a chair, she gulped down a chocolate chip cookie. Soon she reached for another, then still another.

Finally Jamie put the cover back on the cookies. *I can't stand those boys,* she thought again. *But most of all, I can't stand myself.*

Before she could start eating again, Jamie pushed the can back into the farthest corner of the cupboard. Even so, she knew she'd find them the next time she felt upset.

Why do I do this? she asked herself. *Every time something goes wrong, I gobble every sweet thing I find.*

This time Jamie's upset feelings took the form of a prayer. *Lord, I want to start liking myself. I want to change my old eating habits, but I can't do it by myself. Will you help me?*

Let's Talk . . . or Journal

DAY 1

Sometimes there's a medical reason why people are overweight, and we need to understand that. Other times excess weight comes from poor eating habits and/or lack of exercise. Which do you think is true in Jamie's case? Why do you believe that?

The teasing of the boys deeply wounded and humiliated Jamie. What would you like to tell her instead?

DAY 2

Nearly all of us have something about our bodies that we don't like. We have two choices — to accept the way we are or make a change. Is there something about your body that you need to accept? Something you need to change?

DAY 3

During her tween years a girl often goes through a stage where she needs larger-sized clothes. Then in a short period of time she grows taller and thins out. What happens to a girl's self-image if she doesn't understand this may happen?

DAY 4

Sometimes girls think they need to have the extremely thin shape of a professional model. How can it harm your health if you insist on being too thin? How can eating disorders harm your health and threaten your life?

DAY 5

If we are not eating wisely it's important to understand what triggers us. When people get upset, some people, such as Jamie, eat too much and gobble up comfort food. Others eat too little and lose too much weight. Which is it for you? What triggers you to start eating too much or too little?

DAY 6

The Holy Spirit can give Jamie greater willpower and help her change her eating habits. But even though Jamie asks for God's help, what choices will she need to keep making?

Often we fail at losing weight because we set too hard a goal. Then, if we fail, we feel even less able to lose weight. Instead of thinking, "I want to lose 5 pounds this week," make it realistic. "I want to lose one pound a week for 10 weeks until I'm at the right weight." What would be a realistic goal for you?

If you, like Jamie, need to develop new eating habits, there's a practical way to begin. Who are some friends and role models who will help you feel good about yourself? Ask a person who can help you begin and encourage you to keep on.

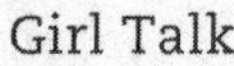

DAY 7

Some things we eat day after day can seem small. But if we are eating too much or too little and need to maintain the right weight we won't be healthy. Think about the different things that can help you succeed in achieving a healthy weight and body. Write down those ideas.

Let's Pray About It

Jesus, you love me so much that I know you want me to take care of myself and value the person I am. I need your self-control to say yes or no about what I take in or don't take in. In your name I ask for all the power of your Holy Spirit to change my unwise eating habits and eat the right foods in the right amounts. In faith I thank you for your help!

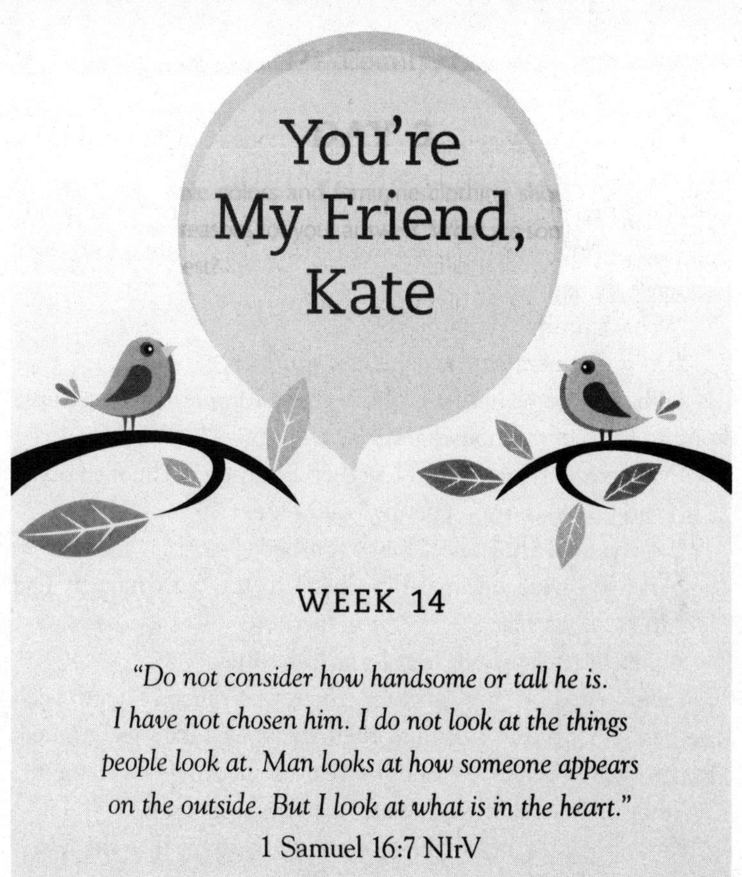

You're My Friend, Kate

WEEK 14

"Do not consider how handsome or tall he is. I have not chosen him. I do not look at the things people look at. Man looks at how someone appears on the outside. But I look at what is in the heart."
1 Samuel 16:7 NIrV

Kate looked down at her skirt. No matter which way she twisted it, she just couldn't make it fit right. Even worse, the material was starting to fade from the many times it had been washed.

Hastily she stuffed her shorts and shoes into her book bag. Up till this year, she had liked gym the best of any class. Now she was starting to hate this moment. It always made her realize the difference between her clothes and those of the other girls.

Across the locker room, her friend Libby stood in front of a mirror. As Kate watched, Libby carefully brushed her long hair until it hung smoothly down her back. But it wasn't Libby's silky auburn hair that made Kate feel out of it. It was her awesome tops and jeans, dangly earrings and flip-flops.

Libby turned, saw Kate watching, and grinned. "Ready to go?"

Kate nodded. Weaving their way through the crowded halls, they reached the great outdoors and started for home. Because they lived only two houses apart, they had known each other for years.

The spring sunshine reminded Kate of a time long ago. Suddenly she laughed.

"What's funny?" Libby asked.

"Do you remember the day I met you?"

Libby's smile lit her face. "How could I forget? I had set up a stand in front of our house, and I was selling—"

"Mud pies!" they shouted together, laughing at the memory.

"I ran home and got a penny," said Kate.

"So you could buy one!" Libby finished.

"And you were smeared from head to toe with mud. It had even dried on your face."

Again Libby laughed. "But I was in business!"

Kate joined in her laughter, then was quiet. They'd been together so long that now and then she took Libby for granted. Though they'd been best friends for years, something was changing.

Libby broke the silence. "Kate, is something wrong?"

Kate shook her head. She didn't want to admit how she felt.

"Are you sure?"

"Yup, I'm sure," Kate said.

"You'd tell me if something was wrong?"

Kate started kicking a stone along the edge of the street. *I'd like to bring back the old days,* she thought. *Sometimes I feel so far away from Libby.* Yet she felt embarrassed to say anything.

"Remember how we always shared secrets?" asked Libby. "Even when I made only one penny—your penny—on mud pies?"

Kate smiled, but the ache didn't leave her heart. *I'm afraid to tell her,* she thought. *Maybe she won't like me anymore.*

But Libby knew her too well. "Spit it out, Kate," she said.

Kate debated with herself, trying to decide what to do. At last she spoke. "You know how my dad got laid off a year ago?"

Libby nodded.

"He still hasn't found work. Mom and Dad don't say much, but they seem different—worried, I guess. Last week I asked if we'll be able to stay here. Dad said, 'We'll keep trying with what your mother makes.'"

"Oh, Kate, I'm so glad! I don't know what I'd do if you moved."

Libby's words gave Kate courage. In spite of the lump in her throat, she went on. "But sometimes I don't feel like your friend anymore. We used to be alike, and now we're different."

"Different?"

When Kate didn't answer, Libby asked, "What do you mean?"

Kate could barely get the words out. "Our clothes," she said.

"Ohhh." Understanding came into Libby's eyes. "And that's why you've been acting strange lately?"

Kate nodded.

"But clothes shouldn't make any difference between us!"

Afraid that Libby would see how she felt, Kate looked off at the house they were passing. "Doesn't it bother you to walk down the hall with me? To have kids see the way I look? My clothes are so *old*."

Kate choked on the words, hardly able to speak. "And you have a whole closet full of wonderful, beautiful tops. The latest style in jeans. Jeweled flip-flops."

When Libby stopped right where she was, Kate had to stop, too. "Is that all that's bothering you?" Libby asked.

Kate blinked, trying to hide her tears. "I don't look like the other kids. There's no money for clothes. There's no money for *anything*!"

For a long moment Libby was silent. When she spoke, she sounded as if she'd been thinking hard. "Kate, what if you had a bunch of nice clothes and I didn't? How would you treat me?"

The question surprised Kate. Her gaze met Libby's. "It wouldn't make any difference."

"What if my house was destroyed in Katrina or some other hurricane?"

"I'd give you whatever you could use."

Libby grinned. "What did you say?"

"I'd give you whatever you could use." Kate stopped, suddenly feeling foolish.

For a moment they walked on without speaking. Then Libby broke the silence. "I've got an idea," she said.

Kate looked at her and waited, afraid to hope.

Let's Talk . . . or Journal

DAY 1

Why does it seem important to dress the way other kids do? Is it important sometimes?

DAY 2

As Libby and Kate talked, both of them discovered something big about clothes. What did Libby need to know how to handle? What did Kate?

DAY 3

Libby showed that she's a true friend by asking Kate what is wrong. What would have happened if Kate hadn't told her? How did Libby help Kate learn something important about self-worth?

DAY 4

What do you think Libby will do?

DAY 5

Are there times when you feel embarrassed because your clothes aren't the same as those worn by other kids? Is it because of the style? Or is it because your clothes no longer fit or look worn-out? What can you do about it?

What if you felt embarrassed about something and a friend *didn't* ask what's bothering you, or try to help? What could *you* do to start talking about what's wrong?

DAY 6

What did Jesus tell us about the clothes that we wear? See Matthew 6:25 – 34 for clues. In what way does Jesus want us to keep looking to him for every need?

DAY 7

In 1 Sam. 16:7 God says, "Man looks at how someone appears on the outside. But I look at what is in the heart." (NIrV) What do you think God is seeing inside your heart?

Let's Pray About It

Help me, Lord, to look my best with what I have. But protect me from thinking I'm worth something only if I have clothes like everyone else. I want to please you with the way I am in my heart. In my day-to-day choices I choose to run close to you.

Like a Porcupine

WEEK 15

When you are angry, do not sin.
Ps. 4:4 NIrV

Do not let the sun go down while you are still angry.
Ephesians 4:26 NIrV

Danielle slammed the door of her locker. "What do you mean, I'll get a bad grade?"

Tina took a step backward. "Well, don't get mad at *me*. I'm just telling you what Mrs. Hernandez said. For each day your paper's late, it gets marked down."

"Aw, forget it!" answered Danielle. "I don't wanna hear about it."

"Hey, c'mon—"

"I said, forget it! You sound just like my mom."

Tina tried again. "Listen! We're friends, remember? I was just trying to help. What's *really* bothering you?"

Unable to speak, Danielle stared at her. *Well, starting with home room. Two boys teased me about my hair. Then at lunch I stood up and had a spot on my jeans. Sure, it was ketchup, but the same dumb boys saw me—*

Their words hurt so much that Danielle would never forget them. She couldn't even tell Tina.

Instead, Danielle started down the hall with Tina calling after her. Halfway to the outside door, Danielle remembered what else had happened.

An F on a theme I really cared about. Finding a big, red zit on the end of my nose right after talking to a boy I like.

As Danielle reached the outside door, she thought about the hurt in Tina's eyes. Turning, Danielle looked back, but Tina had started in the other direction. Instead of going after her, Danielle shrugged and headed out the door.

Fifteen minutes later she dropped her book bag on the kitchen floor. Mom was peeling potatoes and tried to give her a hug. But Danielle brushed her mother aside.

When she asked, "Did you have a nice day?" Danielle answered, "Fine, fine."

As soon as she finished her cookies and milk, Danielle headed upstairs to her room. Half an hour later, Mom knocked on her door.

"What do you want?" Danielle answered.

"May I come in?" Mom asked through the door.

"Guess so," Danielle called back. "It's your house."

Slowly the door opened, and Mom walked in. It was hard finding a place to sit down, but she managed. Picking up a pile of clothes, she cleared off a chair.

For a long moment, Mom was silent. Finally she asked, "How was your day?"

"What do you think?" Danielle sprawled on the bed.

Mom tried again. "Do you want to tell me what happened?"

No, I don't want to tell you. But for Danielle it was like opening a faucet. All the awful things that had happened poured out. Starting from the moment she ran for the bus until she got back home, Danielle told everything that had gone wrong.

"That's pretty awful," Mom said once. And another time she said, "I don't know what you mean. Will you explain again?"

At last Danielle finished by saying, "Even my best friend doesn't understand. Even Tina—"

Afraid the tears would come, Danielle broke off. But in that moment Danielle understood something more. Tina *would* have understood, and she, Danielle, hadn't given her the chance.

Now Mom's voice was gentle. "Danielle, how do you feel on the inside?"

"On the inside? Like crud."

Danielle thought for a moment. "I feel mad," she said. "Stupid. Burned. Hurt. Embarrassed. Like I'm not worth anything. I want to hit back, especially at those two dumb boys. What can I do to get even?"

"You feel like a porcupine?" Mom asked.

Danielle almost smiled. She knew what Mom meant. Last summer they'd seen a porcupine cross a country road. Its quills stuck out in all directions. The end of those quills had barbs that would stay in whatever flesh they touched. Whoever was on the receiving end of a porcupine's quills would feel pain.

Danielle nodded. "Like a porcupine."

"Sometimes things get blown up and aren't as bad as we think. But the things you're telling me about are real. I don't blame you for being upset. For feeling embarrassed. Ketchup on a chair? Do you think the boys put it there?"

Danielle thought about it. "Maybe." She hadn't considered that. "Could be."

She still wanted to get even—to throw quills at anyone who came her way. Those two dumb boys, for instance.

"I'm glad you told me what happened," Mom said. "The feelings you have aren't right or wrong. It's what you do about those feelings that can be right or wrong. You make the choice whether you're going to let your feelings control you."

For the first time Mom smiled. "Do you want to stay like a porcupine? Or do you want to learn more about how to handle your feelings?

As Danielle thought about it, Mom waited. Finally, Danielle

spoke in a low voice. "I woke up grumpy this morning. I was mad at you last night, and I felt the same way when I woke up."

"Okay. Let's talk about the things that made you angry last night."

"Sure!" Danielle jumped at the chance. Sitting up, she faced Mom. "Sometimes you expect too much of me. You think I can do more than I can. Other times you treat me like a little kid."

As Danielle continued, Mom listened without speaking. Once she flinched, and a hurt look entered her eyes. In a moment it disappeared.

When at last Danielle finished, Mom said, "Tonight after supper, let's make a list. We'll decide what we can expect of you at this age. Okay?" Mom paused. "And how do I make you feel like you're still a little kid?"

Suddenly Danielle looked at her and laughed. For the first time she realized how funny it was. Funny sad.

But now Mom looked bewildered. "What did I say?"

"Mom, it's not all you, is it? With some things I've been *acting* like a little kid, haven't I? Times when I want my own way?"

Mom grinned, then looked like she was swallowing her words.

"Go on," Danielle said softly.

Instead, Mom changed the subject. "Danielle, something else is happening. Things that never used to upset you bother you now. Sometimes you feel moody and grumpy when awful things like today *didn't* happen. Other times you're at the top of a mountain. Everything in the whole world seems wonderful."

Danielle nodded. "You're right."

"Your body is changing. The way you think and feel about things is changing. Some of the things you used to like doing seem like kid stuff now. Do you know what I mean when I say that your emotions swing back and forth?"

Danielle nodded. "My moods go up and down."

"That's something that happens to both boys and girls your age. As a girl, you may notice the feeling more just before your period."

That's true, Danielle thought. That's how she felt all day. That's why she thought the ketchup was really—

Danielle felt relieved. "Do you have up-and-down days, too?"

"All of us do," Mom told her. "Sometimes we know what causes our feelings to swing one way or another. A sunny day or bright colors make most of us feel better. And there are lots of reasons for feeling upset. Someone may say something that hurt you or you're too tired, or—"

"Sometimes I don't know why I feel this way."

"Sometimes you *won't* know why," Mom answered. "That's okay. But grumpy moods are something all of us need to fight."

Danielle remembered the hurt look in Tina's eyes. *Yeah, Mom, you're right. I wonder how Tina feels about the way I treated her?*

"Do you think you'd feel better about yourself if you learned some ways to handle your moods?" Mom asked.

When Danielle didn't answer, Mom stood up. "Why don't you think about it for a while?"

As Mom headed for the door, Danielle wanted to reach out for a hug, the way she used to. Instead she said, "I didn't think you'd understand."

Mom came back. "I do, Danielle. Really, I do." Leaning down, Mom gave her a hug, and Danielle returned it. For a long time she lay on her bed thinking.

The next day Danielle was still thinking about what Mom had said. But when Danielle saw Tina again, Tina didn't look happy to see her.

In that moment Danielle felt ashamed. *She's my friend. But she doesn't know how I'll treat her—if I'll be nice or grumpy and mean.*

Seeing herself in that way didn't make Danielle feel good. Suddenly there was something she knew. *Whether something is real or blown up, I want to stop being a porcupine.*

Now, what should I do about Tina?

Let's Talk . . . or Journal

DAY 1

What do you think Danielle did about the way she treated Tina the day before? What does it mean to feel and act like a porcupine? Give examples from Danielle's life and your own.

DAY 2

Why was it important for Danielle to talk about how she felt? Are feelings right or wrong?

What *is* right or wrong? What do you think Danielle would have done if her mother had said, "You shouldn't feel that way"?

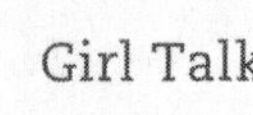

DAY 3

What does it mean to say, "Grumpy moods are something we all have to fight"? Why or why not is that true?

DAY 4

When Danielle comes home from school in an angry mood, she can warn her family by saying, "I feel ..." and finish the sentence with a feeling word like mad, upset, or cranky. Pretend you're Danielle. What would you say?

DAY 5

In what ways can Danielle learn to handle her down moods? You can help her by finishing these sentences:

If she's swamped with homework, she can say, "I feel ..."

If she's angry, she can say, "I feel ..."

If she's hurt, she can say, "I feel ..."

If she thinks kids are picking on her more than she can handle, she can say, "I feel ..."

To handle moods it also helps to do other things. Help Danielle by finishing these sentences too:

If Danielle is cranky because she's tired, she can ...

If she wants to be alone for a while, she can ...

If she needs to forgive someone, she can ...

Instead of continuing to think about how bad she feels, she can ...

If she needs exercise, she can ...

She can do what I do, which is ...

DAY 6

Sometimes people say, "Don't go out the door when you're angry." The Bible puts it this way: "Do not let the sun go down while you are still angry, and do not give the devil a foothold." What does it mean to say, "Do not give the devil a foothold?" Why is it a good idea to not go out the door when you're angry? Or to not let the sun go down without working things out? Give reasons for your answers and examples from your own life.

Whenever you're hurt and upset, Jesus stands with his arms open to you, ready to offer a big hug. Is the way you see yourself based on your own feelings or on God's love? How can you know the difference?

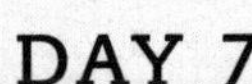

DAY 7

Over 2,000 years ago, when Jesus walked here on earth, he left some really big footprints. No other person has ever been like him because he truly was God living here on earth among us. If you ask him, Jesus will walk right alongside you, helping you again and again.

It will encourage you to notice the way people acted before and after Pentecost. Peter is a good example. Compare Mark 14:66 – 72 with Acts 2:14 – 16 and Acts 4:18 – 20.

If you are a Christian, ask Jesus to give you all the power of his Holy Spirit to help you handle your moods. Then work with him by doing your part.

Let's Pray About It

Jesus, you know my body is changing. You know how often I have up-and-down moods and need your help. Fill me with all the power of your Holy Spirit to help me live as you want me to live. Help me handle my moods in a strong way. Help me to know your love in the midst of whatever happens. And help me to live your love — to reflect your love and caring heart.

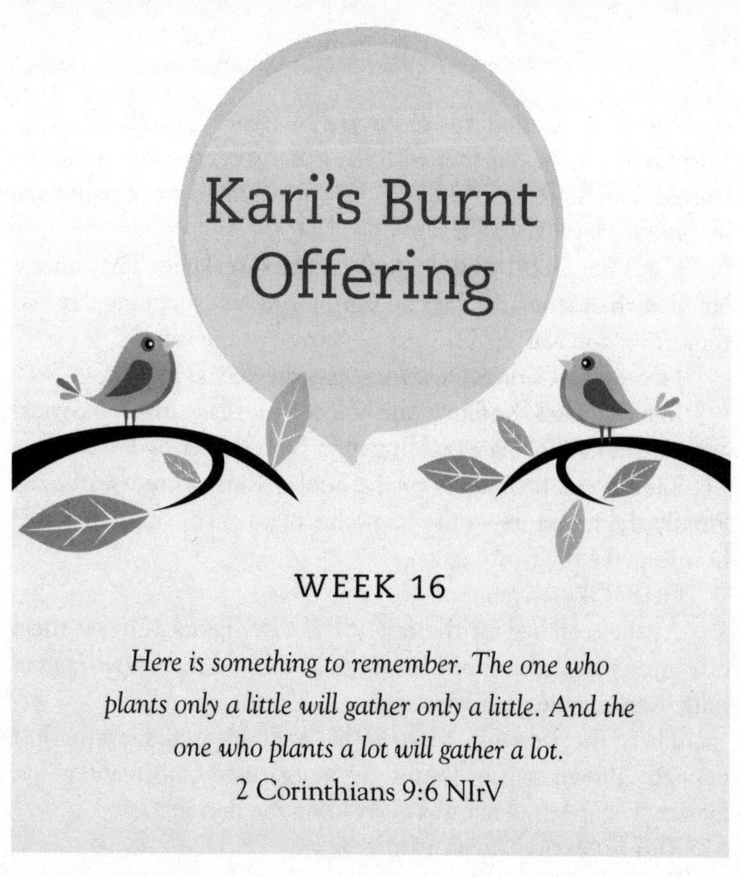

Kari's Burnt Offering

WEEK 16

Here is something to remember. The one who plants only a little will gather only a little. And the one who plants a lot will gather a lot.

2 Corinthians 9:6 NIrV

When the phone call came that winter afternoon, Kari didn't know what to do.

"Hey, Kari," Mom said. "Can you please help me out?"

"How's Grandpa?" Kari quickly asked. Early that afternoon he had fallen, and Mom had gone to help.

"It's a bad sprain and not a break," Mom told her. "But I'm running out of time. Can you bake the cake I'm supposed to bring tonight? Dad will be home in time to drive you there, but I'll need to go straight to the meeting."

"Sure, Mom. I'll be glad to do it."

"Oh, thanks, Kari." Relief filled her mother's voice.

"No problem. Give Grandpa a hug from me. Tell him I hope he feels better soon."

As Kari got off the phone, she thought about the program that evening. The meeting was sponsored by their homeschool group. Kari loved getting together with the other students. But when she started searching for ingredients Kari felt a moment of panic. *Do we have the ingredients I need?*

Kari's boy cousins had visited over the weekend. They always ate as if their stomachs had no bottom. Mom's shopping day was tomorrow, and Kari had no way of getting to the store.

I'll try for a German chocolate cake, she decided.

In a cupboard she found one box of white cake mix. One package of instant chocolate pudding mix. But no frosting mix.

Taking out her mom's recipe books, Kari started searching. Finally she found it—a German chocolate cake recipe that told how to make the frosting.

Good. Okay so far.

As she searched for the rest of the ingredients, Kari set them one by one on the counter. Two eggs. She found three. Two cups of milk. Kari measured. It was close.

Then the frosting. More milk. Kari measured again. Just enough. Brown sugar. Butter or margarine. Chocolate chips. Exactly ½ cup left. That was everything she needed.

Kari felt excited. *I can do it!*

Soon she had the ingredients for the cake blended together, poured into the pan, and in the oven. With the timer set she took out a kettle and started the frosting. As she melted margarine and added brown sugar, she felt good about what she was doing. Mom really needed her help.

Besides, German chocolate cake was Kari's favorite. Even now she imagined her friends gathering around, telling her how great her cake looked and tasted. *I want it to be just perfect!*

But when the timer dinged and Kari opened the oven to take out the cake, she gasped. "Oh, no!"

On one end, the cake was high, nearly reaching the top of the pan. On the other end the cake was low, less than an inch high. At one spot in the middle, the cake rose in a slight mound. Otherwise it was all at a slant.

Kari groaned. *There's my perfect cake, all right. How did I manage to do that?*

Carefully she set the cake down to cool, then opened the oven again. Before her eyes was the rack on which the cake had baked. Only now did Kari remember wiping it off three nights before and putting it back in the oven. She groaned. *I didn't push it in right!* On one side the rack was higher than on the other.

More than that, she should have put the rack in the middle of the oven, instead of its lowest position.

"What on earth will I do?" Kari felt so upset that she spoke aloud.

Frantically she looked through the cupboards again, hoping that somehow there was a cake mix she had missed. Partway through her search, the frosting boiled up and over. Grabbing the kettle, she turned down the heat and went back to her search.

Not one more cake mix. Not one more pudding mix. Maybe she could substitute water for milk, but only one egg.

Swallowing hard, Kari blinked away tears. *So. I can't make another cake.* Grabbing a Kleenex, she blew her nose.

Dad! But he wouldn't be able to leave work until just before the meeting.

Pete and Jo! But their closest neighbors were gone for January and February, basking in the Florida sun. Their other neighbors were too far away. *If I ride my bike—it's cold, but—*

Ice, thought Kari. *Too dangerous. I'd spin out for sure.*

Again Kari blinked away tears. When the frosting finished cooking, she took it from the heat and added the chocolate chips. There was no choice but to use it. Maybe she could heap it up at the low end.

Kari glanced at the clock. No more time to let the cake cool. Spooning out the frosting, she started at the high end of the cake. Like a sled race, the frosting started down hill.

Kari sighed. What a disaster! Standing back, she looked at the cake, then started again. When she finished frosting it, she had done all she could to make the low end look high. But there was still close to an inch difference between the two ends of the cake.

I can keep it at home and pretend I forgot to bring it, Kari told herself. *Or I can sneak it into the kitchen at church. I'll cover it with tinfoil and not put my name on the pan. I'll set it on that counter next to the back door. Maybe no one will see it there. Maybe they won't need to use it.*

But that night when Kari and her family reached the church where the homeschoolers met, none of those things worked.

Mom's friend Sally met Kari at the door of the kitchen. "Oh, Kari, thanks for stepping in!" she exclaimed. "What would we do without you?"

"My cake is really awful— " Kari started to say. But she didn't even get the words out.

"Just set it on the table with the other cakes," Sally told her. "I'll cut it in a minute. We're almost ready to eat."

Kari gulped. As her friends gathered around, she almost panicked. *I have never been so embarrassed in my whole life! They'll think I can't bake a simple cake!*

She was right. When Kari took off the cover, Sally's son, Isaac, looked over her shoulder.

"That's a funny-looking cake," he said. But then he pointed. "If I take from that end, I'll get the biggest piece!"

Already Sally was back with a knife and spatula. Before she began cutting, Kari decided what to do. *I can put myself down and feel bruised all over. Or I can make a joke of it.*

"Just a minute," Kari told Sally. "Before you start cutting, I need to explain how to make this cake."

Kari's friends gathered around, some standing across the table and others looking over her shoulder. Kari pointed to the high end of the cake. "You set the oven rack at an angle," she began.

Looking up, she caught a hint of laughter in the eyes of her friend Jennie. "Then you bake the cake without opening the door to look at it." The girl next to Jennie grinned.

"After it's well set so you can't change anything, you open the oven door and look in."

A second girl giggled. Sally's lips twitched, and a sparkle lit her eyes.

"Let the frosting boil over," Kari went on. "Then heap what's left at the top of the hill and let it slide down."

When Isaac and Jennie started laughing, Kari's other friends joined in. But Kari felt warmed by their laughter. *They're laughing with me, not at me*, she thought, and she, too, began to laugh.

"It's going to be the best cake I've ever eaten," Sally said. "You help serve it, okay?"

As people came through the line, they had their choice of cakes, but every one of Kari's close friends took a piece from her. "I have to try this," said more than one.

The cake was half gone when Kari made another discovery. Under the raised place in the middle lay a dark brown circle of burnt cake.

Kari gulped and remembered the oven rack set too close to the gas flame. But quick as a wink she decided what to do. Pushing in the spatula, she cut the piece off halfway up, leaving the burnt part in the pan. For each person receiving a piece, she offered her biggest smile.

As Kari finished dishing up her hilly burnt offering, Sally brought out still another cake. That one, of course, looked absolutely perfect. For a moment Kari had one twinge of regret, one mountain-high wish that she could have done better. Then she pushed the thought aside.

I did the best I could, she told herself. *That's more important than being perfect.*

Kari's friends seemed to think so, too.

Let's Talk ... or Journal

DAY 1

When Kari wanted to make a cake she felt confident that she could do it well. Yet in spite of her best effort, the cake didn't turn out the way she wanted. What is the difference between doing the best we can and doing something perfectly? Give examples from your own life.

DAY 2

When we put ourselves down through what we say, it's as though we invite others to put us down. Kari looked at her strange cake and made some important choices. How did she help Isaac and the others laugh with her, not against her?

DAY 3

Every one of us has made a mistake or goofed up in some way, in spite of our best intentions. Describe a big mistake you've made. How did you deal with it?

DAY 4

Kari was resourceful. What does it mean to be resourceful? How did Kari turn failure into success?

DAY 5

Jesus told us, "The one who plants only a little will gather only a little. And the one who plants a lot will gather a lot" (2 Corinthians 9:6 NIrV). George Washington Carver was a strong Christian who was born into slavery and worked hard to get an education. Long before African Americans achieved the level of success they can achieve today, he won international fame for his agricultural research and developing over 300 ways to use the peanut. Those products created markets that helped people earn a living by selling more peanuts.

Today the George Washington Carver National Monument near Joplin, Missouri honors his life. And here's something that is very exciting for anyone who wants to be creative. Whenever George Washington Carver went into his laboratory he asked God for ideas. He knew that the Lord would show him the method to use. How did that belief help this very successful researcher plant many seeds?

From what you have just read about George Washington Carver, what do you think was his motivation for working so hard?

DAY 6

George Washington Carver said, "Ninety-nine percent of the failures come from people who have the habit of making excuses." Why do excuses bring failure? Explain. Why do you think Carver's willingness to ask God for guidance helped him succeed?

DAY 7

If you ask for and accept God's guidance in whatever you do, how can that help you be more creative? How can it improve your ability to do something well? George Washington Carver continually asked God for help. In what ways would you like to continually ask Jesus for his help?

Let's Pray About It

Lord Jesus, I want to do the best I can with the gifts and abilities you have given me. But I also want the ability to laugh at myself and get up and go on. Help me to plant good seed—to give good things into the lives of others. Help me to turn my failures into success. When I fail at something I need to know, help me to get up, try again, and learn how to do something better. Because you're my forever Friend, I know you'll help me do that.

Country Cousin

WEEK 17

"Your beauty comes from inside you. It is the beauty of a gentle and quiet spirit. Beauty like that doesn't fade away. God places great value on it."
1 Peter 3:4 NIrV

That summer morning Mitzi came into the city on a train. Living on a Midwestern farm, she hadn't seen her cousin Erica for over two years. Now they would have a whole week of fun together.

Because Mitzi's school year ended earlier, Erica's mom picked her up and drove Mitzi to their house. Soon Erica came in from her last day of school before summer vacation.

As soon as they hugged their hellos, Mitzi stood back. "Look at you! You're all grown up!"

When Erica smiled, Mitzi knew that her words pleased her cousin. But when Erica didn't say a word about how she looked, Mitzi started wondering why.

The first thing she noticed was how much her cousin had changed since they'd seen each other. At home Mitzi was used to being with groups of kids from school. Or her family got together with other families that had kids her age.

And now? Mitzi forgot all that. Taking one look at Erica, she thought, *Wow! Does she ever look cute!* Mitzi especially liked her cousin's cut-offs.

But then Mitzi took a second look. *They're really short. Doesn't her school have a dress code? Or has Erica somehow gotten around it?*

As though still hearing the rules in her school, the words replayed in Mitzi's mind. *Stand up. Put your arms down at your sides. Wear cut-offs the length of your longest finger.*

The next thing Mitzi noticed was Erica's top. Mitzi could almost hear one of her teachers saying, "Hey, people, everything needs to be covered. Two-inch wide straps. No bare midriffs."

Watching Erica, Mitzi felt uneasy, but quickly pushed her thoughts aside.

Their first afternoon together got off to a great start. Erica and her school friends had planned a beginning-of-summer-vacation party for that evening. When Erica's friends dropped over to talk about it, some were nice, but Mitzi didn't feel comfortable with others.

A boy named Ross was different. Fun, and like a brother. He reminded Mitzi of some of the kids she liked at home. As he left, Ross asked, "See you tonight, Mitzi?" She could hardly wait.

The minute all the kids were gone, Mitzi followed her cousin upstairs to figure out what to wear.

Mitzi's half-open suitcase lay on the floor of Erica's bedroom. As Mitzi started taking out clothes, Erica stopped her. "Wait a minute," she said.

Erica pulled open a door. Mitzi had never seen a closet so full of clothes. Jeans, tops, and cutoffs were packed in as tight as they could go. On the floor beneath the clothes lay a jumble of shoes and flip-flops.

"We're almost the same size," Erica said. "Maybe I've got something you can wear."

For a moment Mitzi felt uneasy. Then she pushed her feelings aside. *I'm in the big city now. I need to look like a city girl. If I do, Ross might like me.*

Erica started at one end of her closet, pulling out jeans. One by one Mitzi tried them on. She liked one pair of jeans especially.

Erica walked around her. "Nope. They're too loose on your hips."

"That's how I always wear 'em." Mitzi turned this way and that in front of the mirror. "They feel good that way. Not too loose. Not skin tight. Just right."

But Erica kept looking and soon came up with another pair. "Try these. They'll fit better."

Mitzi pulled them on. The seat and legs were so tight she felt as if she couldn't breathe.

Erica inspected her again. "They're perfect. That's how they're supposed to fit."

"Perfect?" Mitzi hoped she could still walk.

"Now wear this top," Erica said. "It'll go great with those jeans."

Mitzi pulled on a top she knew instantly would be too small, revealing more than she cared to show. Yet she didn't dare tell Erica how uncomfortable she felt. *I'll wear my own blouse over it*, she told herself. *I'll still look like a city girl.*

A smile of satisfaction on her face, Erica walked around Mitzi and the clothes she had loaned her. "Now you look like one of us."

"Like one of *you*." Mitzi's answer spilled out. *Now where did that come from?*

Erica grinned, as though thinking Mitzi's words were a compliment. "Like *two* of me."

When Mitzi saw herself in the mirror, she again felt uneasy. *I'm glad Mom and Dad won't see me. They'd be upset. What if a seam splits when I sit down?*

Aloud she asked, "You're sure these clothes aren't too small?"

When Erica laughed, as though that was the funniest thing she'd ever heard, Mitzi tried to ignore how she felt. *Maybe all the girls dress like Erica.*

No, they don't, said a still small voice.

Mitzi pushed the thought aside.

Remember the other girls this afternoon? Mitzi nodded, as though that inner voice had spoken aloud. *Remember how they dressed?*

Mitzi thought about it. *They* do *have a dress code here. But there's something more I need to understand.*

In that moment Mitzi knew how to describe it. It was like the other girls respected their bodies.

The idea surprised her. *What does it mean for a girl to respect her body?* Mitzi had never thought about it before. But she wasn't able to think long.

Soon it was time to leave, and she and Erica set off down the street. The party was only a few blocks away at Anna's house.

As Mitzi and Erica waited to cross the street, a car wheeled around the corner. Two guys sat in the front. The driver honked.

"You're standing out too far," Mitzi said.

Erica shook her head. "He liked the way we look."

"Liked the way we look?" Mitzi felt scared right down in the pit of her stomach. *So that's why she didn't want me wearing my own jeans.*

Suddenly all the beautiful clothes in Erica's closet seemed totally worthless. A bunch of junk that made her cousin look the wrong way.

Sure, I want to look nice, Mitzi thought. *I want to look like the other kids. But—*

Once again the thought came. *What does it mean for a girl to respect her body?*

As Mitzi looked down at her poured-into jeans and the top that revealed more than she cared to show, she no longer liked herself. *I'm edging too far out—dressing to call attention to my body. How can I look like the person I am?*

When Mitzi breathed deep, the button at her waist popped off. She felt relieved. "I can't go to the party this way."

"Oh, sure you can," Erica told her. "No one will notice. We'll ask Anna's mom for a pin when we get there."

As she looked into her cousin's eyes, Mitzi knew it would never work to explain. "Why don't you go to the party?" she said. "I'll run back and take care of it."

"Well— "

"I know where Anna's house is," Mitzi said quickly. "I was

there last time I visited you. Remember? Her parents had all of us over. Go on! I'll catch up."

Before Erica could say another word, Mitzi jogged off.

As soon as she reached her cousin's house, Mitzi ran up the stairs. In the bedroom she pulled her best jeans and favorite top from her suitcase and changed into them.

It's not whether I live in the country or the city, Mitzi told herself. *It's the kind of person I want to be.*

For a moment she stood in front of the full-length mirror. *I look nice*, she thought, feeling surprised. *I look really nice!*

When Mitzi reached the party, Ross had been looking for her. Something in his grin gave him away.

He likes me the way I am. Mitzi smiled. *And I like myself, too!*

Let's Talk . . . or Journal

DAY 1

Why do kids want to wear clothes that look the same as what other kids wear?

DAY 2

What did Erica want to say through the way she dressed? What did Mitzi want to say? What did Mitzi mean when she decided, "It's not whether I live in the country or the city. It's the kind of person I want to be"? What kind of person do you want to be?

DAY 3

How can attractive colors and feminine clothing show that you enjoy being a girl? Give reasons for your answers. What are some of the colors in which you look best?

DAY 4

What is your motive for how you dress? Explain what kind of clothing gives you self-respect. What is the difference between dressing to look nice and dressing to call attention to your body? Explain.

DAY 5

If you make choices like Erica, how will your choices affect your life and the kind of friends you have? If you make choices like Mitzi, how will your choices affect your life and the kind of friends you have?

DAY 6

Think again about the verse at the beginning of this week's story: "Your beauty comes from inside you. It is the beauty of a gentle and quiet spirit. Beauty like that doesn't fade away. God places great value on it." Why do you think God values the kind of beauty that comes from inside of us? Why does that kind of beauty keep growing instead of fading away? Do you think Mitzi understands what it means to dress in a way that she looks nice and also honors God? Give reasons for your answer.

DAY 7

When Jesus walked on earth, he made clear footprints. We know what he believed and how he wanted to live. Are there ways in which you want to make clear footprints? In what ways do you want to show others what you believe?

Let's Pray About It

Jesus, I don't want to feel out of it with kids because of the way I dress. But I don't want to be an embarrassment to you, either. Help me to dress in an attractive way but also in a way that honors you. Thank you that when I respect who you are I can also respect myself.

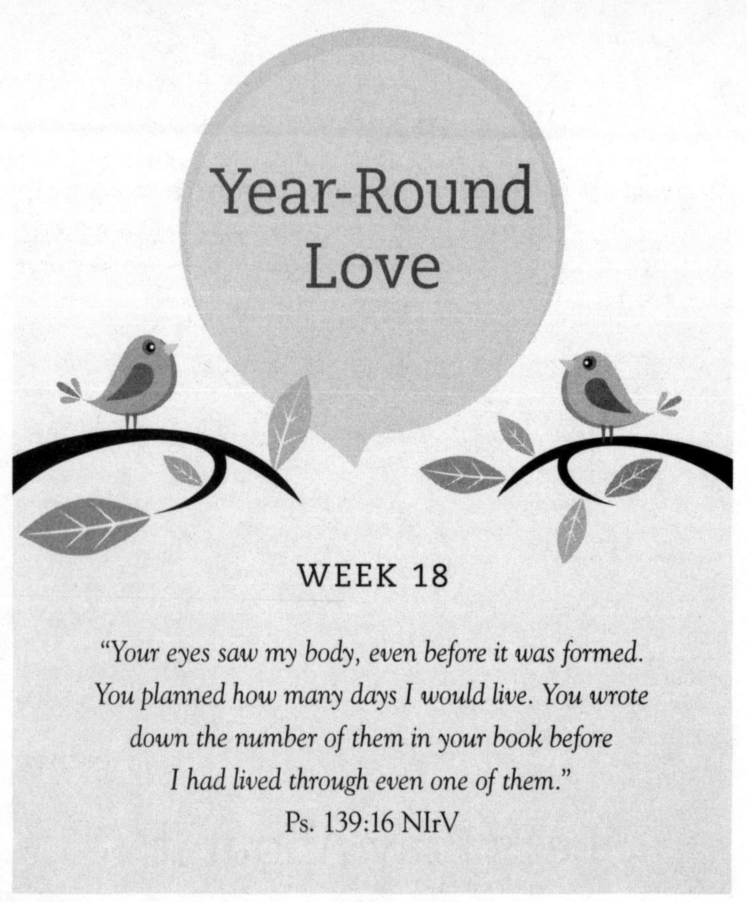

Year-Round Love

WEEK 18

"Your eyes saw my body, even before it was formed. You planned how many days I would live. You wrote down the number of them in your book before I had lived through even one of them."

Ps. 139:16 NIrV

As the kids at school talked, Joanna wanted to put her hands over her ears. She wished she could shut out the sound of their words. Their voices sounded like hammers pounding on steel.

"Your mom dropped you on a doorstep," said one of the girls.

"She didn't want you," added another.

The minute Joanna could get away, she took off for home. By the time she was out of sight from the kids, she could no longer hold back her tears. As they streamed down her cheeks, Joanna broke into a run. When she reached the front door, she was panting.

Joanna stopped long enough to take a deep breath, then quietly slipped inside. *Maybe I can get to my bedroom without anyone seeing me.*

But the little Christmas bells on the door gave her away. As she tiptoed toward the steps, Mom came into the hall.

"Joanna! What's going on?"

Joanna kept moving, but as she passed under the light, Mom stopped her. "What's the matter?" she asked gently.

Joanna wondered if her cheeks were streaked from crying. "Nothing," she said.

"You can tell me, you know," Mom answered.

"I said *nothing*!" snapped Joanna, the hurt inside her changing to anger. "I mean *nothing*!"

But Mom put an arm around her shoulder. "Dad's home, and we've been putting up the tree. Come and see."

Knowing there was no escape, Joanna walked slowly into the family room. The tree was beautiful and the tallest she could remember. Part way up a step ladder, Dad was putting a star at the top of the tree. When he saw Joanna, he climbed down to give her a hug.

"Have a hard day?" he asked.

Joanna shrugged. She didn't want to say what was wrong. But as Dad gave her another hug, the words tumbled out.

"The kids at school said I was adopted."

Joanna saw the look that passed between Mom and Dad, but it was Dad who spoke first.

"You know that. We've talked about it lots of times. Why is it bothering you now?"

"One of the kids said my mother dropped me on a doorstep—"

Joanna's shoulders began to shake. "She said my own mother didn't want me! I wasn't worth anything, not even to her. I'm just—just—"

Joanna broke off and plopped into Dad's big chair. "I am totally nothing!" she wailed.

Dad sat down on the floor, cross-legged, in front of her. As Mom pulled up a chair beside her, Joanna's sobs increased. She needed to know someone loved her. But she didn't know how to say it or how to ask all the things she wanted to know.

As she blew her nose, Dad spoke. "Joanna, do you remember what we've told you about your birth mother?"

Joanna nodded, and Dad went on. "She was very young when

she became pregnant, but she wanted to give you life. She wanted you to be born. That's how much she cared about you."

Tears welled up in Joanna's eyes. As she tried to brush them away they came again.

Leaning forward, Mom took up the story. "Your birth mother didn't have a daddy for you, and she knew how important that is. She wanted you to have a father. Just think—what would you or I do without your daddy?"

As though seeing a new person, Joanna studied her dad's face. His brown-black hair. The kind expression in his brown eyes. The grin that always came just before he laughed. And the many ways he took care of her—

"You always watch out for me, don't you?" It wasn't a question. It was something Joanna knew. "What I eat, what I wear. This house." Joanna looked around, then up to the star her father had placed at the top of the Christmas tree.

"You care about what I learn. What I know about Jesus. You care about my friends. And you care about *me*."

Dad nodded. He needed to clear his voice before he could speak. "Yes, I care about you. I care about everything that happens to you. That's what your birth mom wanted you to have. A daddy. Before you were born, she went to a group of loving people—people who know moms and dads who want to adopt a baby. Your birth mother loved you so much that she made plans for you to have a family."

Joanna drew a deep breath. "That's really true?"

"Really true," echoed Dad. "And that's how we became your adoptive parents. Your mother and I wanted you very much. We chose to have you."

"But you didn't know me," answered Joanna. "I was just a baby. You didn't know what I'd be like."

"We had prayed about you," Dad answered. "We believed that God wanted you to an important part of our family."

Dad grinned. "And we got the best part of the deal!"

Joanna looked into Dad's eyes. Again she searched his face. Something stirred inside her, a deep-down knowing that Dad really meant what he said. As she thought about it, she let the warmth of being loved sink in.

In the next moment Mom echoed that feeling. "Joanna, Dad and I love you very much. I think you're forgetting why we gave you your name. Remember what it means?"

"God is gracious," answered Joanna.

"That means God is kind," Mom said. "You're our special gift from him. Your birth mother gave you the gift of life. It's our job to offer you another gift—to be your adoptive parents. To love you all year round. Every day of the year. Every moment of the day and night. It's our privilege and our desire to do our job well—to help you grow up to know and love the Lord."

Now Mom had tears in her eyes. As they spilled over onto her cheeks, Joanna crawled out of Dad's chair. This time it was Joanna who gave the hugs.

Let's Talk ... or Journal

DAY 1

When Joanna thought her birth mother didn't want her, how did she feel about herself?

DAY 2

What would you like to tell Joanna about the mean things the kids told her?

DAY 3

In what ways did Joanna's birth mother show her love and concern for Joanna? In what ways did Joanna's adoptive parents show their love for her?

DAY 4

Every one of us needs to know that we're loved just the way we are. Do you ever wonder if you're loved? What questions do you have?

DAY 5

It's a big gift to find out how you came into a family, whether by birth, adoption, or marriage. It's fun to hear those stories over and over. What would you like to ask your mom or dad about when you were born?

DAY 6

Were you adopted, either as a baby or when you were older? What are the good things that have happened because you were adopted?

DAY 7

There's someone who always loves you exactly the way you are. Who is that person? How do you know he loves you as a person? Where in the Bible can you find proof? For starters, check out the verse at the beginning of this week. Then take your Bible and read Psalm 139:13–18. No matter what your birth situation was, God the Father saw you before you were born. He is the one who formed and created you. He protected you when you were conceived. If you don't know how much he loves and cares about you, ask him to make his love real to you.

Let's Pray About It

Jesus, I choose to look to you in everything that happens to me. Help me know deep down inside how much you love me. Thank you that even in the moment I was conceived, your Father was my Father and saw and cared about me. Thank you that I'm a valuable person in your sight and in his.

How's My Mom?

WEEK 19

The person who rests in the shadow of the Most High God will be kept safe by the Mighty One. I will say about the Lord, "He is my place of safety. He is like a fort to me. He is my God. I trust in him."
Psalm 91:1 – 2 NIrV

They stood at the church door, ready to leave. Cheri looked at her mom, as if for the first time.

She's really pretty! Cheri thought. Mom's dark brown eyes sparkled, and her lips curved in a smile.

As Mom shook hands with Pastor Evenson, he asked, "How are you doing?"

Mom smiled again. "Fine, just fine," she said.

Yet as Mom and Cheri and two-year-old Rachel walked the short distance home, Cheri noticed the shadow in Mom's eyes. Since Dad stopped living with them, Cheri had seen that shadow of unhappiness often. She dreaded what it meant and hoped she was wrong.

As they ate lunch, Mom said, "Let's go for a bike ride." Soon they were off, Cheri on her own bike and little Rachel in the bicycle seat behind Mom. The September day was perfect, and Mom seemed okay.

Once, she stopped to point out the ducks on a pond. Another time she pulled up the hood on Rachel's sweat shirt to protect her from the wind. Mom had even brought treats along. After a while they sat down by a lake to eat them.

But when they got home that evening, Mom started drinking again.

Did I say something that upset her? Cheri wondered. As her mom downed one glass after another, Cheri blamed herself. *I thought I poured it all out.*

Cheri pretended that she didn't see what was happening. Yet as she watched TV, she kept count of the glasses, and her uneasiness grew. Sometimes when Mom drank, she just got sad and talked strange. Other times she acted mean.

Which way is Mom going to act this time? Cheri wondered, feeling scared.

Soon she found out. In her funny toddler way, Rachel went over to Mom and held up her bottle. Mom pushed the bottle aside.

Rachel tried again.

"Don't bother me!" snapped Mom, shoving the little girl away.

Rachel yowled. Cheri jumped up and pulled her into the kitchen. After filling her bottle, she took Rachel to the bedroom, changed her clothes, and put her to bed.

Feeling as though a giant hand twisted her insides, Cheri crept into her own bed. For a long time, she lay there, afraid to fall asleep. She thought about the last time Mom got like this.

Though the night wasn't cold, Cheri started to shiver, remembering. *Mom is so nice when she's sober—so unhappy when she's drinking.*

Now Cheri wondered as she had a hundred times, *What did I do wrong? Where are you, God? I'm so scared.*

Cheri thought about Sunday school that morning and the Bible verse her class had learned. She remembered how Jesus said, "Do not let your hearts be troubled. Trust in God; trust also in me."

Just thinking about the words, Cheri started to cry. Soon she pulled her blankets over her head. Afraid Mom would hear her sobs, Cheri buried her face in the pillow. "'Do not let your heart be troubled,'" she kept repeating to herself. "I believe in you, God. I believe in you, Jesus."

After a long time, Cheri stopped sobbing, but her heart still cried out, *What should I do, Jesus? What should I do?*

As she finally drifted off to sleep, Cheri wondered if she should tell someone. Just as quickly as the thought came to her mind, she tossed it out. *I don't want anyone to know how Mom acts,* she thought, filled with shame. *I'd be embarrassed to tell them.*

The next morning Mom seemed better. She had the day off, but Cheri had school. *What about Rachel?* Cheri wondered. *If I go to school, will she be okay? If I ask about it, Mom might get mad.*

When she could wait no longer, Cheri finally left for school. Off and on through the day, she thought about Rachel. The minute school was out, Cheri hurried home.

As she walked up the front sidewalk, she heard Rachel crying and broke into a run. The little girl sounded as if she'd been crying for a long time.

Bounding up the porch steps, Cheri tried to open the front door. It was locked. From somewhere Rachel still cried. Cheri's heart tugged at the sound.

Her panic growing, Cheri rattled the door. Then she ran along the porch to the front window. Peering in, Cheri saw Mom sprawled on the sofa, sound asleep. A bottle lay on the floor beside her.

Cheri felt sick. With another bound she was down the steps, heading around the side of the house. Once again she heard Rachel. Her crying seemed closer.

Following the sound, Cheri came to the backyard. There in full sunlight was Rachel's playpen.

As Rachel saw Cheri, the little girl held up her arms and whimpered. Cheri picked her up and hugged her. When she saw Rachel's sunburned arms and face, Cheri broke into sobs.

It's all my fault! If I hadn't gone to school—

Still holding Rachel, Cheri sat down in the shade. Clutching the child in her arms, Cheri cried as she had never cried before.

Rachel nestled close, her arms circling Cheri's neck. Through her tears Cheri looked down at her. *Oh, God, what should I do?* This time her cry for help was a prayer.

Two words dropped into her mind: *Tell someone*. But Cheri still pushed the idea aside.

Then Rachel stirred in her arms. Gently Cheri touched the little girl's skin. It felt hot and dry with sunburn. Her eyelids and cheeks were puffy from crying. Once again Cheri's heart tugged with the pain of it.

In that moment she remembered Pastor Evenson looking at Mom and asking, "How are you doing?"

Could I talk to him? Cheri wondered.

Staggering under Rachel's weight, Cheri stood up and started walking to church.

Let's Talk . . . or Journal

DAY 1

What does it mean to say that someone has a drinking problem? What was Cheri's mom like when she wasn't drinking?

DAY 2

How did Cheri's mom change when she started to drink? Why was Cheri afraid of what her mom would do?

DAY 3

Her mother's drinking had affected Cheri's self-respect. What are some clues that tell you how Cheri felt about herself? Why did Cheri wonder what she did wrong? Was what happened to Rachel really Cheri's fault? Why or why not?

DAY 4

Cheri reached out in faith that she could change what was happening. She made a good choice in going to talk with Pastor Evenson. What do you think he'll do to help Cheri's mom?

DAY 5

Cheri's mom will be okay after she gets help, but will Cheri be okay? Will it be easy for her to forgive her mother for what she's done to the family? Why is forgiveness important?

DAY 6

If you or one of your friends need help because of a problem like Cheri's, there are people you can talk to. Think of a school or Sunday school teacher, a pastor, neighbor, relative, or friend you trust. There are also groups called AA—Alcoholics Anonymous—that help people who have a problem because of drinking. Or your church may have a Celebrate Recovery program. Ask a responsible person how to get help.

If you have hard things in your life, Jesus understands when you hurt. He wants you to ask him for help. He wants to heal you. But you also need to talk with people you trust.

DAY 7

Let's fast-forward the ending of this story to a time after Cheri's mom receives help and makes changes in her life. Imagine another Sunday afternoon when she and Cheri and Rachel have fun. What are some things that the three of them can enjoy doing together?

Let's Pray About It

Thank you, Lord, for caring about what happens to me. If I'm ever in trouble, remind me that I can always ask you for help. Help me to also talk to the right grown-up. Protect me. Take away my scared feelings and heal me. In the strong name of Jesus I pray. Thank you!

Grandma's Story

WEEK 20

"I run in the path of your commands,
for you have set my heart free."
Psalm 119:32

Tiffany was staying with her grandparents for the weekend. She liked being with them. Grandma seemed to know how she felt about things, even when Tiffany didn't tell her. Though Grandma was seventy years old, she still stood tall and straight and slender.

Grandpa was shorter than Grandma, and his square hands were rough from working as a carpenter. His eyes crinkled at the corners, and he always looked ready to laugh. He liked to tease Tiffany.

"Come on, we're going out for a fish dinner," he said now.

Tiffany grinned. Grandpa knew she didn't like fish, and she knew Grandpa and Grandma didn't care much for pizza. But they knew that Tiffany liked it. She felt like laughing as she guessed they had planned a special time for her.

Sure enough, Grandpa pulled up in front of a pizza place and let Tiffany and Grandma out. As they waited on the sidewalk, some of Grandma's friends came by. Grandma introduced them, leaving a boy about Tiffany's age until last. "This is their son Dan," she said.

Tiffany smiled her hello to everyone, and especially to Dan. *He looks nice*, she thought.

But then Tiffany knew her smile had frozen on her lips. She felt tall and awkward, as though she were bending over to talk with him. *I must be a whole head taller than he is.*

Suddenly every thought vanished from Tiffany's mind. She couldn't come up with one thing to say. When Dan asked how long she'd be visiting her grandparents, Tiffany could hardly answer. Letting her shoulders slump, she tried to look smaller.

Tiffany was relieved when Grandpa came, and the three of them went into the restaurant. While Grandpa ordered pizza, Tiffany and Grandma waited in a booth.

For Tiffany the fun had gone out of the day. All she could think about was how awful it felt to look down on Dan. *I'm taller than any girl my age*, she thought with embarrassment. *I'd like to disappear into a hole.*

Instead of sitting straight, Tiffany slid down on the bench. She hoped no one would notice how tall she was, even when sitting.

Grandma broke into her thoughts. "Did I ever tell you how your grandfather and I met?"

Tiffany shook her head. She was still thinking about Dan and how short he was.

"When I was about twenty years old, I went to visit one of my cousins for the weekend. For Saturday night she had invited a bunch of friends for a big treasure hunt."

"Where you have clues and go from place to place until you find the treasure?"

Grandma nodded. "My cousin divided us up as couples. She matched me with your Grandpa Andy. I was upset. There were two tall, good-looking boys in the group. I wanted to be with one of them."

Grandma laughed, remembering that long-ago time. Tiffany knew the feeling, but she didn't feel like laughing about it.

"I thought I was big and awkward and at least a foot taller than Andy. I slumped my shoulders and hoped I could somehow look shorter."

Now Tiffany felt uncomfortable. Once again Grandma had guessed her thoughts. Tiffany straightened, sitting tall, and took a deep breath.

"Andy teased me," Grandma went on. "He called me Skyscraper! I was hopping mad. I didn't want to go around the block with him, let alone on a treasure hunt."

Grandma smiled. "But the teams were ready to start. Your grandpa and I went from clue to clue. We were always just a minute or two ahead of everyone. When we came to the last clue, we were in the lead."

Tiffany leaned forward, listening.

"The clue was tucked in a tin can in the hollow of a tree. When I shone the flashlight, I was tall enough to see the glint of the tin. Andy couldn't see it at all." Grandma paused.

"Go on," Tiffany said.

"I thought, 'If I tell him I see it, he'll know it's because I'm taller. He'll tease me again.'"

"What happened?" Tiffany asked.

"Just then I heard a noise. Another couple was close on our trail. I reached up, grabbed the can, took out one clue, and stuffed the can back in its place. We won the treasure!"

"What was it?"

Grandma laughed. "A fake diamond ring and two tickets to a play. Andy had to take me out. He groaned and pretended that was no treasure. He got me to laugh about being taller than he was. It was the first time I'd ever laughed about being tall."

Tiffany could understand that. She couldn't imagine laughing at something so awful. "And you kept going together?"

A smile curved Grandma's lips. "I started realizing it was probably harder for him to be short than for me to be tall—especially if he liked me. Eventually we got married. I've never been sorry. I've always known how much I mean to Andy."

"It really didn't matter? That you're taller, I mean?"

Grandma shook her head. "You come from a long line of tall people, Tiffany. It's hard now, but many of the boys will catch up. A few will pass you in height. If you slump your shoulders, you'll look tired, or discouraged, or ashamed of how you look."

Just then Grandpa set the pizza on the table. But Grandma kept talking. "If you stand up straight, you'll let people see how nice you are on the inside."

"And you'll get a good-looking husband like me." Grandpa winked.

Tiffany grinned. "I'll have to think about it." She reached for the pizza. But to herself she added, *Maybe that wouldn't be so bad after all.*

Let's Talk . . . or Journal

DAY 1

What happens to your self-esteem when you keep thinking about what you don't like about yourself?

DAY 2

Most of us have something we don't like about the way we're made. We think we're too tall, too short, too fat, or too thin. Our nose is too long or our ears too big. Or perhaps we have a physical, emotional, or mental disability.

But what about those times when you need to accept the way you are? Is Tiffany's height something she can change or something she needs to accept? What are some things about yourself that you need to accept? Explain.

DAY 3

Often girls get a growth spurt before boys. As a result, girls frequently shoot up taller than boys during their middle-school years. In what ways might Tiffany have a special advantage because of her long legs and height?

DAY 4

If tall people stand tall, what happens to their appearance? Does that give a clue about how to handle anything else you don't like about yourself? Give an example.

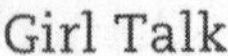

DAY 5

The Bible says that God saw you before you were born, even while you were being made. If you don't like the way you are, what are you telling God about how he made you?

What is something you *do* like about the way you're made? How does it help your self-respect to know the strengths God has given you?

DAY 6

Someone has said, "It's not how you look, but who you are that's important." Is that an excuse for looking sloppy? For not being clean, even if there's water available? Why or why not? What do you think the words just above really say? How can you put that idea into practice? Who are you if you know Jesus? Give your ideas.

DAY 7

Psalm 119:32 tells us, "I run in the path of your commands, for you have set my heart free." What does it mean to have Jesus set your heart free? What does it mean to be a Faithgirl, running in the path of God's commands?

Let's Pray About It

Father, you know that often I don't like the way I'm made. Yet because you created me this way, I choose to accept the way I am. I choose to be a Faithgirl and develop the strengths you have given me. Thank you!

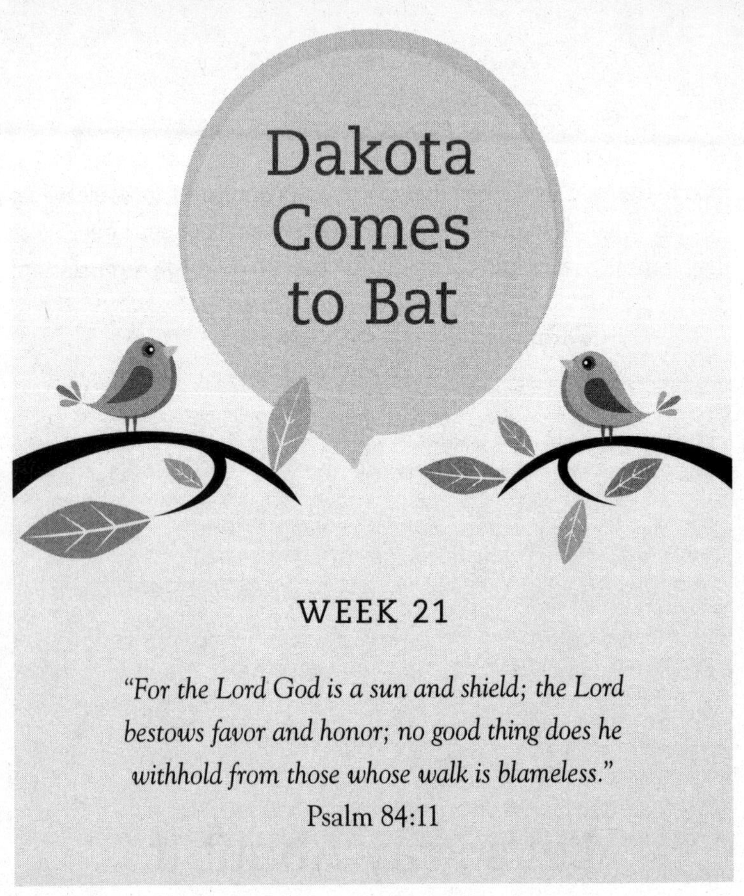

Dakota Comes to Bat

WEEK 21

"For the Lord God is a sun and shield; the Lord bestows favor and honor; no good thing does he withhold from those whose walk is blameless."
Psalm 84:11

Let's go to the baseball diamond at the park," Dakota said.

"Let's not and say we did," answered Mick as he tossed a softball in the air.

Dakota tried again. "My dad said we're not supposed to play in the street."

"Aw, c'mon, the park is too far away."

Dakota still had her doubts. After all, she was the one with the most to lose. She lived here, while the others came from blocks farther away.

"Hey, you two. Do you wanna play or don't ya?" called one of the boys.

"Well— " Dakota started to give in. "Put first base a few more feet that way." She pointed to the curb. "Mrs. O'Rourke is crabby. She doesn't want us on her grass."

They moved first base to the edge of another neighbor's lawn and started playing. Soon Dakota came up to bat. Pushing back her long black hair, she pulled down her baseball cap to keep it in place.

Mick was pitching, and Dakota knew he'd give her his fastest ball. Taking a firm grip on the bat, she waited. Sure enough, there it came—a little low, but right over the plate.

Dakota swung and connected. A fly popped off to the right. Then *C-R-A-A-A-S-S-H!* The sound of broken glass shattered the air.

Dakota looked around and felt sick. Sure enough, it was Mrs. O'Rourke's window.

One moment everyone stared at the house. The next instant every kid scattered in a different direction.

Every kid, that is, except Dakota. She felt frozen to the spot. Then, as she recovered, she headed for the bushes across the street. Just in time she knelt down, hiding behind the leaves and peering through.

Mrs. O'Rourke opened her front door. Cane in hand, she came out on the porch. With her white hair piled on top of her head, she looked slender and tall. But Dakota knew it was difficult for her to walk. Today she leaned on her cane more than usual.

Mrs. O'Rourke looked at the shattered glass, then turned to the empty street. Her face crumpled.

It doesn't matter, Dakota told herself as she tried to ignore the woman's hurt look. Hiding behind the bushes, Dakota knew she could get away. *Mrs. O'Rourke might guess, but she can't prove I did it. A lot of kids were here.*

Then the older woman moved, and her cane slipped on the glass. Dakota caught her breath. *What if she falls?*

As Dakota held her breath, Mrs. O'Rourke stretched out her cane, took a slow step. Then another slow step.

Still Dakota waited. *Why should I get the blame? All the kids were in on it!*

Again the older woman stretched out her cane. Again her feet followed. Step by slow step Mrs. O'Rourke went back into the house.

Dakota backed away from the bushes that hid her. On her hands and knees, she crept to the corner of the nearby house. But instead of edging away to safety, she waited a minute.

Everything within Dakota wanted to run. At the same time, something held her there. Most of all, she felt ashamed.

Finally Dakota stood up. Feeling as if her legs were not her own, she walked into the open. As she crossed the street, her feet dragged. Dreading what she was about to do, Dakota climbed the steps and rang the bell.

I'm crazy! she thought as she waited. *Every other kid will get away free!*

When Mrs. O'Rourke opened the screen door, Dakota waited for the angry words she thought she'd hear. Instead, Mrs. O'Rourke spoke quietly.

"Hello, Dakota."

Feeling even more ashamed, Dakota looked down at the weather-beaten porch. The boards were gray with time, and she wondered if other kids had ever stood in this place. Then she looked up into Mrs. O'Rourke's faded blue eyes.

"I'm sorry," she said. She wanted to tell Mrs. O'Rourke that it wasn't her fault. She wanted to put the blame on the other kids. But only four words came out. "I broke your window."

"I know." Mrs. O'Rourke surprised her. "Just before the ball hit, I saw you out another window."

Again Dakota's gaze fell to the old boards. Panic filled her now. *What if she'd been standing at the window I broke?*

"I was going to call your dad at his office."

Full of misery, Dakota apologized again. "I'm sorry. *Really* sorry. I'm glad you weren't hurt."

"I forgive you," Mrs. O'Rourke answered quietly. "I respect you for coming to talk with me. I know that was hard to do."

Suddenly Dakota's gaze found the older woman's eyes. Something Dakota saw there drew her to Mrs. O'Rourke. *Why have I always thought she's crabby?*

Aloud she asked, "What can I do to pay for the window?"

Mrs. O'Rourke swung the screen door farther open. "Why don't you come in? We'll talk about it."

Dakota drew a deep breath. For some strange reason, she almost felt as if she had a new friend.

Let's Talk ... or Journal

DAY 1

When we make good or bad choices, there are logical consequences. For Dakota and the other kids, what was their first bad choice? What were the consequences?

DAY 2

The story tells some of the feelings Dakota had about the broken window. Give some of the feelings you've had when you do something wrong and don't want to own up to it.

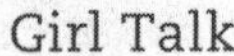

DAY 3

Dakota also made some good choices that had good consequences. Instead of running away, she went to Mrs. O'Rourke. When she apologized she said, "I'm sorry." Sometimes people are just sorry that they got caught, not for what they did wrong. Which way did Dakota feel? How do you know?

DAY 4

Dakota was also very direct. She said, "I broke your window," instead of putting the blame on the other kids. How does this compare with someone who sneaks away? Who do you respect more — Dakota or the kids who kept running? Why?

DAY 5

Mrs. O'Rourke did some special things for Dakota. What were they? Why is it important that Mrs. O'Rourke said, "I forgive you"?

DAY 6

What do you suppose Dakota and Mrs.O'Rourke decided about the broken window?

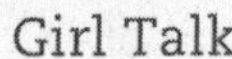

DAY 7

Can you think of a time when you did something wrong but made the right choice? What are some of the feelings you had? What happened? What helped you make the right choice? How do you feel now about what you did? Give reasons for your answer.

In a short story the main character faces a problem and figures out a way to solve it. Can you write a short story about the time when you did something wrong, but then made the right choice?

Let's Pray About It

Jesus, when I've done something wrong, help me to do the right thing. Help me own up to what I did and deal with the consequences. Thank you that whenever I ask forgiveness, you do forgive me. Thank you that you also show me how to learn from wrong choices so I can make better ones.

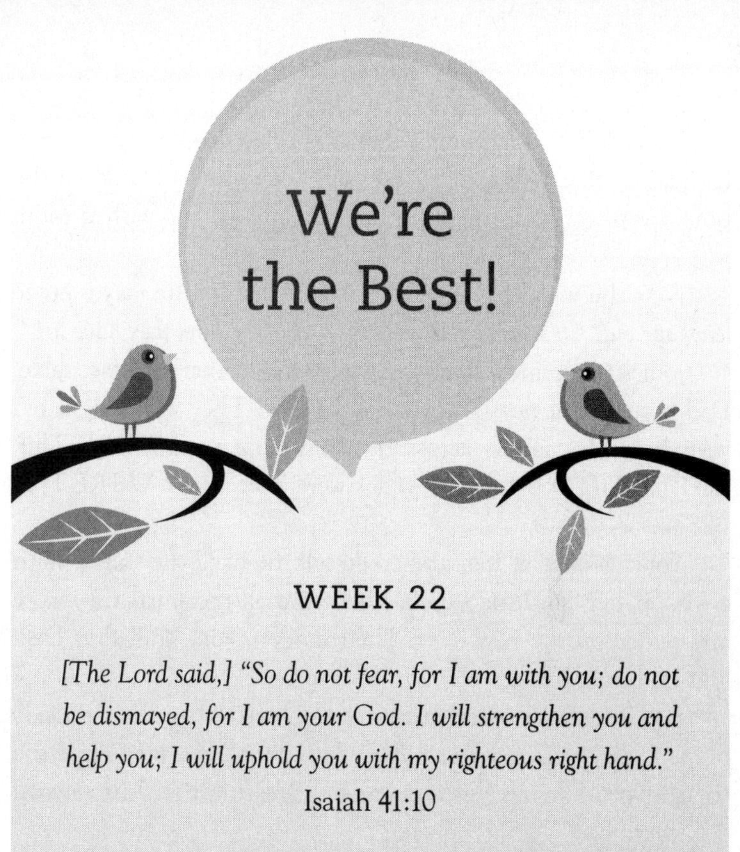

We're the Best!

WEEK 22

[The Lord said,] "So do not fear, for I am with you; do not be dismayed, for I am your God. I will strengthen you and help you; I will uphold you with my righteous right hand."
Isaiah 41:10

Tonya woke to a stream of sunlight coming through the window. For a moment she didn't know where she was. Then she remembered—Dad's new house.

In the other bed, Jodi still slept. *She'd be nice*, Tonya thought. *That is, if she didn't have to be my sister.*

Tonya wished there wasn't a Jodi. She wished there weren't two younger brothers. Most of all, she wished there wasn't Jodi's mom, Rita.

Tonya closed her eyes and tried to go back to sleep. Instead, she remembered how she felt about leaving Mom for this weekend with Dad's new family.

"The divorce is something between Dad and me," Mom had told her. "I don't like it any more than you do. But he's your father. You can love me and still have a good relationship with him."

Instead, Tonya felt angry that there had been a divorce. She felt jealous that Jodi and her brothers got to be with Dad all the time. Even worse, Tonya felt lonely and afraid. She wished Mom was here.

Now she wondered about Dad's new family. *Are they going to leave me out? Or will they act nice because they think they have to?*

Jodi stirred, and the day began. Around the breakfast table, Dad brought out new T-shirts he'd bought. They were bright red with bold blue letters across the front that said, WE'RE THE BUTTERFIELDS. Across the back were more words: WE'RE THE BEST!

Tonya looked at Jodi and could tell she liked the shirts. With a whoop, her two little step-brothers tore off the shirts they wore and pulled on the new ones. Their mother, Rita, smiled at Dad, and Dad smiled back.

But Tonya felt miserable. She remembered when she was Dad's only kid. *Do I still count with him? Does he still love me?* Then she thought of Mom sitting home alone. Wearing the shirt seemed disloyal to her.

"Let's get 'em on and go for a hike," Dad said.

Glad to get away from the table, Tonya jumped up. But she moved slowly up the stairs. Even more slowly, she shut the door to the room she and Jodi shared.

Grateful that Jodi hadn't followed her, Tonya sat down on the floor. She felt mad and sad all at once.

I don't want to wear that stupid shirt. I'm not a Butterfield. Sure, that's my last name. But I'm not part of this *family.*

Unwilling to move, she sat there for a long time. Then someone knocked on the door. "Hey, Tonya!" Dad called out.

Tonya didn't answer, and Dad called again. Finally she stood up and opened the door.

"We're all ready. Let's go." Then Dad saw Tonya's face. "What's the matter?"

Tonya made herself look at Dad. "I don't want to wear the shirt you gave me."

Just in time she caught the hurt look in his eyes. "I've got a new life, Tonya. I want you to be part of it."

But Tonya looked down.

"You're worried about your mother, aren't you?"

Slowly Tonya nodded.

"Why don't we call this a special shirt? Wear it on weekends when you're with us. Leave it here when you go home."

Still Tonya stared at the floor.

"I love you, Tonya," Dad said softly. "Because I have a new family doesn't mean I love you less. My love gets bigger to take in all of you."

Dad gave her a quick hug. As he headed for the stairs, he turned back. "You belong here, too, you know. We'll be waiting in the car for you."

When he left, Tonya picked up the shirt and looked once more at the lettering. With her finger she traced the B, then the U, then the whole name. "I love *you*, Mom," she whispered.

But then, as clearly as if Mom were there, Tonya remembered her words. *"He's your father. You can love me and still have a good relationship with him."*

Tonya turned over the shirt. Through the blur of tears, WE'RE THE BEST! stared up at her.

As Tonya blinked away her tears, she remembered Dad at the breakfast table. *I guess I have to think about his feelings, too.*

Tonya drew a deep breath. *Maybe I have to give up the idea of one family. Like it or not, I'm part of two families now.*

In that moment she made a choice. Slowly she pulled on the shirt. *Maybe someday I'll feel like I belong.*

Let's Talk ... or Journal

DAY 1

What does it mean to be loyal to someone? Why is loyalty a good quality to have?

DAY 2

Why did Tonya's feelings of loyalty make it hard when her parents were divorced? What idea from her mom helped Tonya work out her problem?

DAY 3

Because a dad or mom takes on a new family it doesn't mean they have to leave the first one behind. What did Tonya's dad tell her about his love for her?

DAY 4

When a parent remarries, it may be difficult to see a mom or dad as often. What are some things Tonya can do in the times when she isn't able to be with her dad?

Even though a dad or mom remarries, it doesn't have to change the love they feel for their children. How do you know Tonya's father still loves her? Who promises to be with Tonya no matter where she lives? How do you know?

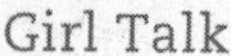

DAY 5

In your daily life you are able to make countless choices about what happens to you. But it's not possible to control everything that happens to you. You especially can't control what grown-ups decide or how they act. In times like that, what counts is what you do about the hard things you face. What are some difficult things in your life that you're able to change? Make a list. What are some difficult things in your life that you can't change? Make another list.

Can your feelings about any of the things on the second list be changed if you talk to a grown-up about what is happening?

DAY 6

In Jeremiah 33:3 the Lord says, "Call to Me and I will answer you, and show you great and mighty things, which you do not know" (NKJV). Look at the lists you've written and ask Jesus to be your forever friend in whatever way you need help. Ask him to give you people who will help you with the things you don't understand and feel you can't change.

DAY 7

Whatever you're facing and no matter where you are, Jesus wants to be with you every moment of the day or night. He promises, "I will not leave you as orphans; I will come to you" (John 14:18). Jesus also promises, "Anyone who loves me will obey my teaching. My Father will love him. We will come to him and make our home with him" (John 14:23 NIrV).

Ask Jesus to come to you and be with you. Ask Jesus and his Father to come and make their home with you.

Let's Pray About It

Thank you, Lord, for my parents. Show me how to have a good relationship with both of them. When I feel mixed up about the difficult things in my life, help me to sort things out. Help me to talk to the right grown-up about my feelings. Thank you that wherever I am and wherever I live, you are always with me.

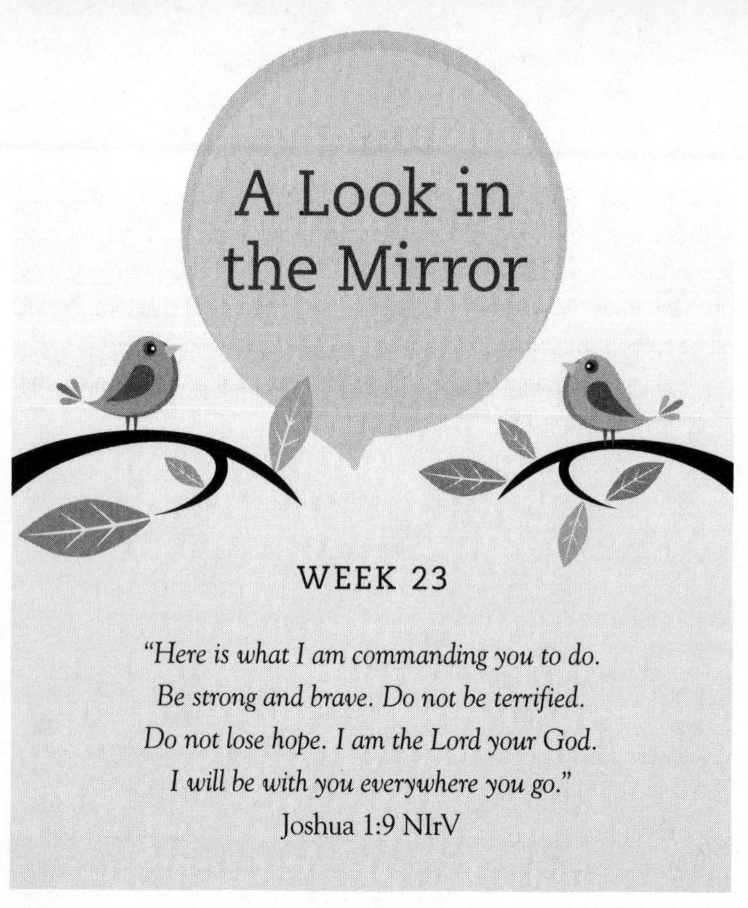

A Look in the Mirror

WEEK 23

"Here is what I am commanding you to do.
Be strong and brave. Do not be terrified.
Do not lose hope. I am the Lord your God.
I will be with you everywhere you go."
Joshua 1:9 NIrV

Brynn hated using the mirror in the school bathroom. The light gave her skin a funny color and every spot and blemish showed.

She was so busy looking at herself that she barely noticed the girl who had come in. A strange movement in the mirror caught her attention. *What's she doing?*

The girl wore a cute hat that fit close around her head. When she twisted it in place, Brynn saw under the brim.

Did I imagine it? she wondered. Then she knew she hadn't. The girl was bald!

Just then Brynn realized she'd been caught staring. Red crept into her face. *There I go again—forgetting how someone else might feel.*

Picking up her books, Brynn turned to leave, but something

clicked in her mind. *The girl with cancer.* She had just changed her schedule to come into two of Brynn's classes.

Everyone had been talking about the girl and how she was taking chemo. Someone said she had lost all her hair. The rumor must be true.

As Brynn turned back, she looked in the mirror in time to see a tear roll down the girl's cheek. Other tears followed. The silent weeping made Brynn feel miserable. *Should I say something? Or pretend I don't notice?*

For a moment Brynn stood there, trying to decide. The girl acted as if she didn't see her. At last Brynn spoke. "I'm Brynn. What's your name?"

The girl's lips quivered. "Yolanda. Yolanda Garcia." Leaning down, she turned on a faucet and splashed cold water on her face. "I'll be all right," she mumbled.

But Brynn felt sure Yolanda was just trying to be brave. "I don't know what's wrong, but can I help?"

Yolanda turned to face her. "Help? I wish you could." If the words hadn't sounded so hopeless, Brynn would have thought the girl was bitter. Instead, she seemed ready to give up.

"What's wrong?" Brynn asked.

As Yolanda turned off the faucet, her tears started again. "I've never been so embarrassed in all my life. Both yesterday and today—"

As if unable to stand up anymore, she braced herself against the sink. Brynn waited, feeling embarrassed herself.

Yolanda drew a long, ragged breath. "Some boys found out—" She struggled to speak. "They found out I've lost my hair. When I walk through the hall, they come up behind me and pull off my hat."

"Oh, no!" Brynn couldn't believe something so cruel.

Yolanda's shoulders shook with sobs, but no sound escaped. "I can't walk down that hall anymore," she finally said. "Taking chemo is bad enough. But I can't handle how the boys laugh when they see my bald head."

Turning on the facet again, Yolanda bent down and splashed

water on her face. When she straightened up, she drew a deep breath.

Her pain pierced Brynn's heart. "Can I help?"

Yolanda shook her head. "I'll be fine."

But now Brynn prayed with her eyes open. *Jesus, I don't know what to do. You're going to have to show me.*

Once more Yolanda turned her hat and settled it on her head. When she tried to smile, her lips trembled. "Well, how do I look?"

"Totally awesome!" But Brynn hurt inside, just thinking how it would feel to have cancer. And stupid boys teasing besides. "Let's figure out what we can do."

"I've tried," Yolanda said. "I don't want to stay home all day. I need something to do. I want to be here with everyone else, but—"

But now Brynn had an idea. "You said the boys come up behind you? Then I'm going to walk behind you!"

"Really?" Hope leaped into Yolanda's eyes. "You mean it? You *really* mean it?"

"Yup." Brynn sounded more confident than she felt. "I'll walk behind you whenever you go through the hall. I'll make sure that none of those big bullies get near you."

Yolanda looked as if she wanted to believe her, but wasn't sure she could.

Brynn kept on. "You're in two of my classes, so I'll walk with you before and after. I'll talk to some other girls, and we'll work out a schedule for the rest of your day."

When Yolanda smiled, it was like the sun coming out after a storm.

"And let's do something else. We need to tell the principal what's going on. She won't like it. Mrs. Erickson doesn't allow *anyone* to get away with acting like a bully. I promise you—she'll make sure it doesn't happen again. And to be *extra* sure I'll still walk a few steps behind you."

Yolanda straightened her shoulders. With Brynn behind her, Yolanda walked into the hall like a soldier going into battle.

Let's Talk . . . or Journal

DAY 1

In real life some bullies really did this to a girl who had cancer. What would you like to say to those boys?

Brynn came up with two good plans. What was her plan for what *she* could do? What was her plan for a way to get help in dealing with bullies? When is it important to ask grownups for help?

DAY 2

There's a difference between showing pity and giving understanding. Showing pity means we act as if we're sorry for someone but don't want to be like them. We offer sweet, kind-sounding words but no real help. What might have happened to Yolanda if Brynn had treated her that way? How do you know?

DAY 3

Giving understanding means that we let someone know we feel sorry about what's happening to them, but we also offer support. In what ways did Brynn give understanding to Yolanda?

DAY 4

Pity takes away whatever hope or self-confidence a hurting person has left. Understanding helps a person go on, even though it's hard. Why was it important to Yolanda that she keep going to school? Would you feel the same way? Give reasons for your answer.

DAY 5

Have there been times when you've made fun of someone because you didn't understand what was happening? If you could go back in time, how would you change that now? Is there anything you can still do to make up for what happened?

DAY 6

Do you know any people — kids your age or grownups — that you could help in some practical way? Draw a line down the center of a page. Make a list of people who could use your help and next to it some ideas for what you could do. Talk with a parent or other adult about a plan you'd like to follow.

DAY 7

When Jesus walked on earth, he showed us that he cared about people and what happened to them. How did he also help them in practical ways? Look for clues in Mark 6:30 – 44 and John 11:32 – 44.

Let's Pray About It

This: *Jesus, it's so easy to be selfish and think only about myself. Sometimes I need your help and sometimes I need to see what is happening to the people around me. In your name I choose to care about the hurts and needs of others. Help me love them with your love and find your practical and creative ways to help. Thanks!*

Or this: *Jesus, I know what it's like to have cancer or something else that is really hard. Help me especially much when I'm discouraged and feel like giving up. I ask in your name for physical, emotional, and spiritual healing. In your name I choose to be a Faithgirl and run close to you. I ask you to give me every place where I set my feet. Make me strong and courageous. Thank you for being with me wherever I go.*

Rosita twisted her flute together and set her music rack next to the open window. As she looked outside, a gentle breeze lifted the pages of her exercise book.

Down the street the kids had a volleyball game going. Through the warm summer air, the sounds came clearly. Rosita wished she were there.

"Mommmm!" she called. "Do I have to practice?"

Mom poked her head in the door. "Put in your half hour, and you'll be free the rest of the day."

Rosita glanced at the clock and sighed, making sure Mom heard her. "Why did I say I wanted to play the flute? I must have had rocks in my head."

"No, you didn't," Mom answered. "Remember how much you liked hearing that flutist at church?"

"But I didn't know it was going to be so hard."

"It can be hard to learn an instrument," her mother said. "But we rented the flute, so give it a fair chance. See how you feel at the end of six months."

As Mom started to leave, she turned, "I'm going to the store in a few minutes. I'll be back in less than an hour."

When her mother disappeared, Rosita again faced her exercise book. "'A note followed by a dot has its value increased one half,'" she read. "Phooey!"

Tapping her foot to keep time, she began playing. One, two, three, rest. One, two, three, rest.

Rosita stopped. The volleyball had rolled this way. As she watched, her friend Marie ran to pick it up, then raced back to the game.

Next Rosita tried her scales—G, A, B, C.

She paused. *How do I go from* C *to D?* Taking out the sheet of fingerings, Rosita stared at the circles her instructor had drawn on a paper.

Just then she heard her mom's car leave the garage. As quickly as she could, Rosita twisted her flute apart, put the instrument in its case, and hurried outside.

Moments later she was playing volleyball with her friends. When she felt uneasy, Rosita pushed it aside. *Mom will never know.*

All through the month of June, Rosita practiced with her music rack next to the window. She longed to be out with the kids. Always she looked forward to that moment when she would finish her thirty minutes.

Then one July morning something inside Rosita changed. After hurrying through the scales, she opened her book of songs. As she played the notes, her mind began thinking the words. "Jingle bells, jingle bells, jingle all the way ..."

The tune was catchy, and she played it several times, surprised that it sounded better with each try.

Next, Rosita found a song she had sung in her music class at school. Soon her lower lip was sore, and she felt lightheaded from blowing. But when she glanced at the clock, she discovered twenty-five minutes had passed.

That day Rosita moved her music rack away from the window. Somehow it didn't seem as important to watch the kids down the street.

The next Sunday morning the flutist was back in church. As she soared to the high notes, Rosita held her breath. *How does she do it?*

By now Rosita knew how hard it was to reach those notes. With her whole heart, she longed to play really well.

Will you help me, God? she whispered during the prayer that followed. *Will you help me play like that?*

Near the end of the service, the flutist swung into a quiet, simple melody. Rosita knew the words. "In my life, Lord, be glorified, be glorified. . . ." She wanted the clear, high notes to last forever.

The next morning the melody was still in Rosita's mind. *I wish I could play it,* she thought. When she searched in her books, she couldn't find the song.

As soon as Rosita finished her scales, she started her other music. But the song from church kept coming back in her thoughts. "In my life, Lord—" As clearly as if she had just heard it, Rosita remembered the tune.

For the first time she began going up and down the scale, listening for the note she needed.

There it is! she thought when she finally stumbled across it. *It's E!* She tried again and found the second note. Now she felt excited. E, G, E, G. As she kept listening, she picked out the rest of the tune. Afraid that she would forget the notes, she played them again and again.

Just then Rosita glanced at the clock. She had gone five minutes over!

It struck her so funny that she laughed out loud.

Let's Talk ... or Journal

DAY 1

When Rosita found it hard to practice, what poor choice did she make?

DAY 2

There's an old saying that tells us, "If at first you don't succeed, try, try again." Why is trying again important?

How do you think Rosita would have felt about herself if she had given up when she found it hard to practice? Give reasons why.

DAY 3

If we ask God to help us learn to play an instrument, does that mean we don't have to practice? Why or why not?

DAY 4

For most people, learning to play an instrument is hard work until they reach a breakthrough. What good choices helped Rosita come to the breakthrough where she liked playing the flute?

What are some skills you've worked hard to learn? Describe what it was like to learn those skills, whatever they are.

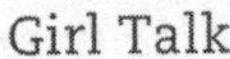

DAY 5

Often we think of a reward as some good, outward thing that happens to us. A reward can also come in the satisfaction we feel about what we've done. How did Rosita receive a reward in both ways?

DAY 6

How do the new things you've learned help you stretch out and do even more? Is there something worthwhile that you've longed to do, but have never had the opportunity to try? How could you get started?

DAY 7

In addition to learning new skills, there are experiences that can help us grow in our ability to know and help people. For instance, going on an outreach with a missions group. In what ways can you honor and serve the Lord by using music, athletic ability, or other skills you might have? Tell or write about those skills and what you could possibly do.

Sometimes the Lord puts a vision on our heart for something we'd like to do some of the time or with our entire life. A vision is something that gives us direction and helps us plan our life and how to use it. If you're wondering how God wants you to use your life, why don't you pray about it? Ask him what he wants you to know.

Let's Pray About It

Jesus, you know I often find it hard to practice. Yet I believe you want me to keep trying. Show me the ways you want me to keep growing, stretching out, and learning new skills. Thank you for the way you help me learn. Thank you for the abilities you have given me. I choose to use them to honor you. I also ask in your name, Jesus, for your vision, your plan for my life. Thank you!

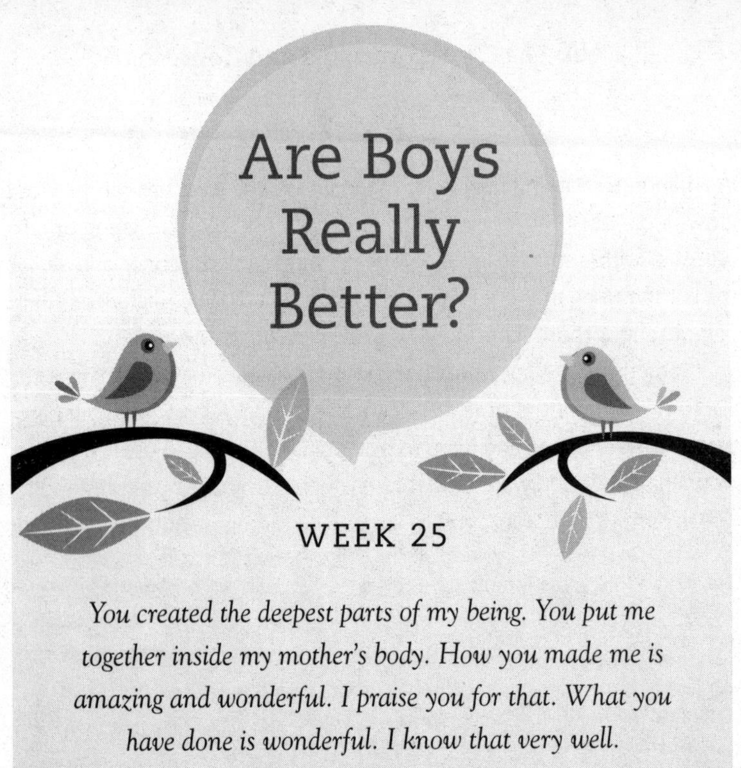

Are Boys Really Better?

WEEK 25

You created the deepest parts of my being. You put me together inside my mother's body. How you made me is amazing and wonderful. I praise you for that. What you have done is wonderful. I know that very well.
Psalm 139:13–14 NIrV

Gerry slid onto the tractor seat. It felt good to curl her fingers around the large steering wheel. When she first started driving the tractor, she'd been afraid of it. Now it had become her friend.

What a great day! she thought. Haying was fun on mornings like this. From a cloudless sky, the sun beat down on the road stretching out before her. If the weather held, they'd get everything in before rain edged over the horizon.

For a moment the breeze lifted Gerry's hair, tossing it in her face. As she pulled the long strands out of her eyes, she wished she'd brushed her hair into a ponytail. Shifting the tractor into gear, she took a quick look at the wagon behind her.

"Either sit down or hang on!" she called.

Her two younger cousins waved, and each slung an arm around the posts on the wagon. Sid and Kenny were there for the summer. Gerry had to admit she was getting mighty tired of their company.

Why does Dad keep asking them back every June? she wondered. *They're almost my age, yet they don't do nearly the work.*

As Gerry drove onto the gravel road, stones kicked up around the tractor. A trail of dust billowed behind the wagon.

When she headed into a field, Dad was already there, using the baler. Gerry watched as one bale after another shot up and then back, falling into the nearly full wagon behind Dad's tractor.

Once again Gerry twisted around to check on her cousins. By now they were wrestling. Sid had Kenny pinned dangerously close to the edge of the wagon.

"Hey, you guys, quit it!" shouted Gerry. "If I start up suddenly, you might fall out."

Facing forward again, she saw Dad motion to her. "Get a move on!" his arms seemed to say.

Gerry pulled up behind Dad's baler. "What took you so long?" he asked.

Without waiting for an answer, Dad hopped down to unhitch Gerry's wagon. She set the brake and went to help, but Dad was still impatient. "You should have been a boy," he grumbled. "You never work the way a boy would."

Hot tears welled up in Gerry's eyes. More than once she had told her dad, "*I can't help the way I was born.*" Instead of trying again, she leaned down, hiding her face as she hooked the chains under the hitch.

All day long, Gerry drove between the field and barn, but her thoughts were elsewhere. As though she was seeing a DVD, one memory after another appeared before her eyes.

Mom telling her, "We didn't have a girl's name picked out for you. You were going to be Gerald instead of Geraldine."

A neighbor saying, "When you were only three years old, you wanted to do boys' work. One day I saw you trying to carry large stones for your dad."

By mid-afternoon Gerry was tired of thinking about the way things were. *I've tried and tried. But does it do any good? Does Dad love me at all? I just want to please him.*

That day, for the first time all summer, they finished work

early. Mom had a good supper fixed. As everyone dug into the roast beef and potatoes, Dad looked at Sid and Kenny. "Want to swim in the pond when we're done eating?"

"Sure thing!" they exclaimed and started eating faster.

Watching them, Gerry thought about how good it would feel to dive into the cool water. She imagined the water closing over her warm body and the pull of her muscles in a long swim.

Left out again! she thought. *It would be fun being with Dad. Maybe just once—*

"Can I go, too?" Gerry asked him.

Dad shook his head. "This is only for boys."

Like the rush of water ready to spill over a dam, Gerry felt anger and despair rise within her. She wanted to cry out, "I'm worth something, Dad! I'm worth something, even though I'm a girl!"

But she had said those things before, and it hadn't helped.

Without a word Gerry stood up and carried her dishes to the sink. As she set them down, she turned and looked back at Dad, still sitting at the table. *I'm going to try once more!*

Soon Mom finished her coffee and went to find the boys' swimsuits. Sid and Kenny left to change clothes, and Gerry sat down across the table from Dad.

"I want to tell you something," she said, facing Dad squarely. "I want you to know how I feel."

Dad looked at Gerry, as though surprised at the tone of her voice.

A nervous feeling started in Gerry's stomach, but she kept on. "All my life you've wanted me to be something I'm not. I'm *not* a boy. I'm a girl! I can't help that. But you make me feel like I'm no good!"

As though he didn't believe what he heard, Dad stared at Gerry. For the first time in her life, Gerry stared back instead of looking at the floor.

Dad was the first to look away. As he set down his coffee mug, his hand shook, and the cup rattled on the table.

For a long moment, Dad sat with his head bowed. When he finally spoke, his voice sounded strange and far away. "I'm sorry, Gerry," he said, still looking down. "That's what my ma and pa always told me. No matter what I did, they'd say, 'You're no good. You're no good.'"

Dad's broad shoulders began to shake, and Gerry felt scared. She'd never seen Dad cry before. When he looked up, there were tears in his eyes.

"I heard it so often, I always thought I was no good. I've passed that feeling on to you."

Wondering what to say, Gerry searched his eyes. The pain in Dad's face was like the pain she had felt all these years.

"I'm sorry, Gerry. Forgive me. I'm very sorry."

In the quiet room Gerry heard the ticking of the clock. The moment seemed to stretch out forever. But at last Gerry knew what to do.

Standing up, she slowly circled the table. For the first time since she was a little girl, she gave her dad a big hug. And they wept together.

Then her dad spoke. "Gerry, I can't change what I've done up till now. But can we do something special? Say that today is your new birthday?"

Gerry stared at him. "You mean, say that you like my being a girl?"

Dad took out a big hanky, blew his nose. "Say that I not only like it, I'm *glad* you're a girl. And I'm glad you're a girl who speaks up and is honest so you help your old dad change."

Gerry felt sure she was hearing things, but her father went on.

"Gerry, I'm not good with words, but I want you to help me." Dad wiped his eyes, then his cheeks. "If I forget to tell you how important you are to me, I want you to remind me."

Dad paused, blew his nose again. "It's hard for me to say, but I'm going to keep on saying it till I get it right. Gerry, I don't want you to ever again think you're no good. You're good all the way through. You're important to me not only because you're a girl, but because of the kind of person you are."

As tears welled up in Gerry's eyes, she could not speak. But when the tears spilled over, streaming down her cheeks, her dad could. "Happy Birthday, Gerry. Happy Birthday!"

Let's Talk ... or Journal

DAY 1

What clues tell you that Gerry's dad valued boys more than girls? Because of the way Gerry's dad treated her, how did she feel about being a girl?

DAY 2

How do you think God feels about Gerry being a girl?

DAY 3

Why did it take courage for Gerry to tell her dad what was wrong?

DAY 4

When Gerry's dad talked about feeling no good, he said, "I've passed that feeling on to you." What does it mean to pass a feeling on to someone else?

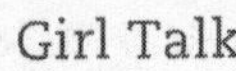

DAY 5

Why is it important for every one of us to know that we are valuable the way we are? Explain why you think the way you do.

DAY 6

Sometimes it's not possible to change the way other people treat us. Yet if we ask God, he can help us change the way we feel about what is happening to us. Are there ways in which you hurt because of how people have treated you? Talk with an adult you trust about it. That person can pray with you and ask God to show you good things about yourself.

DAY 7

In God's sight is your being a girl ever an accident? Give reasons for your answer.

Let's Pray About It

Father God, thank you for creating me just the way I am. Thank you that long before I was born you were the one who decided whether I would be male or female. Because you care deeply about who I am, I choose to value myself as the girl I am now and the young woman I will become. Thank you that in your eyes I am worthwhile. Thank you that I am important to you. Thank you that you love me very much.

Shae's Gift

WEEK 26

Always think about what is true. Think about what is noble, right and pure. Think about what is lovely and worthy of respect. If anything is excellent or worthy of praise, think about those kinds of things.
Philippians 4:8 NIrV

On the bus ride to her friend's house, Shae took a good look at Toni. *Something's wrong,* she decided. *Toni is changing.*

The change bothered Shae. Since third grade the two had been good friends. Even on that first day of school they had ridden the bus together. But now Shae didn't understand what was happening. *We're both growing up, but it's not that. With Toni it's something more.*

When Toni laughed it didn't reach her eyes. Instead, the laugh that was once full of fun had a hard ring to it.

Just thinking about it, Shae twisted a strand of her long blonde hair. What made Toni seem so hard? So turned off to the things she used to like?

For a moment Shae stared out the window, but she was really praying. *Jesus, I care about my friend. Will you show me what's wrong?*

When their bus squealed to a stop, Shae and Toni climbed

down and walked to the house. In the kitchen they found Toni's dad sitting at the table.

"Hi, Toni. Hi, Shae. Have a good day?"

Toni shrugged.

"How did your test go?" her dad asked.

"Same as always." Toni's dark eyes were angry. Turning her back to her dad, she seemed to say, *What's it to you?*

Her dad started to speak, then stopped, as if wanting to wait until Shae wasn't there. Instead, he offered them a snack. But Toni shook her head.

Did they have a fight? Shae wondered. She doubted it. If they had, Toni's dad would have done his best to straighten it out before Toni left in the morning. Now his eyes looked as troubled as Shae felt.

Without another word Toni headed down the steps to her bedroom in the basement. Shae accepted a bowl of munchies and then followed her friend.

Already Toni was listening to her mp3 player, clicking her fingers and swaying with the music. As Shae watched, Toni ripped off her headphones and held them out. "Listen up! You'll like it!"

Even before Shae slipped the headphones over her ears, she heard and felt the beat of the music. Toni flopped onto her bed, but her foot still moved up and down, keeping time.

Lying on her back, hands behind her head, Toni stared up at the posters on her ceiling. Though the singer's music sounded upbeat and peppy, Shae knew the female singer didn't send the right message. Just looking at her photo, Shae felt uneasy.

Dropping down on the rug, her back against the wall, Shae made herself comfortable. A second large poster showed a band. As Shae listened, their music came on.

At first the sound felt good, like the kind of day Shae wished she could have had, but didn't. Then she began hearing the words. As she started to guess what the singers were saying through their music, her thoughts headed in the wrong direction.

Feeling confused, she pulled off the headphones. How could her feelings say one thing—"I like this"—and her mind and spirit say the opposite? It was confusing.

Instantly words she had memorized came to her mind. "God is not the author of confusion, but of peace."

Putting the headphones back on, Shae closed her eyes. Listened. Concentrated. Prayed. *Jesus, help me understand. What do you want me to know?*

At first Shae heard only the music. Then she listened only for the words. This time Shae understood their meaning. Instantly she turned down the volume, and shut off the player.

Swear words, yes. Profane. And also more. Demeaning.

As the word popped into her mind Shae felt surprised. Demeaning wasn't a word she normally used. But she had no doubt about what it meant. The words did not represent girls in a good way. Instead the song degraded them.

Is this the singer's way of selling lots of CDs?

Of one thing Shae felt sure. The music would negatively affect a girl who listened. That was exactly what she had seen in her friend.

And Shae felt certain of something else. She didn't want any part of it.

My best friend likes this? The words of the song showed a life exactly opposite from the one Shae wanted to live.

Tearing off the headphones again, Shae leaned forward, tucked her face into her hands, and started praying.

For a moment everything else fell away. She knew only that she wanted to get clean, free of the wrong thoughts she had heard.

Jesus, clean me up. Take those thoughts from me.

Just then Toni noticed her. "Shae, what are you *doing*?"

But in that same moment Shae felt peaceful deep inside. Sitting up, she drew a deep breath. As she pushed her long hair behind her ears, Shae knew where to start.

"Toni, we've been good friends for a long time. Remember what we promised each other? That we'd always tell each other stuff, even if it's hard?"

When Toni met her eyes and nodded, Shae began. "Do you know what the words of these songs really say?"

Let's Talk . . . or Journal

DAY 1

God created the gift of music. He gave us not only the ability to create and perform music, but also created the song of birds and the sound of a fast-moving stream running over stones. Why do you think God wanted us to have music? Give reasons for your answer.

DAY 2

How had the music and words on the CDs become part of Toni? In what ways had she changed?

The name Shae means *gift*. How can Shae be a gift to her friend?

DAY 3

Shae could have just shrugged her shoulders and decided the message in the songs didn't matter. Instead, she prayed in two different ways. Once with her eyes open. Once on her knees. What are some different ways you pray? What happens when you do?

DAY 4

If Toni keeps listening to the same kind of CDs she could become an entirely different person from the one Shae has known. If that happens, what do you think will happen to their friendship?

What kind of person does Shae want to be? What kind of person do *you* want to be?

DAY 5

Sometimes kids want to see how close to the edge they can get in the things they like and the way they behave. What do you think will happen to a girl if she keeps trying to get away with as much as possible, thinking it doesn't matter or she won't be caught? Give reasons for your answer.

If you were Toni, what would you do about what Shae says? Why?

DAY 6

We love a holy God. That holy God loves us so much that he sent his only Son to earth to die for us. Because of his suffering and death, we can come to him and say, "Jesus, I ask forgiveness for my sin. I ask forgiveness for my sinful thoughts. Thoughts that lead me in the wrong direction. Thoughts that can someday lead me to sinful actions."

Whatever our sin is, it separates us from God. When we ask forgiveness, it removes the barrier, the high wall between us and Jesus. We know when that wall goes down because we receive his peace. As David prayed, "Restore to me the joy of my salvation."

In what ways do you think Toni's fascination with demeaning music has hurt her spiritual life? How can Toni remove the wall she has put up between herself and God?

DAY 7

Whatever we allow into our thinking becomes a part of us and affects our minds, emotions, and spiritual lives. Give an example of each of the following:

What is true?

noble?

right?

pure?

lovely?

worthy of respect?

Why is each of these excellent? Worthy of praise? What happens to your thoughts and spirit when you think about such things? Give examples.

Let's Pray About It

Protect me, Jesus, from harmful thoughts that would enter my mind through what I see, hear, and read. Forgive me when I think sinful thoughts. Take those sinful thoughts from me. Set me free.

In your name I choose to think about the good things that are true and noble and right and pure and lovely. Most of all, I choose to think about you being the truth. Being all that is honorable and good. Being totally free of sin. Thank you, Jesus. Thank you for setting me free!

All My Problems?

WEEK 27

This is what the Lord says. . . . "Fear not, for I have redeemed you; I have called you by name; you are mine. When you pass through the waters, I will be with you; and when you pass through the rivers, they will not sweep over you. . . . For I am the Lord your God, the Holy One of Israel, your Savior."
Isaiah 43:1 – 3a

Emily's church had brought a busload of junior high kids to hear a well-known Christian singer. As the kids emptied out of the bus, Emily looked around.

Some of the older girls and boys walked together. Emily watched them talking and laughing. All of them seemed so sure of themselves.

I wish I could feel that way, Emily thought.

She and her new friend Rachel followed José, the youth leader, and his wife, Maria, into the auditorium. Seats were filling up fast.

José turned and called out to the kids. "If we can't sit together, meet here at the end of the concert!"

When they needed to split up, Emily and Rachel found themselves down near the front, two rows away from the other kids. Listening to the excited talk all around them, Emily felt lonely again. *I bet if I had more friends, I'd always feel good inside.*

Soon the concert began. The music was great. Often the audience clapped along, stomped their feet, and called out. Before long, Emily forgot about herself. After a number of songs, the singer started telling how he had come to know Jesus.

As he described his past sinful life, Emily felt uncomfortable. *Is there something wrong with me?* she wondered. *I don't have a very exciting testimony.*

"Accept Jesus, and all your problems will be over," the singer said.

Now Emily felt really confused. *I've already invited Jesus into my life. But I still have problems. Is there something I didn't do right?*

All around Emily, kids began standing up and going forward. One minute Emily wanted to join them; the next she felt as if her feet wouldn't move. *Should I go forward again?* she wondered. *Didn't I really accept Jesus?*

Instead of moving, Emily sat there. *I want to be a Christian, but I'm afraid to ask someone if I am. They'll think I'm dumb if I don't know.*

Finally Emily bowed her head. "Help me, Jesus," she prayed. "I really want to know where I'm at."

At the end of the concert, Emily followed her friend Rachel to the place where they were to meet the others. Their youth leader, José, and his wife, Maria, were already there. Hoping for a chance to talk but scared to try, Emily went over and waited beside Maria.

As soon as José counted noses they started toward the door. When kids poured out of the building, Emily stayed close. At last she worked up the courage to begin. "Maria—"

Just then, someone grabbed Maria's arm and kept talking all the way to the parking lot. When Emily climbed onto the bus, she found an empty seat next to Maria and sat down.

On the ride back to church, Emily tried again. "Maria, the singer said that if I became a Christian, all my problems would be over. But they aren't!"

"Are you confused?" Maria asked. "I'm glad you told me. The

singer didn't explain that very well. He should have said, 'If you accept Jesus, he'll be *with you* in your problems.'"

Whew! Emily felt as if a heavy bag of books had fallen off her back.

"Have you found that's true since you asked Jesus to be your Savior?"

Emily thought about it for a moment and nodded. "But when the singer talked about how he was before he became a Christian, I thought—"

"That maybe you haven't been sinful enough?" As the bus passed under a street light, Maria's smile shone in her dark eyes. "I know. When I hear testimonies, I sometimes wonder that myself. But do you know what? You and I haven't gone through all the suffering that comes with the kind of sin he talked about. We don't have to have a colorful past life. It's exciting to be sheltered by God and become a Christian without that suffering."

"He explained it in a different way—the singer, I mean."

"Did you wonder if you needed to go forward again?" Maria asked.

Emily nodded.

"Sometimes that happens. Different speakers use different ways to explain how to receive salvation. But when José and I prayed with you a few months ago, you told Jesus you were sorry for your sins and asked forgiveness. You asked him to be your Savior and Lord. That's what's important. When you did that, you became a Christian."

"But—" Emily hesitated. "Sometimes I'm not sure. Sometimes I don't *feel* like I'm a Christian."

"If you believed what you were saying when you prayed that prayer, you *are* a Christian," Maria told her. "You can't depend on your feelings. You have to go by what God promises."

Digging in a pocket of her jacket, Maria pulled out a small Bible and flashlight. When she found the right place, she turned the Bible toward Emily. "Read this."

Just then, someone spoke to Maria and she turned away. Emily looked down and started reading. Suddenly the words were so real that they seemed to jump off the page. "I write these things to you who believe in the name of the Son of God so that you may *know* that you have eternal life ..." In Maria's Bible the word *know* was underlined.

Emily took a deep breath, then let it out. All around her, the bus was noisy, but deep inside Emily, there was something steady and quiet. All the confusion she had felt slipped away. The words she had read in the Bible gave her the certainty she needed.

Snapping off the flashlight, Emily sat there, not wanting to talk with anyone. Silently she prayed. "I asked you, Jesus, to be my Savior and Lord. So you are! Thank you! And thank you for your promise. Thanks for your promise that because I believe in you I *know* that I have eternal life!

In that moment Emily had a surprising new thought. No one had ever told her, but Emily knew. *Jesus is the* only *one who can fill* every *empty space in my heart!*

Let's Talk ... or Journal

DAY 1

Why did Emily wonder if she had been sinful enough?

DAY 2

Has Jesus promised to take away all of your problems? Why or why not? What does it mean to say, "Jesus will be with you in your problems"? How can Jesus give you the power to deal with hard things in your life?

DAY 3

What did Maria mean when she said, "You can't depend on your feelings. You have to go by what God promises." Explain. If possible, give an example from your own life.

DAY 4

Do you have questions like the ones Emily had? Are you wondering whether you're a Christian? Receiving the salvation that Jesus offers as a free gift is the most important decision you will ever make. If you would like to ask Jesus to be your Savior and Lord, you can do this:

Thank Jesus for loving you. Believe that he died on the cross for your sin. In the Bible Jesus says, "I am the way and the truth and the life. No one comes to the Father except through me." The Bible also promises "But here is how God has shown his love for us. While we were still sinners Christ died for us."

Tell Jesus that you're sorry for your sins and ask him to forgive you. The Bible tells us, "Suppose we claim we are without sin. Then we are fooling ourselves. The truth is not in us. But God is faithful and fair. If we admit that we have sinned, he will forgive us our sins. He will forgive every wrong thing we have done. He will make us pure."

Ask Jesus to be your Savior and Lord. The Bible promises that "Everyone who calls upon the name of the Lord will be saved."

Thank Jesus for the salvation you received in the moment you asked. The Bible says, "I write these things to you who believe in the name of the Son of God so that you may *know* you have eternal life."

You can pray like this: "Thank you, Jesus, for dying on the cross for me. I'm sorry for my sins and ask your forgiveness. I ask you to be my Savior and to be Lord over every part of my life. Thank you for your salvation and your eternal life beginning right now. Amen!"

If you have asked Jesus for his salvation, it will seem more real if you fill in these words or write them in your Bible. It's important to see what you believe written in your own handwriting: "On this day ________________________________ (give the date and year), at this time________________, I told Jesus that I am sorry for my sin. I believe he has died to save me from my sin and that he has forgiven me. I have asked him to be my Savior and to be Lord over every part of my life. Because of his death on the cross and his resurrection from the dead, I believe he has given me his salvation and eternal life, beginning right now. Thank you, Jesus!"

Now sign your name____

Here are the verses that Emily read from 1 John 5:11 – 13: "I'm writing these things to you who believe in the name of the Son of God. I'm doing it so you will *know* that you have eternal life. There is one thing we can be sure of when we come to God in prayer. If we ask anything in keeping with what he wants, he hears us. If we know that God hears what we ask for, we *know* that we have it." (NIrV)

DAY 5

If you are reading this book by yourself, tell a parent, teacher, pastor, church youth leader, or another Christian about the prayer you've prayed. Your salvation will seem more real to you. If you aren't attending a church now ask a grownup you trust to recommend one for you. Ask Jesus to guide you to the church that will help you keep growing in him.

DAY 6

If you don't have a Bible, tell another Christian or a church about it. Decide on a time when you can read the Bible every day. Many people like to read from the Bible the first thing in the morning. Before going to bed at night is another good time.

The book of John is a good place to start reading. In the front of the Bible find a page called *Contents*. Then look for *The New Testament*. John is the fourth book in the New Testament.

The verses given in Day 4 are special promises for you. If you'd like to read them in the Bible, check near the front for a page called Contents. Then look at the books listed under The New Testament. If needed, ask someone to help you find the verses. They are given in this order: Romans 10:9; John 14:6; Romans 5:8; I John 1:8 – 9; Romans 10:13; I John 5:13.

DAY 7

Decide what you want to do to read the Bible every day. Write down what you've decided here.

In the days ahead come back to this page and write down what you're learning about Jesus.

Let's Pray About It

Thank you, Jesus, that when I ask you to forgive my sins, you do forgive them. Thank you that through your death on the cross, you give me salvation and eternal life, beginning right now. Thank you for making it real to me. I want to run close to you all the days of my life and forever.

Oreo Goes to the Fair

WEEK 28

When the way you live pleases the Lord, he makes even your enemies live at peace with you.
Proverbs 16:7 NIrV

At the county fair Cassidy led her calf inside a shed. As she tied Oreo's lead rope to a rail, she saw Paula heading her way. *Hope she doesn't come here*, Cassidy thought.

But Paula did. Bringing over her heifer, a young cow that has never given birth, Paula took the space next to Oreo. As Cassidy said hi and tried to smile, she took a good look at Princess. Paula's entry in the fair competition could give Cassidy a good run for her money.

Feeling uneasy, she turned back to her own calf. Named Oreo because she was a black-and-white Holstein, the heifer acted as if she wasn't sure about her new surroundings. Cassidy kept talking to her. "It's okay, girl," she said, stroking her neck. "Settle down."

Born in January, Oreo would be one of the largest in her class. Cassidy felt proud of the calf's shiny coat and the straight line of her back.

But Paula looked toward Oreo and said, "She's got a back like a camel."

Cassidy felt a hot flush go to her face. *How mean can you get?* she thought.

"A rea-a-al winner!" Paula drawled the words, and Cassidy knew she meant just the opposite.

Still Cassidy didn't answer. She and Paula were members of the same 4-H Club. Usually members worked together at fair time and helped each other. But Paula always picked on Cassidy. Last year their entries had been the same age and class. Now they were competing against each other again.

"Her eyes are too close together," Paula went on. "Looks like she has a brain the size of a peanut."

Cassidy's anger boiled up and spilled over. "What about Princess? She doesn't look so great!"

A half smile formed on Paula's lips, as if she was glad she had made Cassidy angry. Turning away, Paula got Princess a bucket of feed.

Cassidy washed down Oreo, then started to groom her. She'd taken care of the heifer since she was a newborn calf with wobbly legs and hair that was still wet. When Cassidy chose Oreo for her 4-H project, she began leading the calf around, teaching her to follow.

Cassidy's kindness to the young calf paid off. They became friends. Whenever Cassidy entered the pasture, Oreo came close and waited for Cassidy to scratch her neck and behind her ears.

Now Paula broke into Cassidy's thoughts. "Just because you won a blue ribbon last year doesn't mean you'll do it again."

"Is that what's bothering you? Because you got second place—a red ribbon?"

Paula tossed her head. "Of course not. The judge was playing favorites, and you know it."

Once more Cassidy's anger boiled up. As she brushed Oreo until her coat shone, she couldn't get Paula out of her mind. Cassidy didn't like being enemies with anyone. Usually she found it easy to make friends. She'd even done it with a calf.

Just then an idea dropped into her mind. *Aha!* Cassidy bent down to hide her grin from Paula. *I'll be as nice to her as I am to Oreo.*

While clipping the hair around Oreo's ears, Cassidy decided

what to do. She felt as if she'd be spitting through her teeth, but she'd give it a try.

When Paula finished brushing Princess, Cassidy turned to her. "Her coat looks nice and shiny."

Paula looked surprised, but didn't say anything.

"You've done a good job of grooming her."

Still Paula looked surprised, as though she didn't trust Cassidy. But this time she mumbled thanks.

As Cassidy worked the end of Oreo's tail into many small braids, she felt different inside. She still didn't like being next to Paula, but at least she didn't feel as upset.

The next day Cassidy unbraided Oreo's tail and back-combed the kinky ends. As she fluffed them up, Cassidy looked over at Paula. "Your heifer looks great."

Again Paula looked as if she didn't know whether Cassidy was teasing. After a moment Paula seemed to decide Cassidy meant it. "So does yours," she said, her voice low.

When it was time for the judging, Cassidy changed into white clothes. If there was a tie between entries, even the appearance of the one showing an animal could make a difference in winning or losing. Then she attached a lead to Oreo's halter and fell into line. Paula and Princess followed them into the large, open space surrounded by bleachers.

As they walked in a circle, the judge called out, "Stop your heifers!" Then, "Pose them!"

Oreo stood with her front legs firmly beneath her. With the back leg closest to the judge forward, she kept the other leg straight.

Soon the judge began pulling animals out of the circle and placing them in lines—one line for the blue ribbons, another for the red, and so on. When the judge placed Oreo at the front of the blue ribbon line, Cassidy felt excited. *Maybe she'll get Grand Champion of our class!*

Paula's turn was next. The judge circled Princess, and Paula kept moving to the opposite side so she wouldn't block the judge's view. She looked sure of herself and Princess.

Cassidy caught her breath. For the first time she wondered, *Was Paula being mean so I'd feel jumpy and not do as well?*

A moment later the judge led Paula forward, putting her and Princess in front of Cassidy.

Outwardly Cassidy stood at attention, but inside she felt sick. *Paula's first, and I'm second. She'll get Grand Champion.*

Then Cassidy had an even worse thought. *Did I help Paula win by being nice to her? She looks so sure of herself.* In close competition Paula's attitude could make a difference.

As the judge circled the other calves, the awful question stayed with Cassidy. Watching the judge, Cassidy kept Oreo alert. But Paula glanced toward the stands and smiled.

In that moment the judge glanced her way. *He must have seen Paula,* Cassidy thought. *She shouldn't have looked at the stands. She looks too sure of herself.*

The judge returned to their line and asked Cassidy more questions. When he told her to move in front of Paula, Cassidy hardly dared breathe.

A moment later the judge brought out the Grand Champion ribbon. "I place Oreo at the top of the class," he called out. "She's an outstanding heifer and responds well to her owner."

Then the judge handed the ribbon and trophy to Cassidy.

Grand Champion? Best in show? Cassidy felt like crying and laughing at the same time.

The judge moved on and gave Paula a blue ribbon. Watching her, Cassidy wondered, *How's she going to feel—missing it by one wrong move?*

Soon the 4-H'ers began leading their heifers back to the shed. Cassidy felt like shouting, but Paula was quiet the whole way. When they finally stopped their calves at a rail, Paula looked at Cassidy. "Congratulations," Paula told her. "You deserved it."

"Thanks!" Cassidy felt relieved that the competition between them was gone. "But you were just a hair's breadth away. It was really close."

Then Cassidy flung her arms around Oreo. When she looked up, she saw Paula's grin. *I've won more than a trophy*, Cassidy decided.

Let's Talk . . . or Journal

DAY 1

What did Cassidy mean when she thought *I've won more than a trophy*?

DAY 2

Why can it be especially hard to be nice to someone you compete against? Explain.

DAY 3

Cassidy learned something from Oreo that helped her decide how to act toward Paula. What was it?

DAY 4

How does putting down another person hurt a friendship? Give examples from the story or your own life.

When you compete against others, there can be hard lessons to learn. At the end of a game, players go down a line, shaking hands with players on the other team. Why do they do this? What do you think they're saying?

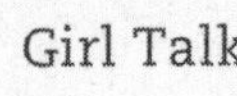

DAY 5

Why does encouragement help a friendship grow? Why can encouragement be called a put-up instead of a put-down?

DAY 6

Do you have a pet that you love very much? If so, explain why that animal means a lot to you. How does your pet encourage you? Tell about ways your pet has helped you know how to treat people

DAY 7

Did Jesus ever give people put-downs? Why? Give reasons for your answer, then check out Matthew 22:34 – 39. In what way does Jesus want us to give people put-ups?

Give examples of ways that Jesus has given you put-ups that encouraged you when you were having a hard time.

Let's Pray About It

Thank you, God, for creating all kinds of animals for us to enjoy. Thanks for how much my special pet means to me. When kids upset me, help me act in a way that pleases you. Thanks that you can turn even my enemies into friends.

Jackie Comes Home

WEEK 29

Don't let love and truth ever leave you. Tie them around your neck. Write them on the tablet of your heart. Then you will find favor and a good name in the eyes of God and people.
Proverbs 3:3–4 NIrV

It took only a moment, and it was done. "I want to come home later tonight," said Jackie. "I'd like to go to Deb's after school."

Dad looked her straight in the eyes. "You'll be at Deb's? And you'll be home by 5:30?"

For a split second Jackie thought about her answer. Yet when she told the lie, it seemed easy. "Sure, Dad, at Deb's. I'll be home at 5:30. Just in time for supper."

Jackie's dad had been both mom and dad since her mom died. Now he was telecommuting so he could work at home.

Avoiding his eyes, Jackie gave her dad a hug. A moment later she was out the door. As the below-freezing air hit her face, her cheeks began to tingle. Squinting her eyes against the blinding white snow, Jackie started the four long blocks to school.

Halfway there she met Margrit. "Can you come after school, Jackie?" she asked. "The boys said they could."

"Sure, I'll see you then. Dad didn't catch on. I told him I'm going to Deb's."

Hours later, Jackie reached Margrit's front door. Chad and his friend were already there, and a strong bass thumped from a boom box.

For a moment Jackie felt a twinge of uneasiness. More than once her dad had said, "You can't go to Margrit's after school. I don't want you there, especially when her mother is at work."

"Yeah, Dad, sure," Jackie had promised just as often. Now she pushed down her uneasiness. *Dad will never find out,* she told herself. *I know how to handle older boys. I can take care of myself.*

Turning on her brightest smile, Jackie entered the family room. Chad stood up. "Hi, Jackie."

The way he said her name made Jackie uncomfortable, but she tried to ignore the feeling. Soon she slipped into the beat of the music and forgot the whispers of her conscience. *Sure is more fun dancing with Chad than being at Deb's.*

But Chad kept moving closer. Each time Jackie stepped back, he followed. *I don't like this,* Jackie thought. Uneasy feelings clutched at her stomach. *Dad was right. I shouldn't be here!*

Just then the music stopped. Feeling desperate, Jackie glanced at a clock.

Ten minutes after five. Suddenly she knew what to do.

"I said I'd be home at 5:30. Gotta go." Before anyone could answer, she picked up her coat and headed out the door.

Whew! I'll never try that again! Jackie felt grateful for the two blocks she had to walk in the cold fresh air. But Dad was waiting for her.

"Where have you been, Jackie?"

"I told you this morning where I was going. Don't you remember I said I was going to Deb's?"

Dad's gaze held steady. "I called, and you weren't there. Too bad you missed your cousins. The furnace at their school broke down, so they had a day off. Your aunt Laura drove them over. They thought it'd be fun to see you."

In that moment Jackie felt like throwing up. Okay, so Dad had learned the truth. She was in for it now. But Jackie also felt relieved.

Hiding the truth, her awful feelings, the lies—all the telling herself it was okay when it wasn't. And she had missed her favorite cousins!

Who have I been lying to? Jackie asked herself. *To my dad or to myself?*

Let's Talk . . . or Journal

DAY 1

Why did Jackie try to hide what she was doing? How did one lie lead to another? What are some dangers for anyone who tries to hide what he or she is doing?

DAY 2

What did Jackie mean when she asked herself, "Who have I been lying to? My dad or myself?" Do you think her dad had figured out what Jackie was doing? Give reasons for your answer.

DAY 3

What are some of the dangers of hanging out with older kids?

DAY 4

How did Jackie's choices keep getting her into deeper trouble? What were the consequences of her lies?

DAY 5

Because Jackie lied to her dad, she set aside safeguards that could help her. She also took herself out from under his protection. In the same way that earthly parents want to keep us from harm, God our Heavenly Father wants to protect us. But he has given us free will. If we deliberately make wrong choices it's the same as telling him, "I don't want you to protect me. I want to do it my own way."

How do you think God feels about our telling him we don't want his help? Give reasons to support your answer.

DAY 6

If you're going to a party at a friend's house, it's easy for your mom or dad to make one phone call. Your parent can say to your friend's parent, "I understand there's going to be a party at your house. Will you be home?"

How would your mom or dad feel if they asked such a question and learned that you had lied to them? How do you think your friend's parent would react when learning about a party being planned for a time when they're not home?

DAY 7

Parents are people who want to give their help whenever you need it. In what ways can you work together as a family to make life easier for all of you? In Week 8, we started a list that would have helped Bobbi at her sleepover. Review that, then keep making a list of other practical ideas.

Here are some starters. You can always say:

- "My mom said I have to be home at a certain time."
- "My parents don't want me to go there."
- "My dad says that isn't safe. I've promised him I wouldn't do that."

Always remember:

- When you don't feel comfortable with a crowd it might be time to leave.
- You can call your parents any time your want. No matter where they are or what they're doing, they can tell you what to do.
- God is the biggest protector of all. You can pray his name—Jesus! at any time. You can ask for his help at any moment. But you also need to be smart and not purposely do something you know is wrong.
- You can repeat verses that remind you of the Lord's help.

Let's Pray About It

Jesus, when I'm tempted to lie, give me the power of your Holy Spirit to be truthful. I don't want to ever let your love and truth leave me. Help me so my words and actions are honest before you, my loved ones, and others. Thank you that when I'm honest I can respect myself and run close to you. And Jesus, I ask in your name for your protection and blessing over me, my friends, and our families. Thank you!

I'd Rather Do It Myself!

WEEK 30

"I will give all of you every place you walk on, just as I promised Moses."

Jos.1:3 NIrV

"None of you should look out just for your own good. You should also look out for the good of others."

Phil. 2:4 NIrV

When they began to sing, Christa leaned forward to watch the excitement on Karyn's face.

"Happy birthday to you. Happy birthday to you. Happy birthday, dear Karyn—"

For a moment Karyn waited, deciding about her wish. Then with a mighty *whoooof* she blew out every candle.

The girls clapped. "You got your wish!" someone said.

The party with girls from the neighborhood had been fun. As Karyn's mom cut the cake, Christa looked around the table. Several girls were laughing. One was ready to pop a balloon. Close by, Christa saw the heads of two girls reflected in a mirror. One of them was April, the girl sitting next to her.

As Christa watched, April leaned forward. Turning this way and that, she studied her face in the mirror. Then her hand went up, rubbing the zits on her nose.

It wasn't hard for Christa to figure out what April was thinking. *She's wondering if anyone can possibly like her when she's got a few pimples.*

Deep inside, Christa sighed. Though she made no sound, it felt like the wind rustling the autumn leaves. *I wish I had April's problems.*

Restless now, Christa wished the party would end. Just then April stretched her legs under the table and bumped the brace on Christa's leg. Christa jumped.

Turning, April apologized. "I'm sorry. Did I hurt you?"

Christa smiled. "I'm good. Don't worry about it." Moving her leg, Christa bent down and pushed her crutches farther under her chair.

Soon the party was over, and all the girls crowded into Karyn's room to pick up their coats. Once again Christa caught April looking in a mirror as though thinking, *What can I do? How can I hide my zits?*

Leaning her crutches against the wall, Christa shrugged into her coat. As she thanked Karyn's mom, she saw that everyone was already ahead of her. *Always the last,* thought Crista. She wished she could move more quickly.

After stuffing her belongings into a book bag, she picked up her crutches again. As the outside door closed behind her, Christa saw the other girls set out.

They'll have fun walking home. And I'll walk alone again.

In the next minute, Christa realized that the dropping temperature had changed the light rain to sleet—a sleet so fine that not even Karyn's mom had noticed it. A thin layer of ice coated the sidewalk.

Ahead of Christa one of the girls took a flying run. "Wheeee! Race you!"

When April followed in a long slide, Christa wished she could do the same. She dreaded the short walk home. Though she lived only a short distance away, the ice would make the trip seem like miles.

For a moment Christa thought of turning back to ask Karyn's mom for help. In the next instant Christa pushed the idea away. Not for anything would she admit how scared she felt.

I can make it, she promised herself. *I'll make it just like any other kid.*

Standing on the wide top step, Christa set her crutches on the narrower step below. As she swung forward, one of her crutches slid.

Christa gasped. In the next instant, she landed hard on the second step. Her crutches clattered out of reach.

April whirled around. With a long slide, she was by Christa's side. "Here, let me help you," she said.

Christa shook her head. "I'm okay," she answered quickly. But her whole body felt the jolt. Panic tightened her muscles. *How will I ever make it home?*

"The sidewalk is icy, too." April gave her a hand up, then held out Christa's crutches.

By now April's friends had stopped. "Hey, hurry up!" they called.

Instead, April slid her hand under Christa's arm. As Christa once more started down the steps, April's grip tightened.

When they reached the sidewalk, Christa still felt afraid. Here, too, her crutches slid on the ice.

"I'll walk home with you," April said quickly.

"Thanks," Christa told her, "but I live the opposite way from you. I'll be okay."

As if wondering what to do, April glanced toward her friends.

"Go ahead," Christa said. "They're waiting for you."

Instead, April waved toward the other kids. "Go on without me!"

Then she turned back to Christa. "Just tell me what to do. I've wanted to help you before but didn't know how."

Startled, Christa's words spilled out. "You didn't know how?"

April shook her head. "You always seem so independent. Like you don't need anyone's help."

Like I don't want *anyone's help.* The thought amazed Christa. *Really?*

But now April asked, "Would it be easier walking on the grass? It wouldn't be so slippery."

As they set out together, Christa's thoughts raced ahead. *Maybe I try too hard to do everything on my own. Maybe I push kids away. I wonder if they're afraid to be friends?*

By the time she and April reached Christa's house, they were laughing and talking together. Christa had also noticed something. *April forgot about her zits.*

Just thinking about it, Christa felt glad. *Maybe I helped* her *today. Maybe I have a new friend.*

Let's Talk . . . or Journal

DAY 1

What do you think was worse—April's zits or how she felt about them? How do you know?

Are there ways in which you feel sorry for yourself? Describe what they are. Are these important reasons for not liking what is happening to you? Or do they involve something you can change?

DAY 2

What did Christa mean when she thought, *I wish I had April's problems*? Instead of trying to walk home, Christa could have gone back inside. Why did she want to make it on her own?

DAY 3

At one time or another, nearly everyone needs to ask for help. What are some ways in which you sometimes need help? Why is it important to ask for help when you need it?

DAY 4

How did April forget about herself? When you make a choice to care about the needs of others, how does it help you?

DAY 5

While Jesus was here on earth, he often went to a quiet place. How did he receive help from his Father in heaven?

DAY 6

What are some ways Jesus forgot about himself in order to help the people who came to him?

Because the Gospel writer Luke was a doctor it's especially fun to see what he writes about the ways Jesus reached out and healed people. For a small sampling of what Jesus did, see Luke 5:12- 26; Luke 7:1 – 17; and Luke 8:40 – 53.

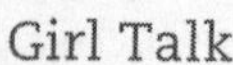

Girl Talk

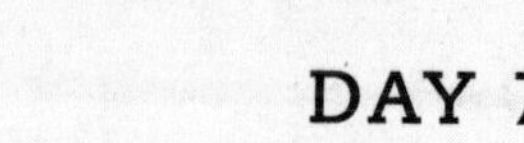

DAY 7

What are some everyday things you can do because you are a Faithgirl and want to walk close to Jesus?

Let's Pray About It

This: *Forgive me, Lord, for thinking so much about myself that sometimes I don't even see the needs of others. Help me to notice ways in which other people need help. Give me a heart that reaches out to them and practical ideas for what to do. I want to keep my eyes on you, Jesus, and live as you lived.*

Or this: *Lord, you know that every day I struggle with not being able to do what other girls can do. Help me in the ways I need to compensate—to make up for what I can't do.*

Help me find ways to do the best I can with the abilities you've given me. And help me to sense that you are with me, always ready to help when I need you. Thank you, Lord!

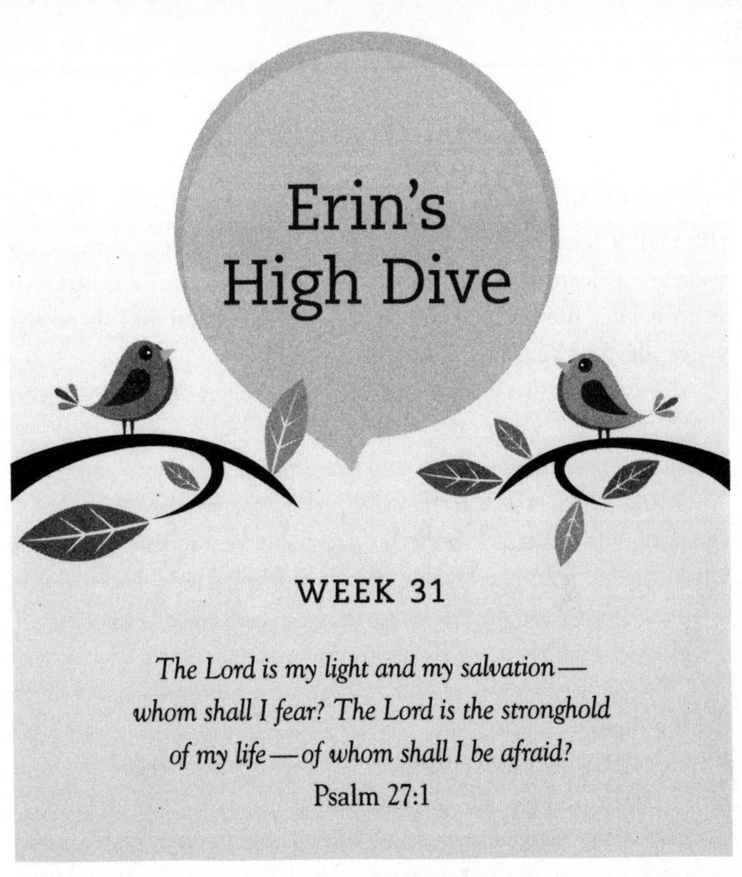

Erin's High Dive

WEEK 31

The Lord is my light and my salvation— whom shall I fear? The Lord is the stronghold of my life—of whom shall I be afraid?
Psalm 27:1

Step by step, Erin climbed the ladder to the high dive. When she reached the board, she looked down. At one side of the pool Tad and Monica lay sunning themselves.

The three of them had come to the pool together, and Erin liked both of them. They always seemed more exciting than the kids she knew at church. But Erin often wondered how the two of them felt about her. *Do they really like me? I don't feel like I fit in.*

Then Erin thought about her dive. She never grew tired of those seconds between leaving the board and breaking the water. Most of the time she loved diving, but sometimes she also felt scared that she wouldn't do it right.

"When you get started, keep going," Mom told her once. "Don't change your mind in the middle of the air."

Whenever Mom and Dad could, they cheered Erin on. Just thinking about them helped her sometimes.

Now Erin took three quick steps and a jump and pushed off the end of the board. Springing into the air, she spread her arms wide in a swan dive. Her body made the arc, swung down. An instant later she brought her arms above her head and sliced the water like a knife.

As Erin rose to the surface, she felt excited. *That was a good one!* Wiping the water out of her eyes, she looked around. Tad and Monica were sitting up. *They're so busy talking. Did they see my dive?*

Erin's strokes slowed, then stopped, as she reached the edge of the pool. Pulling herself from the water, she tried to shrug aside her left-out feeling. As she lay down on her towel, she looked like one of them. But inside she felt set apart. She wanted to belong.

Tad looked her way. "Ready to go?"

"We've only been here half an hour," Erin blurted out. "What's the big rush?"

But Tad's eyes looked bored. He was ready to move on, and Erin knew Monica would go with him. She'd do whatever Tad did.

Is this like another high dive? Erin asked herself. She wanted to go with them, but felt uncomfortable. Trying to push aside her uneasiness, Erin picked up her towel and sunglasses and stood up.

As they left the pool, Tad led the way. Soon he swung onto a path leading to the trees on the far side of the park. His lazy smile creased his face. "Good dive you made."

Erin warmed to his praise. "Oh, thanks!" But a moment later her wondering returned. "Where're we going?" she asked.

Without answering, Tad kept moving, and Monica stayed at his side. Suddenly Erin guessed why they were heading for the trees. Was it their new meeting place? Her steps slowed.

Tad turned. "Come on. What's taking you so long?"

Looking at him, Erin thought again how much she liked Tad and Monica and their friends. She thought about how much she'd like to fit in with them. Yet she also felt as if a mysterious hand pushed her toward something that made her afraid. *What will it be this time?*

As she looked ahead, Erin saw some kids gathered near the

trees. In that moment one of the boys glanced around, as though checking whether anyone was nearby.

Erin's fingers tightened into fists. Her stomach lurched with the worry she felt.

"What are they doing?" she asked Tad.

"Nothing. Just hangin' out."

But Erin caught his quick glance toward the trees. Then she caught the scent of marijuana.

"I don't want anything to do with pot—"

"It won't hurt you any."

"That's not true," Erin told him. "It can hurt both my body and my mind. I don't want to get dependent on any drug."

Tad's laugh broke into her words. "You're crazy. Dumb, dumb, dumb."

Erin hated his laugh. It had a hard sound to it and always made her feel left out. *Maybe I should give it a try*, she thought. *Maybe I would finally fit in.*

"Everybody does it," Tad said as though he had heard her thoughts. Monica looked as if she agreed.

I know pot can start a habit, Erin thought with one part of her mind. Then the other part of her mind tried to push those thoughts aside. *Maybe Tad is right. Nothing will happen to me.*

But Erin's heart seemed to lurch. *Really*? she asked herself. *Or will one thing lead to another?*

Just then she remembered Mom's words about diving: "*Don't change your mind in the middle of the air.*"

Erin drew a deep breath. "I don't want to try it," she said again. "I'm going back to the pool."

"What are you, a wimp or something?" When Tad spoke, his words had a cruel edge. "Or do you think you're better than we are?"

The words cut, but Erin looked Tad in the eye. "I said no, and I mean no. Don't ask me again."

Turning, she started back to the pool—half running, half walking so Tad wouldn't see the tears in her eyes.

Then she heard a voice behind her. "Hey, just a minute," Monica called out. "I'm coming with you."

As Monica caught up, Erin slowed her steps and blinked away

Let's Talk . . . or Journal

the tears. Relieved now, she also felt surprised. *What if I* hadn't *said no? Right now Monica would be saying yes to whatever they offered.*

DAY 1

Why do you suppose Tad and Monica seemed more exciting to Erin than the kids at church?

DAY 2

Why do you think kids get involved with substances that seem okay but lead to something habit-forming?

DAY 3

What was Tad offering to Erin—friendship or the pressure to do something that would hurt her?

DAY 4

If you desperately want to be popular, how can it affect the choices you make? If you don't have a dad or mom who supports you in making right choices, where can you find friends and adults who will help you?

DAY 5

Do you think Erin stuck to her decision to say no? What does it mean to stand firm in a choice? In what ways can you say no so that kids know you really mean it?

DAY 6

Someone who is really a friend won't ask you to do something that will hurt you. Do you feel Tad was a true friend? Is it worth having a friend like Tad? Why or why not? What qualities do you want your friends to have?

DAY 7

Erin wanted to fit in with Tad and his friends, but she felt uneasy. A feeling of uneasiness can be the Holy Spirit's warning. Why is it good if you feel uncomfortable with some kids? How can that feeling protect you?

Courage is going beyond your fear of what others think in order to do the right thing. If you have memorized Bible verses, the Holy Spirit can remind you of those verses at the moment you need them. If you repeat those words when you're tempted to do something wrong, you'll have a laser sword against the enemy that would hurt you. Check out the verse at the beginning of this section and other verses that will help you gain courage. Look up 2 Kings 6:16 and Hebrews 13:5 – 6 and write the words here:

At the back of most Bibles is a concordance, an alphabetical listing of words that will help you find a verse on a topic you'd like to read about. For example, if you look for the word *fear,* you'll find a verse such as Isaiah 41:13. Then you'll see a short phrase to help you recognize which one of the verses on fear you'd like to read.

How about picking out a verse right now and memorizing it?

Let's Pray About It

Thank you, Jesus, that I don't feel comfortable with some kids. Thanks for protecting me that way. Whenever I face something that would hurt me, give me the strength to say no and stick to it. In your name I ask for Christian friends who live the way you want all of us to live. And help me to be that kind of friend to others. Thank you!

Runaway Secret

WEEK 32

[Jesus said,] "I have called you friends, for everything that I learned from my Father I have made known to you. You did not choose me, but I chose you to go and bear fruit—fruit that will last."
John 15:15b–16

When Alyssa stayed overnight with Holly, they talked and giggled all evening long. Now it was late. As they stretched out on their sleeping bags, Holly had a question.

"Alyssa, do you tell me all your secrets?"

Alyssa thought for a moment. "Wel-l-l-l—"

"Well, you should," Holly said. "After all, we're really good friends."

Alyssa was quiet, not sure she wanted to tell Holly everything she thought and felt.

But Holly kept on. "When I tell you a secret, I know you won't tell anyone. And I wouldn't tell anyone your secrets."

"You're sure?" asked Alyssa.

"For *sure*," answered Holly. "I wouldn't give away a secret for *anything*. Especially a secret that's yours."

Alyssa still felt uneasy. What if Holly didn't understand?

Holly rolled over onto her stomach. "I've told you all my secrets. Why haven't you told me yours?"

Alyssa's secret was so special that she didn't want to tell anyone. Talking about it might spoil the special way she felt.

"Come on, Alyssa. That's what friends are for!"

Can I really count on you? Alyssa wondered.

"I promise not to tell a soul," said Holly, as though reading Alyssa's thoughts.

"Promise?" Alyssa asked.

"Promise," answered Holly in her most solemn cross-your-heart-and-hope-to-die-I-will-not-tell-a-lie voice.

So Alyssa told Holly about how much she liked Devin. She told Holly how cute he was when he smiled. How he often sat down with her on the bus ride to or from school. How whenever they had the same class Devin paid attention to whatever she said. And how maybe—just maybe—he liked her.

"You won't tell anyone? You promise?" asked Alyssa.

"I said *promise*, didn't I?" said Holly. "Your secret's safe with me."

Soon after, they fell asleep. The next morning Alyssa wondered if she'd done the right thing in telling Holly her secret. *But I can trust her,* Alyssa decided. *After all, we're best friends.*

Two days later Alyssa started to worry. As she walked down the hall at school, she saw three girls in a huddle, talking and giggling.

Seeing Alyssa, they stopped talking. As if a thin sliver of light shone through a window, Alyssa felt uneasy deep inside.

Later that day she knew for sure. When she ran outside for gym, the other girls started teasing her.

"Alyssa loves Devin! Alyssa loves Devin!" In a singsong chant the words rose all around her.

Alyssa's face grew hot with embarrassment. She tried to pretend she didn't hear. But the girls kept chanting, their voices growing louder all the time.

What if Devin hears them? In panic Alyssa looked around to see where the boys were. Sure enough, Devin was far down the field, playing soccer. As Alyssa watched, his team took a time out.

"Shhhhhh!" Alyssa begged. "Be quiet! He'll hear you!"

But the girls chanted louder, and Devin turned in their direction.

Alyssa wished she could be a turtle and crawl inside a shell. She ached now, ached with the hurt of it. *I'll never be able to look Devin in the face again.*

As soon as school was over, Alyssa hunted down Holly. "You said you were my best friend!"

"I am!" answered Holly.

"And you spread it all over school that I like Devin. I've never been more embarrassed in my life!"

"What? All over school? No, I didn't!"

"Yes, you did!"

"Says who?"

"Says me. How else could the whole school know?"

"You're kidding!" Holly looked upset. "Really?"

"Really."

"I only told one person. Samantha promised—"

"That she would never say a word?"

"Oh, Alyssa! I'm so sorry! I really, really am. Will you forgive me?"

But Alyssa wasn't ready to forgive. "Holly, you promised. And now you just say two little words—*I'm sorry*. I'm left with all the mess—all the hurt. Forever and ever!"

Holly's blue eyes filled with tears. "Alyssa, I really am sorry. I'm sorry I told. I'm sorry I hurt you."

Alyssa glared at her. *What should I say?* she wondered. *Can I ever count on Holly again?*

Let's Talk . . . or Journal

DAY 1

Why is it hard to keep a secret?

DAY 2

Why do most of us feel more important if we have a secret to tell?

DAY 3

What does it mean to trust someone? Why did Alyssa trust Holly? How did Holly destroy Alyssa's trust in her? Think of other ways in which a girl sometimes destroys the trust of another girl.

DAY 4

Do you think Alyssa should forgive Holly? Why or why not? Do you think Alyssa should show her love and forgiveness to Holly by telling her another secret? Give reasons for your answer.

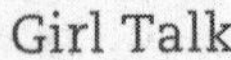

DAY 5

If you lose trust in someone, why is it hard to believe in that person again?

DAY 6

Some secrets should not be kept. When is it important to tell a parent or another adult a secret between kids?

How can talking at the right time and to the right person keep someone from getting hurt?

DAY 7

Here's a big truth: While we can't always trust people to act the way they should, there is someone we can always trust. If you ask him to be with you, he will be. Jesus is the best promise keeper of all.

That doesn't mean he will always answer our prayers exactly the way we'd like. And it doesn't mean he will always answer as fast as we want. But here's what it does mean:

If we ask him to be with us, he will.

And whenever we pray to Jesus, we can trust him with our lives, thoughts, feelings, and all that we are. We can trust him with knowing what is best for us.

Why is he worthy of our trust? Think about it, then make a list, or write about a way in which he has been trustworthy for you. Then check out Hebrews 13:8.

Let's Pray About It

Dear Jesus, help me to be wise and discerning—to know whether it's okay to put my trust in someone and tell that person a special secret. When I need to forgive someone, remind me of how often you have forgiven me, but protect me from making another mistake.

Help me also, Jesus, to be a true friend—a girl others can trust because I keep a secret at the right time. Thank you that I can pray to you, my best Friend, whenever I want. Thank you that I can tell you everything, and it's safe with you. But show me, too, when I need to talk to an adult about something that should not be kept secret. Thank you!

The Hidden Puzzle Piece

WEEK 33

Jesus said, "And you can be sure that I am always with you, to the very end."
Matthew 28:20b NIrV

For many years Elise's older brother Nate has been there for her in tough times, funny times, and times when she just needed help.

He was there when she learned how to snowboard for the first time. That was also her last time snowboarding!

He was there when she was having tough times in school.

Nate was simply always there.

Nate was one of the puzzle pieces that completed her life. Her life would be one part less if he wasn't there.

But it wasn't until she and Nate decided to do a song in her school talent show that Elise started wondering, *What will happen when Nate leaves for college next year? Will he still be the puzzle piece that completes my life? I think that piece will always be there, but who really knows?*

The morning of the talent show was a sunny, humid day. Kids

were laughing, birds chirping, and the scent of lilacs filled the air. But Elise wasn't laughing. As she thought about the talent show, she felt anxious.

She and Nate would be first in the show. While she sang, he would play the guitar. But it was also the night of his senior prom. After having their pictures taken, Nate and his date would come to Elise's school, then go on to dinner and the prom.

Now Elise sat on a kitchen stool, staring out the window at their large tree with the old bird house in it. As she sat there, looking outside and thinking about the talent show, she started shaking.

It seemed impossible to sing in the show! What if she embarrassed herself in front of everyone? She wished that everything would be okay. That she'd have nothing to worry about. But she had never sung in front of anyone besides her family and close friends.

Except for figure skating competitions, she had never done anything in front of an audience. Now she would sing in front of all her peers. For someone as shy as she was — or so she had been told — singing at the show was impossible!

In that moment her brother stomped up the carpeted stairs. *Thump, thump, thump.* Entering the kitchen, he flashed a big, bright, gleaming smile. "Elise, it's going to be ok."

"No, it won't." Her voice trembled.

"Elise, come on." Nate's blue eyes looked directly into hers. "You'll be great. If you mess up, nobody will notice."

"But I can't do it. My friends will be there. What if I make a *huge* mistake?

"Elise, it doesn't matter. High five!"

Elise slapped his hand hard, then took a deep breath. *Maybe, just maybe I can do this.*

When it was time to go to the talent show, Elise took more deep breaths, drank lots of water, and went the bathroom at least six times. Going outside, she sat down in the car, and clenched her hands into fists. Her mom was driving, and Nate had taken his own car.

"Mom," Elise said as they pulled out of the driveway. "I'm nervous."

An instant later she thought, *"Well, duh," I would say if I were Mom.* But instead her mother answered, "You'll do great."

When her mom pulled up at school, Elise's brother and his prom date waited in a parking place. Elise opened the car door. Sweat dripped down her face like rain drops on a window. Wearing jeans for the show, Nate stepped out of his red mini van with the cracked windshield.

As Nate and Elise walked into the building, she saw her friends and classmates arriving. Elise shivered, just seeing all the people. When she tried to open the inner door, her sweaty hands slid off the handle. But then she led Nate through the hallway to the gym where the talent show would take place.

Grabbing the wooden stools they would use, they brought them onto the stage. There, behind closed curtains, Elise wouldn't see all the people. Silently she sat on her stool, staring at the curtains.

"Are you ok?" Nate asked.

"Not really. I can't sing in front of that many people."

Sitting there, waiting, she felt like a bird ready to hatch out of its shell. It wanted to stay safe—hidden by the shell, instead of stepping into a harsh world.

I'm that bird, she thought. *I want to stay backstage. I don't want to sing in front of a crowd of people.*

"Elise, we've practiced a bunch of times." Her brother seemed to guess her thoughts. "You have absolutely nothing to worry about."

As Nate looked into her eyes, his eyes were stern, but friendly and sympathetic. "And just remember, I am always here for you."

"Oh," she said, and lightened up a bit. A feeble smile broke through.

Knowing that her brother was there for her was an amazing feeling. It was a feeling that not many kids get when their brother was a cool eighteen-year-old who didn't want anything to do with his little sister. But his feeling of acceptance changed the way Elise felt before she sang.

Thinking about it more, she offered a big smile, then jumped off her stool. "Does my hair look ok?"

"Good," he said. "What about mine?"

"It's flipping out." Elise patted down his long blond hair. "Now you're good."

"Cool! High five!"

Elise slapped his hand hard.

"Are you ready?" her brother asked.

"Yes," she said with a confident smile.

Then the house lights dimmed, and the announcers introduced Elise and Nate.

As the dark red curtains opened, Elise caught a glimpse of all the people. Taking a deep breath, she thought about her brother's words. *"Remember I'm always here for you."*

Then she caught Nate's look. Yes, she was ready. Slowly he began strumming his guitar.

Elise gulped, closed her eyes, and imagined nobody was there. It seemed like forever, but then she began singing. As Nate accompanied her, she kept on. To her surprise she loved the feeling of being on stage, singing in front of everyone. The longer she sang, the more she loved it.

Throughout the whole song Elise stumbled only a little. When she and Nate finished, applause rose around them. As they walked off the stage, Elise tried to hold in the smile she had been keeping inside.

Backstage, both she and Nate were silent. But then he reached out for her. "Elise," Nate said, "give me a hug."

As she gave her brother an immense hug Elise smiled. "Thanks," she said softly.

It wasn't until then that deep down Elise truly realized her brother was going to be in college next year. *It won't be the same,* she thought. *We can't make another moment like this, or at least not a lot more of these moments.*

I'll see my brother, and all, but part of him will be missing. The part of him that was always there, even when everything crumbled. Soon there will be that missing puzzle piece, the piece that completed my life. The piece that was always there, but I didn't know it until the talent show.

Lifting her head, Elise smiled again. As Nate left for his senior prom she knew something she wanted to hold in her heart forever—her memory of this night.

Nate saying, "Remember, Elise, I'm always here for you."

Her older brother saying, "Give me a hug, Elise. Hug."

Let's Talk . . . or Journal

DAY 1

This is a true story that Elise wrote in first person when she was eleven years old. To introduce her story she said, "There is a hidden puzzle piece in all of us, but you never know it until it seems like it isn't there anymore. But it always is." What was the hidden puzzle piece in Elise's life? What is the hidden puzzle piece in your life?

DAY 2

What do you especially like about Elise's story?

DAY 3

Elise said that her brother Nate gave her a puzzle piece that she would remember forever. Why is it important that we remember our special moments and hug them to ourselves?

DAY 4

Do you have a family member who has always been there for you, even though you didn't realize it? Who is that person and why? Or is there someone outside your immediate family who has been there for you—someone like a teacher, uncle or aunt, grandparents, pastor, or friend?

Tell some of the fun or funny things you've done with one of the special people in your life. Talk about the good times and also about the times when you needed encouragement.

DAY 5

In one or two sentences write what you especially remember about a person who has encouraged you. Then take that sentence and write a paragraph or a story about what happened.

DAY 6

If you don't have a younger brother or sister is there some other person to whom you can offer the gift of being like an encouraging older sister?

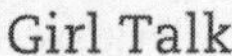

DAY 7

How are you doing on memorizing God's great promises? Here's one that's especially good if you need to give a speech or sing in public: "Now go; I will help you speak and teach you what to say" Exodus 4:12.

In the puzzle of our lives Jesus can be special to every one of us. Remember this promise? "Jesus said, 'And you can be sure that I am always with you, to the very end.'" If you memorize those words you can repeat them back to yourself at any time of the day or night.

Let's Pray About It

Thank you, Jesus, that you want to be the most important piece in the puzzle of my life. Thank you for the special people you have given me. And thank you that if I need someone to help me, I can ask you for that special person. Most of all, thank you for promising to be with me always. By faith I choose to believe that you are with me, even when I can't feel it.

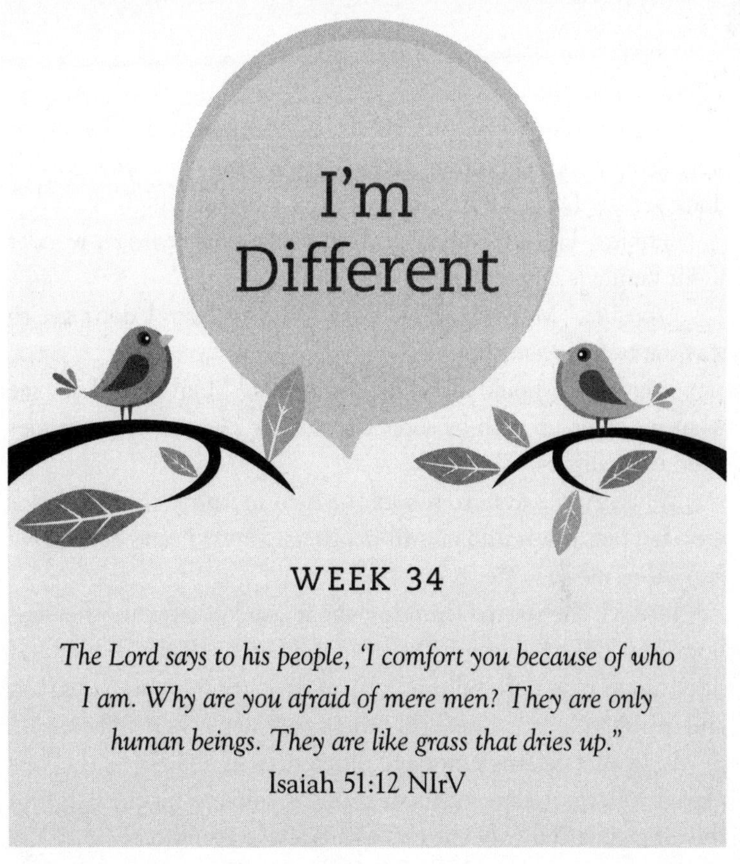

I'm Different

WEEK 34

The Lord says to his people, 'I comfort you because of who I am. Why are you afraid of mere men? They are only human beings. They are like grass that dries up."

Isaiah 51:12 NIrV

I want to go," Angie said.

"I *don't* want you to go," answered her father.

Looking around the supper table, Angie wondered if she could get help from her older brother, Mark, or her younger sister, Peanuts. Right now neither of them looked ready to come to her rescue.

"Angie, why do you want to go to this party?" asked Mom.

"It'll be fun to be with the other kids."

"That's a good reason," Dad said. "But the last time you went to Carly's house, you saw a DVD we didn't want you to see. The one you're talking about is no better."

"Aw, Dad, all my friends are gonna see it. If I don't, I won't know what to talk about at school."

"You'll feel out of it," Mom said.

Angie turned to her, surprised that Mom seemed to be on her side. "Right! All the other parents are letting their kids go. If I don't see the DVD, I'll be different from everyone else."

"Hmm." Thinking about it, Dad stroked his beard. "I wonder if our family is different in other ways?"

"You bet," Mark answered. "I'm different, too. I don't get to stay out as late as my friends."

"Maybe we should all think about this," Mom said. "Let's see what we come up with by supper tomorrow night. Is it sometimes good to be different?"

When Angie went to school the next morning, she looked for ways her family was different from others. *Maybe I can still talk Dad into letting me go to the party.*

Instead, she started thinking about one kid after another and how they looked. In math she saw all different shades of hair and skin. Some kids were tall and others short. Some were very thin and others weighed more. Still others were somewhere in between.

In gym class Angie noticed differences in ability. As the kids played volleyball, some of them always seemed to hit the ball into the air or smash it over the net. Other kids never did.

Between classes Angie stood at her locker listening as kids called to each other. "See ya, J.J.!" Or "Hey, Frog, coming over to my house tonight?" Almost everyone had a different name. Then in her last class Angie paid attention to something she seldom thought about. How hard some kids worked. How others didn't care what grades they got.

Late that afternoon when Mom called her for supper, Angie thought of another way her family was different. It would take her longer than other kids to get back out to play ball in the circle. During supper her family always talked about what had happened that day.

Angie decided to put that time to good use. *Maybe I can still change Dad's mind,* she thought as she took a big bite of her hamburger. *I'll tell him that every family is different, so he might as well let me go to the party like everyone else.*

Partway through the meal, Dad asked, "Well, how did you come out? What are some ways our family is different?"

Angie started off. "When the parents of other kids drive us somewhere, they almost always play rock music. You listen to a Christian station or classical stuff. Kids think I have a nutty family."

Angie glanced at Peanuts as she chimed in. "I'm different 'cause we go to church and some of the kids don't."

"I'm different because lots of my friends are good in sports," Mark said. "But I'm better in music."

Mom stood up and brought more hot rolls to the table. "I'm different because I turn down promotions instead of taking a job where I'd have to travel. If I took the promotions, I couldn't work while you're in school and be home when you're home."

Uh-oh! Angie felt uneasy now. *Maybe this isn't gonna work after all.* More that that, she was starting to feel uneasy.

Dad pushed back his chair. "I'm different because I choose to be honest in business. A lot of people don't."

Suddenly Angie realized she wasn't going to get her way. In her disappointment she wanted to lash out and hurt Dad. "I'm different because this family wants to gab and gab and gab," she said. "Other kids get back out right after supper. They can do whatever they want."

But somehow her words didn't sound as angry as they could have. As Angie spoke, she realized she really did like the times the family talked around the table.

"That's right," Dad said. "We *are* different. But don't some differences hurt a family and others help a family?"

Angie didn't want to meet Dad's eyes or answer his question. In fact, seeing the DVD didn't seem as important anymore. *Strange.* She was almost glad when Dad said no because she kept thinking about Mom's question.

Maybe if she got away from the table she could push it aside. She sure didn't want to tell anyone what she was wondering. After all, what would other kids think?

But in the days that followed, Mom's question didn't go away. Every now and then it came back, and she started wondering again. *Is it sometimes* good *to be different?*

The more she thought about how her family was different because they were Christians, the more thankful she felt.

Let's Talk ... or Journal

DAY 1

What do you think about Mom's question? Is it sometimes good to be different? Explain.

DAY 2

Some kids act differently and do stupid things because they want attention and don't know how to get it in good ways. Sometimes a kid that acts that way is known as a class clown. What do you think that class clown is really doing when he or she acts up?

DAY 3

Other times kids feel different because they refuse to do something that is wrong or something that would hurt them. Describe a time when you saw that happen or it happened to you.

Angie felt different because her parents expected her to make good choices. What do you think would happen to Angie if her mom or dad didn't care about the choices she makes? Why?

DAY 4

If it bothers you to be different, you may be afraid of what other kids think. If you are, how will that fear affect the choices you make?

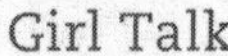

DAY 5

How would you answer Mom's question, "Is it sometimes good to be different?" Tell your reasons why or why not.

How can feeling different from other kids sometimes protect you?

DAY 6

It's okay to be different when it's for a good reason. What are some ways you personally have been different for your own sake or the sake of your family? This might include the way you as an older child take care of younger children in your family or what you do for fun together as a family.

Is your family different because of the kind of schooling you have chosen? Tell what you like about that schooling.

Can you think of other ways you and your family are different for good reasons? If you've needed to make sacrifices for your choices as a family in *any* area, give reasons why that has become important to you.

DAY 7

When Jesus was here on earth he was different from any other person who ever lived. How does it help you to know that Jesus was willing to be different for your sake? Explain why that is especially meaningful to you.

Let's Pray About It

Thank you, Jesus, for being willing to be different from every other person who ever lived. When I'm afraid to be different and afraid of what other kids think, help me remember that it's your approval that counts. Thank you that it's okay to be different for a good reason. When I need to run close to you, help me to stand up and be counted. And help me, Jesus, to help my family have good talk and fun times together. Thank you!

What Should I Do?

WEEK 35

If sinners tempt you, don't give in to them.
Proverbs 1:10 NIrV

For a long time Janie had wanted to be friends with Sheila. She and the girls she hung out with always seemed to have something to do. They always seemed to be having fun.

Janie, on the other hand, felt lonely. She didn't have any close friends. Every day felt the same.

What could I do to make Sheila like me? Janie wondered more than once. As often as she asked herself that question she hadn't come up with an answer.

Then one July morning, as Janie was on her way to get groceries for Mom, Sheila caught up with her. "Where you going?" she asked.

Janie felt glad Sheila wanted to talk. It didn't sound very exciting to pick up a gallon of milk, but that didn't seem to bother Sheila. "If you're headed that way, let's get a sundae."

That was another thing Janie had noticed about Sheila. She always seemed to have money. Just last week Sheila had worn three new tops.

A few days later, Janie met Sheila's friend Colleen. Janie had been right—Sheila *did* think up things to do. But sometimes she said things that puzzled Janie.

"We'll find a way to do that," Sheila would say. When Colleen laughed, Janie didn't understand what was supposed to be funny.

But whenever Sheila said, "I can outsmart anyone I want," Janie felt uneasy. *What does Sheila really mean?*

Just the same, most of the time Janie liked being with Sheila and Colleen. Best of all, she started to feel she belonged in their group.

Then one hot afternoon, Sheila sent Janie a text message. "Wanna do something?"

"What's it going to be?" Janie asked.

For the first time Sheila sounded as if she didn't have a plan. "Oh, I don't know," she texted. "We'll find something. Meet you outside the shopping mall, okay?"

For some reason Janie felt uneasy again, the way she had when Sheila talked about being able to outsmart anyone. On her way to the mall, Janie tried to figure it out. Were Sheila and Colleen hiding something from her?

Then Janie pushed her questions to the back of her mind and felt glad she'd been asked to go.

"Colleen needs a new swimsuit," Sheila said when they met.

There was only one place to go for that—the Fashion Rack. As they left the hot sidewalk for the cool store, Sheila moved closer to Janie. "Colleen doesn't have enough money for the swimsuit," she said in a low voice. "We're gonna help her."

"What do you mean?" Janie asked. "I don't have much money, either."

"That's not what I'm saying." Sheila sounded as though she thought Janie wasn't very smart.

Startled, Janie stared at her. "Hey, count me out! I'm not shoplifting!" She turned, ready to walk out the door.

"Not so fast," Sheila said. "You like being along, don't you? Stick with us, and you'll have lots of fun."

Janie knew that was true. Already she'd had good times with Sheila and her friends.

"Tell you what," Sheila said. "Instead of getting a swimsuit for Colleen, let's get something for you today. What do you want?"

Again Janie stared at Sheila, not liking what she heard. That wasn't Janie's way of thinking. She seldom got things she wanted, only what she needed. Nor did she go into a store planning to shoplift.

"What do I *want?*" Janie asked.

"Sure," answered Sheila, still in a low voice. "What do you want? Look around."

Well, Janie thought. *It won't hurt to look. But I won't take anything.*

Spreading out, the girls moved throughout the store. Janie started looking through a rack of jackets. Sure enough, there was just the jacket she'd like to have. She glanced at the price tag and knew that was out.

From there she went to the jeans. She hadn't bought a pair in what seemed forever. *Maybe I deserve them,* Janie thought.

Pushing away the idea, she wished it hadn't entered her head. But at the next rack she saw a top just like one of the new tops Sheila had worn. *I wonder—*

Janie didn't finish the thought, even to herself.

A moment later Sheila was at her side. "Everybody does it," she said as though there hadn't been a break in the conversation. "You wanna be like the rest of us, don't you?"

Sure, Janie thought, then hated herself.

Sheila moved closer and lowered her voice. "I'll tell you how."

As a clerk came to help them, Sheila said, "Right now we're just looking, thank you."

The clerk moved away, and Sheila began talking again. Soon Janie knew the plan. She felt scared inside, but she listened, knowing she wouldn't really do what Sheila said.

Sheila started edging away. "I'll give you the signal."

"Hey, wait!" Now Janie was more than scared. Inside her

mind, a tug-of-war had started. One part of Janie wanted the top. The other part knew it was wrong.

I'd have to save my allowance a long time to get it, she told herself.

From three racks away Sheila gave the signal. Seeing her, Janie froze. *What should I do?* she asked herself. She looked down, not wanting to meet Sheila's glance.

If I take it, will I get caught? Janie wondered. Then she came back to the same question. *What should I do?*

Let's Talk ... or Journal

DAY 1

Why did Janie want to be Sheila's friend? Why did she like being friends with Sheila and Colleen?

DAY 2

When someone is lonely or has a negative self-image, it can be more tempting to do something wrong. How did Janie's thinking change after she entered the store? Go back to the story and figure out the steps she went through.

What do you think Janie decided to do? Give reasons for your answer.

DAY 3

When we make a good or bad choice, there are logical consequences. If Janie steals the top, what kind of consequences might there be?

If Janie steals the top and gets away with it, how will Janie feel about herself? What is the difference between self-esteem and self-respect? Which is more important?

DAY 4

In Week 30, "Erin's High Dive", Erin discovered something. Someone who is really a friend won't ask you to do something that will hurt you. How can shoplifting hurt Janie now and in the future? If you feel pressure from kids to do something wrong, what can you do about it?

DAY 5

Deep down, there's something that Janie really needs — a place to belong. Jesus is the only one who can truly meet her deepest needs and yours. If you don't know him, you too may have a longing you don't understand and a loneliness deep inside. Do you ever feel this way? If so, what can you do about it?

DAY 6

Besides shoplifting, there are many other ways to steal. Think, for instance, of cheating on a test. You're stealing answers from someone else. Or someone is giving you the correct answers in some way. But whenever we go through school there's a permanent record we leave behind. That record tells other people many of the things we did or didn't do.

What would you like to see on your permanent record before Jesus?

DAY 7

In addition to being your around-the-clock friend, Jesus wants to give you human friends with whom you feel you belong. If you need friends, ask Jesus for kids who will help you live as he wants. Ask in the strong name of Jesus and thank him right now, while you wait to see what he does. Then ask that you can be that kind of friend to others.

How can you help the kids you know to be honest?

Let's Pray About It

Jesus, I want to be liked, and it's easy to go along with what other kids do. Show me how to say no so strongly that kids don't bother me again. Give me Christian friends who help and support me in living as you want. But help me, Lord, through my life and example, to help others be strong. Thanks, Jesus!

From the Pitcher's Mound

WEEK 36

[Jesus said,] "If you forgive anyone his sins, they are forgiven; if you do not forgive them, they are not forgiven."
John 20:23

Jennie plopped down on the bench, rested her chin on her hands, and stared at the ground. *What's happening to me, anyway?* she asked herself.

Only last week she had pitched a no-hit game for her team, the Cardinals. Each time she threw the ball, it went exactly where she wanted. When they won, the coach and team hugged her, saying over and over, "Great game, Jennie!"

But today—wow! What a difference! First she'd let a player walk. Next she fumbled a fly. Finally the other team batted a home run, bringing in three players and ending the game.

Now Jennie felt dusty and tired. A shower would help, but it wouldn't wash off the feeling that she had let down her team. That would probably never leave.

Taking a deep breath, Jennie started toward the parking lot. *Days like this I hate myself. What's wrong with me?*

As she reached the parking lot, Jennie stopped and waited for her family to catch up. Just then she heard someone talking on the other side of a van.

"She's too sure of herself," the voice said. "She's letting her game slide."

A low mumble answered, and Jennie couldn't pick out the words. Then the first voice spoke again. "If Coach had let me in, I would have turned it around. I'm a better pitcher any day."

Tara! thought Jennie. *My old friend Tara! Or my used-to-be friend. Used-to-be before she wanted to be a pitcher!*

Jennie's anger churned. *If that's my friend, I don't need an enemy!*

She felt like stomping around to the other side of the van. *I'd like to walk right up to Tara and tell her what I think. I'd make her take back every word!*

Losing the game was bad enough. Now this! Jennie felt completely wiped out.

A moment later her parents caught up with her. As soon as they reached the car Mom gave Jennie a hug. "You tried your hardest," Mom said. "You did your best."

Usually she and Dad could cheer Jennie up, but nothing seemed to help today. Jennie felt like a softball splitting apart at the seams.

The next time her team played, Jennie discovered the last game wasn't really over. She saw kids look at her, then glance away without meeting her eyes. Once she heard a whisper, "Taking her game for granted."

Suddenly Jennie knew. Tara had started a whispering campaign.

An anger unlike any Jennie had ever known shot through her. Whenever she thought of Tara, the sparks fanned into flames. Her feelings added fuel to the fire.

That anger still blazed when Jennie took the pitcher's mound. As she faced the first batter, Jennie bit her lip and tried to stay calm. Yet it wasn't long until the ump shouted, "Ball four!"

The second batter got off a long hit between second and third. The crowd groaned. Jennie knew she was losing her grip.

Taking a deep breath, she tried again. The windup. The pitch. Oh no! The batter hit a home run! The roar from the crowd was deafening.

"See? You're no good!" it seemed to say.

Jennie wasn't surprised when the coach pulled her out. Nor was she surprised to see Tara take her place. Jennie's anger flared up, this time like a forest fire.

Sitting on the bench, elbows on her knees, Jennie stared straight ahead. As the Cardinals fell further behind the Blue Jays, she watched every move of the game. Yet her thoughts churned round and round.

She felt desperate. Lately Jennie hadn't prayed much, but she started now. Even so, her prayers didn't seem to get off the ground. Something seemed to stand in the way between her and God.

The second inning passed. Then the third. Jennie still sat on the bench. By the beginning of the fourth, she started sorting out her choices. One word dropped into her mind.

Forgive? You gotta be kidding, God. Tara was the one who started it.

Through the first half of that inning, Jennie argued with herself and with God. *See? I* am *a better pitcher. Tara's losing the game. They're three runs ahead of us. We might never catch up!*

But the word stayed in her mind. *Forgive? You want* me *to forgive Tara? I don't* want *to forgive her!*

One minute Jennie felt ashamed of herself. The next minute she decided she didn't want to change the way she felt. *If I stop being mad, it will seem like Tara was right.*

Out on the field the game wasn't going well. By now the Blue Jays were four runs ahead with bases loaded. Until the last game, the Cardinals hadn't lost all season.

Then a thought struck Jennie. *Here I sit, wanting Tara to lose so I look better. I'm almost rooting for the other team!*

Forgive? Suddenly Jennie knew what choice to make. Eyes wide open, she stared ahead, praying silently. She used only seven words. "Jesus, in your name I forgive her."

In the next moment, Jennie felt the weight she'd carried all week drop off her back. "Yaaaay!" she called out the next time something went right. But it was more than a cheer for the Cardinals. She was cheering herself on.

At the top of the fifth the Blue Jays came to bat. "Jennie!" called the coach. "Go on in."

This time the ball felt sweet in Jennie's hands. Thoughts of Tara were gone. Thoughts of how good she herself might look fell away. Even the crowd didn't seem important.

Glove high above her head, Jennie snagged the ball, then caught the catcher's signal. *I'll do my best*, she thought. *But I just want to play ball.*

Facing the batter, Jennie wound up. *It's just a game*, she told herself. *Just a game.*

The ball looked great sailing across the plate.

Let's Talk ... or Journal

DAY 1

What did Jennie mean when she decided, "I just want to play ball"? What had changed in her thinking? Whether her team won or lost, Jennie won in a number of ways. What were they?

DAY 2

Strong kids can't be stopped by the hard things they face. Instead, they figure out a way to do their best in spite of what happens. How did Jennie learn to be strong?

DAY 3

When she chose to forgive Tara, Jennie prayed with her will in the strong name of Jesus. Praying with the will means you choose to forgive even though you don't feel like it in your emotions. Why does praying in the name of Jesus have special power?

What does Jesus tell us about praying in his name? See John 15:16. Does that promise mean we can ask for anything we want and get it? What does our relationship with Jesus need to be?

DAY 4

If you forgive someone who hurt you, does that mean the person was right in what he or she did? Give reasons for your answer.

DAY 5

Forgiveness gives you a way to stop hurting and go on with your life. If you want to feel peaceful about yourself and others, do you have any choice but to forgive? Why or why not?

After she forgave Tara, Jennie felt she no longer carried a heavy weight. You may forgive someone and not "feel" any different. Yet your prayer of forgiveness still counts. How do you know?

DAY 6

Sometimes when a person hurts you, it's important to talk with that person about it. Other times it makes matters worse to say something. Do you think Jennie should talk with Tara about the things she said? Why or why not?

DAY 7

As a Faithgirl, you can look to Jesus and follow his example. What example did he give us about forgiving others? What were his words from the cross?

Name some of the people that Jesus forgave when he hung on the cross. Why do you suppose he forgave them?

Let's Pray About It

Jesus, when someone hurts me, I want to hate that person. Yet even on the cross you prayed, "Father, forgive them, for they do not know what they are doing." Because of what you did, I forgive the person who hurt me. I ask you to bless that person. Take away my bitter and angry feelings. Help me to run close to you. Thanks, Jesus!

Secrets of the Heart

WEEK 37

"The King [Jesus] will reply, 'What I'm about to tell you is true. Anything you did for one of the least important of these brothers of mine, you did for me.' "
Matthew 25:40 NIrV

On that Friday morning in July, Jill sat in the kitchen, putting on nail polish. When the phone rang, she thought, *It won't be for me,* and kept on with her nails.

But the phone kept ringing, and her older sister, Sabrina, called out, "Will you get it, Jill? I'm in the tub."

Jill sighed. Always younger sister Jill running the errands. She took her time about getting to the phone.

"Hello?" Jill was right, of course. It was for her sister.

As Sabrina hung up the phone, she glowed. "Do you know who *that* was?" In an unbelievably short time she was out the door on a date.

Always Sabrina, Jill thought. *Sure, Mom says I'm too young to go out with boys. But even when I'm older, will I ever get any dates?*

On a shelf above the sink were two pictures: Sabrina—slender and lovely, long blonde hair blowing in the wind. *Then there's me,*

Jill thought. *Skinny legs. Mousy hair. Chest like a boy.* Jill blinked away tears.

In that instant she remembered the sleepover that night. *Well, at least I can go to Rachel's. She's still my best friend.*

Just then the phone rang, and Jill picked it up again.

"Hi there!" said a warm voice on the other end of the line.

"Hey, Aunt Mickey!" Something inside Jill jumped, just hearing the voice of her favorite aunt. Mickey was Mom's youngest sister. She had never married and was a social worker who lived almost 200 miles away.

"Just found out I need to come your way tonight to pick up a runaway girl," Mickey told her. "How about if I stay overnight? Then we can talk before I have to leave in the morning. How does that sound?"

"Sabrina has a date," Jill answered. "Mom isn't here, but I'm sure it'll be okay with her."

The moment the words were out, Jill felt uneasy. *Will it* really *be okay with Mom?* After Dad left them, Mom started dating. Often she had even more dates than Sabrina.

But Jill pushed her uneasiness aside. "It'll be great to have you! We haven't seen you for a long time."

"I know. I'm lonesome for you, Jill. I'm not sure exactly when I'll be there, but probably around seven, okay?"

As she got off the phone, Jill felt good just thinking about Mickey. Her aunt's name was really Michelle, but when Jill was little, she started calling her Mickey. The name had stuck, just like the special relationship between them.

Then Jill remembered she had a sleepover at her friend Rachel's that night. Mom would have to take care of Mickey.

But when Jill's mother got home from work, she said, "I can't be here. I've got a dinner date."

"Aw, Mom!" Jill told her. "You're always going out. Can't you change it to another night?"

Mom shook her head. "Nope. You told my sister she could come. You take care of her. I've got only an hour to get ready."

"But I'm supposed to go to Rachel's!" Jill wailed. "Can't Mickey go out to eat with you?"

Jill wasn't surprised that Mom didn't like that idea. "Just leave a key for her. Mickey can come in and go to bed early. She won't mind."

When her mother left, Jill got ready for Rachel's. She had everything in her overnight bag when she wondered how Aunt Mickey would feel coming into an empty house. *It'll be worse than when I'm alone. Mickey doesn't know anyone around here.*

Since Dad left, Jill had been alone a lot. She thought about it. *Even though I'd rather be at Rachel's, it's not fair. Mickey's nice.*

Inside, Jill felt torn, wanting to treat her aunt the way Mickey always treated her. Yet, even more, Jill wanted to be at the sleepover.

Then Jill remembered how Aunt Mickey always managed to laugh about something. Now Jill tried to laugh, but it didn't work. Taking her overnight bag up to her room, she dropped it in a corner with her sleeping bag. Then she called Rachel and said she wasn't coming.

An hour later, Jill was still waiting. *Maybe Mickey won't show up.* Just thinking about that possibility, Jill felt disappointed. At the same time, she felt torn. She still wanted to go to the sleepover.

Finally she went back to her room and picked up her overnight bag and sleeping bag. In the next moment she dropped them again. *Mickey's never broken a promise.* That was one of the things Jill liked about her.

Just then a car door slammed. Jill hurried to a front window. Sure enough, it was her aunt!

Jill ran down the stairs and out the door. She threw herself into Mickey's arms.

"Hey, there! Good to see you!" Mickey held Jill out for a long look. "Wow! What a lovely grown-up person you've become!"

"I'm grown-up?" Jill felt afraid to hope. She didn't dare believe the rest of it. "And lovely besides?"

A smile spread across Mickey's face. "You sure are! I like your hair that way. And you still give a wonderful hug!"

"Thanks!" Jill felt grateful. Mickey hadn't changed. She had the same blond hair Mom used to have before coloring it. And

Mickey's eyes were warm and caring. Jill knew that Mickey was a Christian and wondered if that was why she was so nice.

Jill helped Mickey bring her bag into the house. As she looked around, Mickey asked, "Your mom and Sabrina are gone? They both have dates?"

"Yeah," Jill answered. "Sorry about that." She felt embarrassed that neither of them had tried to change their plans when Mickey came so seldom.

"Then let's celebrate that you and I are together," Mickey said. "Let's go out to eat somewhere. Somewhere really nice, okay?"

In a few minutes they were off. For the first time since she'd seen Mickey a year ago, Jill talked without stopping. There was something about her aunt that made Jill feel she could tell her anything.

They went to a country inn, and it was fun being in such a nice place. It was even more fun to talk, just the two of them. But when they were having dessert, Mickey asked, "Jill, how are you *really* doing?"

Jill blinked with surprise and tried to hold back the tears. When they came anyway, Mickey waited until Jill could speak. It took three tries before she said, "Mickey, do you ever feel like you don't matter?"

Mickey laughed, and Jill felt sorry she'd asked. But when Mickey answered, her voice was soft. "Lots of times. You see, I have a good-looking older sister, too."

Jill smiled through her tears.

"And lots of times I thought I'd *never* be asked out."

"You really thought that?"

"I really thought that."

"But you were—I mean, you *have* been—" Jill broke off, not wanting to hurt her aunt.

"Not much in high school," Mickey said. "Boys always asked your mom. But later on, yes, when they started looking for a wife."

She winked. "They think I'm good wife material."

"But you haven't gotten married."

"And I'm not sorry. Some people feel sorry for me, but that's their problem. It's not mine."

"How come? I mean, why haven't you gotten married?"

"So far I haven't felt that God put me together with the right man. It's much better *not* to marry than to marry the wrong person."

"But do you ever feel like you're—" Again Jill stopped.

"Like I'm not worth anything? Like I'm not cute or worth being with?" Mickey grinned, but her eyes were serious. "You know, Jill, it can be really fun to find the right person at the right time. But it isn't *all* there is to life. Sometimes girls make wrong choices because they think it's a way to get dates. It never works—not in the long run."

Mickey set down her iced tea. "I don't want to spend my life looking around every corner for a man. If God wants me to marry, he'll show me who the person should be. But if he *doesn't* want me to marry, that's okay. It's okay to *not* get married.

"I have a full life," Mickey went on. "And I'm doing new, fun things all the time. Because I don't have a family, there are ways in which I'm free to help other people. But you see, if I'm married or not married, I'm a whole person. I'm a person valued by God."

"Do you ever get lonely?" Jill asked.

"Sure," Mickey told her. "Times like that I try to reach out to others—to see if there's a way I can help them. Times like that I come and see you."

Jill grinned. "And take me out for supper."

"I'm taking you? Oops!" Mickey laughed. "Better see if I have enough money."

In that moment Jill felt glad she'd skipped the sleepover. But it wasn't until they returned home that Mickey discovered what had happened. When she went into Jill's room, she saw the stuffed overnight bag and sleeping bag. "Were you going somewhere?"

Jill had never lied to Mickey, and she didn't want to start. But when she answered Mickey's question, tears came to her aunt's eyes.

"Jill, honey, I'm so glad that you were here when I came."

"Me too," Jill said.

"I'm glad to know you're still the kind of person you are. Keep on being that way, okay?"

Jill nodded. "I'll try."

"But it's getting late, and I have a long drive tomorrow. I really need a good night's sleep. Couldn't you still go to your sleepover? You'll stay up a long time talking, won't you?"

Again Jill nodded. Her thoughts jumped ahead to the fun she could have.

"I'll drive you there, okay?" Mickey asked.

This time it was Jill's turn to feel tears in her eyes. *Wow! I get to do* both *things!* She hugged her aunt so tight that Mickey squealed.

Let's Talk ... or Journal

DAY 1

What were some of the things that bothered Jill about her sister, Sabrina? In what ways was Sabrina acting like her mother?

DAY 2

What did you like about Mickey? What did you like about the relationship between Jill and Mickey?

DAY 3

So far, Mickey had chosen not to marry. She said, "I'm a whole person." What does it mean to be a whole person? What does it mean to be a person valued by God?

What are some good things about being single? Have you thought about the fact that both Jesus and the apostle Paul were single? Does being single mean you have to be lonely? Why or why not?

DAY 4

Jill wanted to go to the sleepover, yet she also wanted to be at home when Mickey arrived. Have you ever been torn between feeling you should do something and wanting to do something else? Explain how you felt. What happened?

DAY 5

Jill saw her mother and sister dating and thought it would be fun. Instead, Jill learned a secret of the heart. What was that secret?

DAY 6

Every one of us needs to know it's okay to be the way God created us. In what ways did Mickey give Jill that message? What miracle did Jill experience in how she felt about herself?

Mickey has accepted the way she is. She helped Jill accept the way Jill is. Is there some way you need to say, "It's okay to be what I am"? Explain what you mean.

DAY 7

When you feel happy with who you are and how God created you, you can also feel free to grow in ways that will help you. Think of how you have grown in your ability to do things. What are those things? In addition to skills and abilities, think of character qualities—perhaps the kind of qualities that Mickey saw in Jill. How about making a list?

Let's Pray About It

You know what, God? When I compare myself with someone else, I always compare who I am to someone older. Or I compare the weakest part of me to someone's strengths. Then I feel sorry for ME. In the name of your Son, Jesus, I choose to accept the way you made me. Thanks for the skills you've helped me learn and the character qualities you've helped me develop.

I choose to be glad for all *of your good gifts. I give them to you and ask you to help me think about the feelings of others. Thanks!*

Jasmine's Special Friend

WEEK 38

[Jesus said,] "I will never send away anyone who comes to me."
John 6:37b NIrV

Jasmine felt nervous as she entered the long hallway. Since moving to a new school, she had dreaded Monday mornings. It seemed everyone had plenty to talk about. Everyone had a special friend. Everyone belonged to a group.

Everyone, that is, except me.

Already a cluster of girls had formed around Dena's locker. Jasmine knew they'd be talking about all that had happened that weekend. As she pushed back her brown hair she wished she could join them. It'd be fun to listen, even if she didn't have much to say.

At the same time, Jasmine felt afraid to walk past the girls. They all seemed especially well dressed. They all acted very sure of themselves, and they all made her feel left out. Yet her locker was a short way down the hall, just beyond Dena's.

Trying to comfort herself, Jasmine remembered how great she had looked as she started for school that morning. *Maybe someone will notice my new jacket. Maybe they'll think I'm worth having in their group.*

A tiny spark of hope came to life. *There's Kacie. She knows me. She'll say hi.*

Trying to look more confident than she felt, Jasmine drew a deep breath. *If I smile, she'll have to smile back.* But even as the thought came, Jasmine started feeling shaky inside.

As she drew close to the girls, Kacie looked up. Jasmine stopped. "Hi, Kacie!" But the words felt stiff on her lips.

For a moment Jasmine thought Kacie would answer. Instead, she raised her chin and turned back to the others. The other girls laughed.

Feeling the hot blush of embarrassment rush to her face, Jasmine wanted to run. Instead, she felt frozen to the spot. Finally, she somehow put one foot in front of the other. *Were they laughing at me? Or just making sure I feel left out?*

Either way, Jasmine knew it made no difference. Instead of going to her locker, she headed for the bathroom.

To her relief it was empty. She'd been spending a lot of time there. She knew every crack in the floor, every faucet that didn't quite turn off. She wished she could hide there forever.

Dropping her books on a ledge, Jasmine went to the mirror. Her new jacket didn't seem nice anymore. Feeling the material, Jasmine tried to believe it was still important. It wasn't. Instead, the mirror reflected the tears in her brown eyes.

Jasmine blinked the tears away, but her lips trembled. *I'm not going to cry,* she promised herself. But tears streamed down her cheeks. The loneliness she felt was too deep. *It's no use. They'll never accept me. I'll never be part of their clique.*

It wasn't the first time Jasmine prayed about it, but now she meant every word. *Jesus, they make me feel worthless. Awful. Thrown in the mud and walked on. I need friends. I forgive them for the lousy way they act. But what can I do?*

Just then the warning bell rang. Jasmine picked up her books and started for her first hour class.

In the next two days nothing seemed different. Would God ever answer her prayer? Did he even hear what she'd asked?

Then, before school on the third day Jasmine headed for her locker. As she passed Dena and her friends, all the girls ignored her. But at that moment an idea dropped into Jasmine's mind.

Keep your eyes and ears open. Look for kids who think and believe the way you do.

Jasmine gasped. Clapped her hands over her mouth. Raced to her locker, tossed in her book bag, and hung up her jacket.

She had all of ten minutes before her first class. Feeling like a private detective, she walked up and down the halls. Looking. Keeping her eyes and ears open. As she passed Dena's locker, the girls still laughed or looked away. Jasmine pasted on a smile, but no longer tried to say hi.

For the first time, Jasmine saw Dena's friends as they really were. For the first time she saw them without feeling an ache deep inside. *I don't need a bunch of stuck-up friends! I don't need kids who shut out anyone who isn't just like them. It's their problem, not mine!*

Jasmine drew a long, deep breath. *If that's how they treat me, that's the way they treat other kids too.*

But now Jasmine smiled, just thinking about the words that had dropped into her mind. The rest of the day Jasmine kept her eyes and ears open. Between classes she started recognizing girls she had barely seen before. Some of them spent a lot of time in the bathroom, hiding out the way she had. Others hurried through the halls as though they wanted to escape.

Before leaving school that that afternoon, Jasmine knew she had found one girl who looked as lonely as she was. The next morning Jasmine found another. And then, as she walked past Dena's locker, Jasmine had the strangest feeling—as though she didn't walk alone.

Not quite sure what had happened, Jasmine thought about it. *Nothing's changed.*

An instant later she knew that wasn't true. *I forgave Dena and her friends. Is that what made the difference?*

Standing by her locker, Jasmine tried to figure it out. *It felt like an invisible bubble around me. Their meanness didn't get through.*

In that moment Jasmine remembered Jesus and his long lonely walk to the cross. Could it possibly be? Had he really been there with her, right in the hallway of the school?

Now Jasmine knew what to do, and she felt good about trying. The minute she hung up her jacket, she headed for the bathroom. Sure enough, the girl who brushed her hair at least a thousand times was there.

"Hi, I'm Jasmine," she began. "What grade are you in?"

It felt good to start making friends. Later that day Jasmine found the second girl hanging out as close to the outside door as she could stand.

Jasmine started out the same way—with a "Hi, I'm Jasmine." When the girl smiled back, her face looked warm with friendship. She talked even faster than the first girl had.

Keep your eyes and ears open, Jasmine thought. *Look for kids who think and believe the way you do.*

In that moment Jasmine started getting excited about what she had discovered. Could she really make a difference in her school?

It didn't take long to find out. On Wednesday a new girl named Haley started school. Dena and her friends gave Haley the same treatment they had given Jasmine.

But now Jasmine knew what to do, and she felt good about trying. Instead of worrying about herself, she'd do everything she could to help the new girl.

And Jasmine did.

Let's Talk ... or Journal

DAY 1

Sometimes kids think they show their popularity and power by shutting other kids out. How was Jasmine shut out by the "in" group? What do you think of a clique that treats someone the way they treated Jasmine? Explain why you think that way.

DAY 2

Can you think of a time when you were shut out of a group? How did it feel? Can you think of a time when you left someone out? Tell what happened. How did you feel about it later?

DAY 3

When people hurt you, you don't have to wait until you feel good about them or like what they're doing before you forgive them. That might never happen! Forgiveness gives you a way to stop hurting. You can choose to pray, "Jesus, I forgive them." After Jasmine's prayer, what changes did God bring?

DAY 4

What was Jasmine's big discovery? How can you use Jasmine's discovery to fix something hard in your own life? What do you think is more important — the clothes you and an in-group have or how you treat others? Explain why you think the way you do, giving examples, if possible.

DAY 5

Why does Jesus understand when we feel lonely and left out? For clues read Isaiah 53, a chapter that was written about Jesus hundreds of years before he came to earth.

God always hears your prayers. Yet he may not suddenly make everything right in the way you hope. Instead, he might give you a sense of being loved. He might change how you feel about what happened. Or he might want you to grow in some way before he answers your prayers. Have you felt Jesus with you in one of those ways? Explain.

DAY 6

How has God helped you accept something hard, even though you didn't like it? What happened?

DAY 7

Jesus loves you, even if you can't "feel" that he does. How do you know that he loves you? Write down some verses that remind you of that promise.

Start with John 3:15.

How many of these verses can you memorize?

Let's Pray About It

Jesus, I don't like feeling lonely and left out. But I forgive the kids who make me feel that way. I'm glad that you have called me a friend and will never turn me away. Thanks for always loving me. Help me know deep inside that you do. And help me reach out to other people and help those who are hurting. Thank you!

Tagalong Trudy

WEEK 39

Love each other deeply. Honor others more than yourselves.
Romans 12:10 NIrV

As Brooke brushed her hair, she caught a movement in the mirror. Her little sister stood right behind her. Wobbling forward on tiptoes, Trudy tried to see herself. Turning this way and that, she managed to brush her hair just the way Brooke did hers.

Brooke groaned. *Will it never end?* she asked herself. *Whatever I do, Trudy wants to do it, too. Well, at least she can't tag along to the sleepover tonight.*

As soon as Brooke finished breakfast, she tried to sneak out. Maybe she could meet her friend Amber at the tennis courts without having Trudy along.

But Trudy guessed where Brooke was headed. "Can I go, too?" she asked Mom.

"Well, you can't go by yourself," Mom answered. "Will you take her, Brooke? And see that she gets home okay?"

"Aw, Mom! Does Trudy always have to tag along?"

"She can play with her friends while you play with yours."

To Brooke's surprise it wasn't as bad as she thought. While she played tennis, Trudy found some girls her age on the nearby monkey bars.

A few hours later Brooke started home. As she and her friend Amber walked together, Trudy fell behind. Wondering what had happened to her, Brooke turned around. Trudy had her head down, as if she were looking for invisible footprints. What on earth was she doing?

"What's the matter?" Amber asked, and Brooke shrugged her shoulders.

Soon she felt curious and glanced back again. Trudy still walked strangely. Stretching out her legs, she took much bigger strides than usual. *Aha!* Brooke thought. *She's trying to walk in my footsteps!*

When Brooke started walking as fast as she could, Amber looked at her. "What are you doing?"

Brooke put her finger to her lips, whispered, "Shh," and tipped her head backward.

Amber looked at Trudy and grinned. She, too, began walking in long, giant strides. Still trying to stay in Brooke's steps, Trudy started running. Soon she was gasping for breath.

Brooke stopped, ready to say, "You're sure acting stupid, Trudy." But something inside Brooke made her hold back the words. *Does she really care that much about being like me? Even in the way I walk?*

Seconds later Brooke was glad she hadn't said anything. As Amber turned off for her own house, Trudy reached out for Brooke's hand.

Brooke looked down. For the first time she caught a glimpse of how much her little sister loved her. *It's kind of scary*, Brooke thought. *What if I do something to hurt her?* Somehow Trudy wasn't just a tagalong anymore.

When Brooke and Trudy reached home, Mom met them in the kitchen. "I have a problem. Your dad and I are supposed to go to a concert tonight. Our babysitter just canceled. Do you know anyone who won't be going to your sleepover?"

Brooke thought for a minute, then shook her head.

"I know what you can do with me," Trudy said. "You can take me to Amber's sleepover!"

"Mo-o-o-mmm!" Brooke cried out. In that moment all of her good feelings about Trudy vanished.

Then, as though she were seeing a DVD, Brooke remembered Trudy trying to walk in her footsteps. Instead of blurting out her feelings, Brooke waited until her little sister went into the bathroom.

The moment the door shut, Brooke drew a deep breath and plunged in, telling Mom how she felt.

Let's Talk ... or Journal

DAY 1

Thoughtlessness tears relationships down. Thoughtfulness builds them up. What are some thoughtful things Brooke did in her relationships with Trudy?

DAY 2

When you belong to a family, you sometimes need to give up what you want in order to work things out. Other times it's important to hold onto something you want and explain why you feel the way you do. Which kind of time is this for Brooke?

When Brooke explains how she feels about Trudy tagging along, she should tell her mom two things: 1) what the problem is, and 2) how she feels about the problem. Pretend you're Brooke. What would you say to your mom?

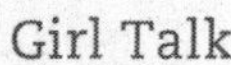

DAY 3

Whose idea was it for Trudy to go to the sleepover? What's the difference between Brooke taking Trudy to the park and taking her to a sleepover? How would Brooke's friends feel about inviting her if she always took Trudy along?

DAY 4

Use your imagination. What do you think Brooke and her mom figured out about who should take care of Trudy?

DAY 5

Often things don't seem as hard if you talk about them with the right person. When you tell how you feel about something that happens in your family, you help your mom or dad understand things they may not have thought about. It also helps you feel better because you get your feelings out in the open. What problems are you facing that you'd like to talk about? A good way to begin talking is to say, "I feel ..." Use feeling words such as angry or sad or glad, and then tell what you feel angry, sad, or some other emotion about. If you can think of ways to solve your problem, be sure to mention your ideas.

DAY 6

In addition to talking with the right grown-up, you can talk with Jesus whenever you want. What are some words you can use to begin?

Do you think it's okay to be honest with Jesus? How do you know? Check out Matthew 7:7 – 8.

DAY 7

When you're honest with Jesus, it's another way of saying that you pray to him. The more you talk with Jesus, the better you get to know him. In what ways have you learned to know Jesus through your prayers?

Let's Pray About It

Help me, Jesus, to be thoughtful about the feelings of others. Help me know when I should help someone else, and when I should explain what I need. Help our family to have good talk times together. Help us figure things out when we have different ideas about what to do. Thank you that we are part of your family!

WEEK 40

"Everything that is secret will be brought out into the open. Everything that is hidden will be uncovered."
Matthew 10:26b NIrV

On that sunny June morning, Gina could hardly wait to get to the beach. All through the winter she had thought about returning for a week of camp. Best of all, her cabin counselor from last year would be back. More than once Megan had made Gina feel like a special person. She remembered their talks well.

"You're a special person in God's sight," Megan told her one night as they talked about self-respect. "He'll help you become all that you can be."

Now Megan was one of the lifeguards. All through the activities of the morning and lunchtime, Gina looked forward to talking with her again.

This year I can swim to the raft, Gina thought. In her mind's eye she could see it well. The raft was in deep water, out beyond the ropes that kept younger children within a safer area. It was part of growing up to swim to the raft and dive off. Gina could hardly wait.

When the time finally came, she hurried to get into her swimsuit and down to the beach.

"Hi, Gina!" Megan called to her.

While Gina told about her school year, Megan listened to every word. It was just as good seeing her as Gina had hoped.

Soon other kids filled the wide expanse of waterfront, and Megan welcomed each of them. As she explained the rules, she pointed to the raft out beyond the safety ropes for young swimmers. While Megan watched from a high lifeguard's chair on the beach, another lifeguard would watch from a rowboat closer to the raft.

"No one swims to the raft without first passing a test," Megan said.

She told them what to do. "Walk far enough into the water to swim, but stay along the shore."

Megan pointed to a nearby post. "Start there. Go across the front of the beach to that post." Again she pointed. "Without stopping, return to the first post. If you can swim that far without touching bottom, we'll let you swim to the raft."

Piece of cake! Gina thought. Starting at the first post, she swam across the front from one side to the other of the beach. As she started back, she felt tired. Before long she was winded and needed to stop and stand up.

As soon as she drew in great gulps of air, Gina dropped onto her stomach again. A few minutes later she reached the final post. But Megan was waiting.

"Go up on the beach, Gina," she said.

"I'm going to be really upset if I can't go to the raft," Gina told her.

But Megan paid no attention. Instead, she divided the kids into two groups. The boys and girls who passed the test paired off as swimming buddies. The rest waited on shore.

As she watched her friends start for the raft, Gina felt sick inside. When Megan paired her with a girl two years younger, Gina became angry.

"I can swim better than Bailey!" she told Megan.

"If you can, you have to show me," Megan said. "You haven't gone swimming all winter, have you?"

Scowling, Gina shook her head. In spite of what Megan said, Gina wanted to be out on the raft, not swimming with a kid half her size.

"All your big talk about self-respect!" she told Megan. "If you really meant what you said last year, you'd let me prove myself. I'm ready for the raft!"

Megan flushed but turned to the kids waiting on shore. "If one of you gets out of the water for some reason, you both get out. Okay? No swimming without a buddy."

For the first half hour Gina swam with Bailey. When the younger girl left for the bathroom, Gina made up her mind.

Megan's my friend. If I head for the raft, she won't stop me. In fact, she won't even know.

Passing quickly through the crowded part of the beach, Gina swam under the ropes. As she struck out for the raft, her swimming went well. Each time she looked up, she checked the distance. Closer. Closer. Closer. But she still had a ways to go when she started feeling tired.

It wasn't long before her arms felt heavy. Soon Gina started gasping for air. *Can I make it?* Desperate now, she stretched down a leg. Unable to touch bottom, she panicked. Taking in a great gulp of water, she choked.

As she started to sink, she heard a sharp whistle. A voice through a megaphone. Oars dipping in water. Then a hand reached down, grabbing Gina under the arm.

A lifeguard pulled Gina next to the boat. "Hang on to the end of the boat," he said. "I'm taking you in."

Gina took two deep breaths. "I'm going to the raft."

"No, you're not."

When the boat reached the ropes, Megan was waiting for Gina. "You're beached," Megan said. "Wait up on shore for me."

When Gina walked out of the water, Bailey stood on the sand.

"So you're the one who told on me!" Gina exclaimed.

Bailey's eyes flashed. "I'm supposed to let you drown instead? You're my swimming buddy!"

Gina was really angry now. But when she turned around to stomp off, she found Megan behind her.

"Bailey stuck to the rules," Megan said. "It could have meant that she saved your life. But I had also seen you. So did the other lifeguard. Did you even hear my whistle?"

Gina dug her toes into the sand. "I could have made it!"

Megan shook her head. "No swimming the rest of the afternoon."

"What?" Gina glared at Megan. "You gotta be kidding!"

"For the next three days you can swim along shore. On Thursday I'll test you again. Maybe you'll be ready for the raft. That is, if you don't bend the rules again before then."

Gina stared at her. "I thought you were my friend!"

"I am," Megan said. "Believe me, Gina, I am."

Let's Talk ... or Journal

DAY 1

Have you ever been disappointed because you didn't get what you wanted? Describe what happened.

DAY 2

How did you feel about the shortcut that Gina tried to take around what was expected? Why is it important to follow rules? What does it mean to bend the rules? Give examples that you've seen on a beach or other places where kids try to get away with something.

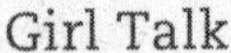

DAY 3

What did Megan care about most—Gina's getting her own way or her safety? How do you know? Do you think Megan was Gina's friend? Give reasons for your answer.

DAY 4

We develop self-respect by learning what is needed, passing some kind of test, and earning new privileges. Will a person who bends the rules have self-respect in that area? Give reasons for your answer.

DAY 5

If we follow God's leading for our lives he often teaches us step by step. If we learn according to his best plan for us and are faithful in doing that well, he often leads us from doing easier things to something harder. Describe a time when God prepared you with something easy and led you on to something more difficult.

What privileges have you earned because you were willing to take the small steps that led to big steps?

DAY 6

In Luke 16:10 Jesus says, "Whoever can be trusted with very little can also be trusted with much." What does it mean to be someone who can be trusted with very little? Look up the second half of the verse and explain what you think about both parts of this verse.

Can you give an example of someone who did something that seemed small, but it was very important?

Can you give an example of someone who was careless in something that seemed small, and could then not be trusted with something more difficult?

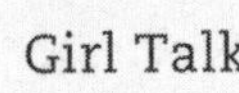

DAY 7

Did Jesus ever bend the rules to get what he wanted? Explain why you think the way you do.

How was Jesus a person of integrity — a person who could be trusted to do what was right, even when there was a cost? Give examples.

Let's Pray About It

Thank you, Jesus, that you teach me step by step. Help me to be honest in each step so that I'm ready to go on to new privileges. Help me to have integrity — to do what is right, even when you and I are the only ones who know about it. Thank you!

Surfing the Web

WEEK 41

"For I know the plans I have for you," announces the Lord. "I want you to enjoy success. I do not plan to harm you. I will give you hope for the years to come."
Jeremiah 29:11 NIrV

When Allison walked in from school, the boxes were in the family room.

"Way to go!" she exclaimed. "You bought the computer today!"

Her grandmother smiled. "When I got off work, I stopped by for it. But let's wait for Gramps to get home so he can set it up."

During the past week Allison's grandparents had been shopping for a computer. Recently she had come to live with them because her mom was overseas with the military. Tears still came to Allison's eyes every time she thought about the day Mom received her orders.

"What will I ever do without you?" Allison had wailed. Her mom started crying too. With both of them sobbing they clung to each other.

In the days that followed, Gran and Gramps invited Allison to live with them while her mom was gone. But Allison had to stuff down her feelings about it. Mom had been single for so long that Allison had often been on her own. When her mom worked, she did her best to watch out for her, but Allison knew she had more independence than most kids her age.

And she still felt angry. Deep inside she felt a big hole where she missed her mom. In one way it was a relief to be here. Gran was a good cook. But Allison didn't want *anyone* breathing down her neck.

"You'll be able to e-mail your mother," Gran said now as though trying to encourage her.

Yeh. A whole year of e-mails. Maybe more. Not the same as a hug at night when you want to see your mom.

Gran was watching her face, and Allison made sure her blank look was in place. Right now she didn't want anyone—let alone Gran—invading her private space. Not only had her mom left the country. She, Allison, who had promised herself she would never move away from her friends, now lived far away from all the kids she knew.

As soon as Gramps got home he started unpacking the boxes. For years he had used a computer at work and knew exactly what to do. But when he set a table in a corner of the kitchen, Allison asked, "Aren't you going to put the computer in my room?"

Gramps shook his head. "Nope." Taking the monitor from the box, he set it on the table.

Allison tried again. "But I'll be the one using the computer. My room is a great place for me to do homework." *And I can surf the net any time I want*, she told herself.

Without looking up, Gramps kept unpacking the computer. Next came the mouse and keyboard.

"Gran won't use it," Allison argued. "She doesn't even know how to turn it on."

Gran looked up from the hamburgers she was browing. "I'll learn. I'm not in the grave yet." A smile took the edge off her words. "And I'll be right here if you need help."

Need help? Allison thought about her computer classes at school. *I know a whole lot more than you do, Gran!*

"You're not going to watch over my shoulder, are you?" Allison asked. "You're not going to check everything I say to my friends?"

"Nope," Gran said. "Remember? I *want* you to be able to e-mail your friends back home."

While they were eating supper, Gramps talked with Allison about the screen name she'd like to use. As Allison helped Gran clear the table, he chose the parental controls.

"What password did you use?" Allison asked when she finished dishes.

But Gramps didn't tell her. "If it isn't in your head, you won't be tempted to use it the wrong way. I've set the controls so you can access the kids' chat rooms, but not the adult ones."

"So you don't trust me!"

"I don't trust everyone else," Gramps said. "The school computers you use have controls. We'll have them too."

When Allison dropped down on a chair next to him he went on. "Both you and I know that with chat rooms you can meet anyone in the world who decides to come online. It can be exciting to meet new people if safeguards are in place. But we want to do our best to protect you. We don't want you talking with adults who pretend to be kids."

"No big deal!" Allison scoffed. "Wherever they are, they're far away, not here in this room."

Gramps shook his head. "It might seem that way, but you know better than to talk to a stranger you meet at the mall or in a park, don't you?"

Allison nodded.

"Same thing here. Did you ever use your mom's computer?"

Allison shook her head. "It was at work. She bought her own laptop to take on tour."

"If you're going to use the Internet, we need to agree on the rules."

"Rules, rules, rules!" *Everything my grandparents do have rules wrapped around them!* Allison sighed so loudly that no one could miss how she felt.

Gramps paid no attention. "Allison, we want you to enjoy the many good sites you can visit. But as all of us know, if you click at the wrong place or type a wrong address, you can come up with some pretty weird stuff. If you feel scared, or uncomfortable, or confused about something you see, we want you to tell us."

When they logged on, Gramps showed her how to turn off the power switch on the monitor. "If something upsets you, just block the image," he said. "The switch on the monitor doesn't shut off the computer. I can turn the monitor back on, see the screen, and understand why you're upset."

As Allison pulled her chair closer, her grandfather explained why he felt the way he did. "A lot of people put things on the Internet that I don't want to see, even as an adult. I don't want those things to enter my mind. It's not your fault if you see something that scares you or makes you uncomfortable. But tell me or Gran, and I'll take care of it."

When Gramps entered the NetSmartz website, he printed the Internet Safety Pledge for Allison's age level. "We'll stop here," Gramps said. "Let's see if we agree on what it says."

After he, Allison, and Gran talked about the rules, Allison signed the agreement. Gran taped it to the wall next to the computer, and Gramps explained something else.

"Soon you'll make new friends here in town. In the same way that we'll know them, we want to know your online friends. And just like we want to know the TV programs you watch, we'll visit Web sites with you. It's something we can do together."

Allison wasn't so sure about that, but then she realized something. Gramps was trying hard to be a parent. It couldn't be easy for him and Gran to give up their freedom and take her in.

"If you spend too much time online, we'll handle it like TV," Gramps told her. "We want you to have time for getting to know new friends in the neighborhood. You can't substitute a computer for real people."

Again Allison felt resentment rising within her. But then something else caught her attention. The caring in her grandfather's voice. "Just be wise, Allison," he said. "Just be wise."

His gravelly voice brought back a memory — a time long past when she was very young. During a walk with him Allison saw a big dog that frightened her and she took her grandfather's hand. Now she wanted to take her mom's hand instead.

Again Allison felt that hole deep down inside where she missed her mom. *Will I ever stop hurting?* she wondered.

Without warning, tears welled up in Allison's eyes. Impatiently she brushed them away. But Gran had seen them. Coming over, she put her arm around Allison in a quick hug.

"We love you," Gran said softly.

Allison drew a long shaky breath. "I know you do. I love *you*, Gran. And Gramps too."

As she and her grandfather visited websites, Allison came to a place where kids could offer their ideas about a topic. She clicked a subject called "My Hero."

She liked seeing what other kids wrote about sports heroes, famous people, and friends. Suddenly Allison stopped scrolling and read an answer a second time. *Hmmm. I never thought about it that way!*

She made sure that both Gran and Gramps read the message:

> *My heroes are my grandparents. They love me so much that they care about everything I do.*

As Allison went to bed that night, she started thinking about the power of the Internet for good or evil. *It's no wonder Gran and Gramps want to protect me. Maybe they know more than I give them credit for.*

To Allison's surprise she had learned something even bigger than online safety. *If I stick with the right rules I'll have the freedom to travel around the world!*

She could hardly wait to write to her mom. Her friends back home would be next.

For more about Internet guidelines and NetSmartz safety pledges, see the NetSmartz Workshop at www.NetSmartz.org. This site

Let's Talk . . . or Journal

offers additional information for parents, educators, and children, tweens, and teens.

DAY 1

What do you think Allison needed more than anything else? Why do you think that?

DAY 2

What did it mean for Allison to feel that she had a big hole way down deep inside?

DAY 3

Why is it important that your parents, grandparents, or other adults decide what you can do on the computer? Give reasons for your answer.

DAY 4

Gramps talked about not wanting to let some things enter his mind. How could that be important for each one of us?

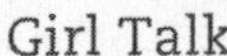

DAY 5

In the same way as there are bullies in your school, there can be kids who are bullies on the Internet. When you use the Internet do other kids ever say mean things to you? What will you do if this happens?

Do the risks of what you might see or hear apply only to the Internet? In what other areas do you want to be on guard? Why?

DAY 6

How can you follow your family's safety rules wherever you use the Internet, whether at home, school, the library, or a friend's house? Though your mom or dad, grandparents, or other adults use parental controls, there's an even more important control — when your own brain and heart say no. How can your own ability to say no protect and help you? Give examples.

DAY 7

In Jeremiah 29:11 God says, "I know the plans I have for you ... I want you to enjoy success.... I will give you hope for the years to come." In what ways would you like to receive God's success? How does he give you hope for the years to come?

Let's Pray About It

Lord, you know that often I get upset about rules. Help me remember that usually there's a good reason for them. Protect me, Jesus, in all that I do and see and take in. And give me an inward control where my heart and my brain and my spirit say no to the wrong things. I trust you to help me! Thanks!

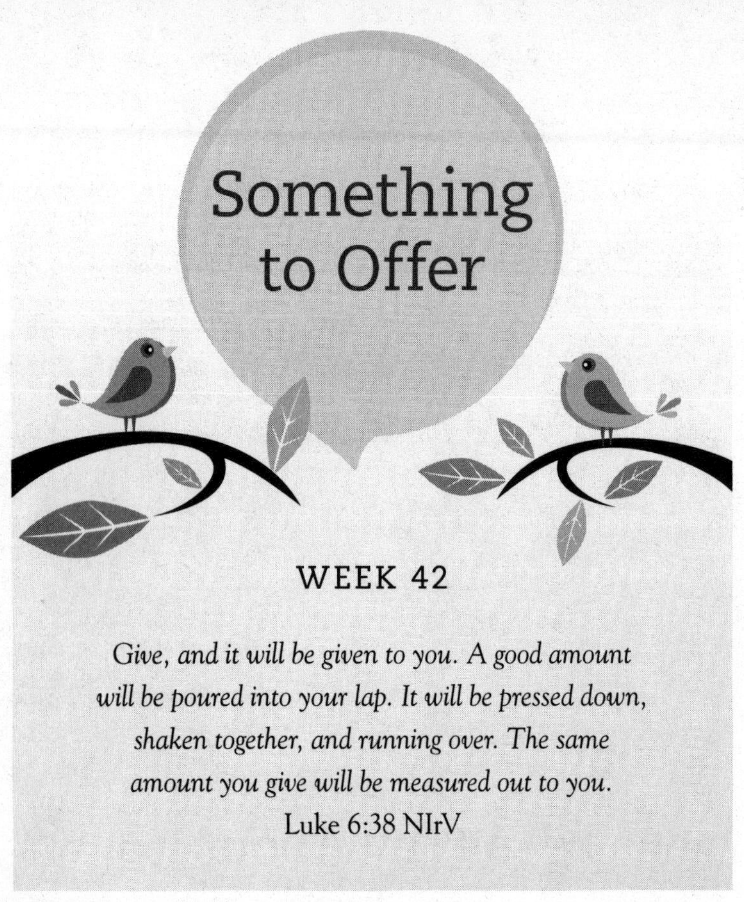

Something to Offer

WEEK 42

Give, and it will be given to you. A good amount will be poured into your lap. It will be pressed down, shaken together, and running over. The same amount you give will be measured out to you.
Luke 6:38 NIrV

Spring sunlight warmed Heather's face as she leaned against the wall of the school. Yet the warmth of the sun was not in her heart.

She always dreaded this moment. Whenever the girls in her class played softball, Heather relived her fear of being chosen last.

As she watched, Lindsey and Skye took their places. *Why do they always get to be captains?* Heather asked herself. Of course she knew. They were the best players. Yet she felt upset over something that never seemed to change.

Soon the choosing of sides began. "Caitlin!" called out Lindsey.

"Brianna!" shouted Skye.

And so it went. One moment Heather pressed hard against the wall, wishing she could disappear forever. The next she stood as tall as possible, hoping Lindsey or Skye would notice her.

If I could at least be somewhere in the middle, thought Heather. *I can't stand it if I'm last again.*

But she was. When no one else was left, Lindsey called her name. Full of misery, Heather went forward, hating even the ground she had to cross.

I'll show 'em, she thought. *I'll play so well that next time they'll* want *me on their team.*

Trying to walk as if she knew what she was doing, Heather hurried to her usual place in right field. For a long time nothing happened. Heather stood there, kicking blades of grass and squinting against the sun. Then a long, slow fly ball headed her way.

Heather ran forward. *If only I can—* She reached for it. The ball hit her mitt and dropped to the ground.

Grabbing wildly, Heather stumbled and fell on the ball. As she scrambled up, two runners crossed home plate. Desperately she threw the ball to second, but she was too late. Moments later the runner touched third.

"Way to go, butterfingers!" someone called.

Heather's face felt as if it had caught fire. The rest of the afternoon it burned. When she returned to school the next morning, Heather still felt the flames of embarrassment.

She was glad when Mr. Johnson asked them to take out their math books. Heather flew through the problems. As she finished, she looked up. Everyone else was still working.

Across the aisle, Lindsey was doodling with a pencil. Today she didn't seem like a softball captain. One look told Heather that Lindsey was as confused as ever.

Secretly Heather felt glad. *Nice to know I can beat her at something!*

But a moment later Lindsey looked her way. "Can you help me, Heather?" she whispered. "My head feels like it's tied in knots."

Forget it! Heather nearly spit out. *When you always choose me last? I should help* you?

In the next instant, Heather felt ashamed of her thoughts. Raising her hand, she got permission from Mr. Johnson, then slid her desk closer to Lindsey's.

"I just don't get it at all," Lindsey said in a low voice.

Step by slow step, Heather started to explain. Each time she saw a confused look in Lindsey's face, Heather backed up a bit, then worked forward again.

At last a light seemed to turn on behind Lindsey's eyes. "I can't believe it, Heather! How do you do it? How come it's so easy for you?"

In that moment Mr. Johnson asked for their attention. "I just received a note from the office about why Skye isn't in school today. It's really bad news. Her house caught fire last night. By the time the firemen got there, it had burned to the ground."

"Oh, no!" The gasp went through the room. Heather saw the shock in the faces around her.

"All of Skye's family got out safely," Mr. Johnson went on. "But they have nothing left but the clothes they were wearing."

Again Heather looked around the classroom. She wondered if her face looked as scared as everyone else's. *How awful! What if someone* hadn't *gotten out?*

Then Heather remembered how she had felt about Skye being one of the captains. Somehow being chosen last didn't matter anymore. Instead, Heather felt relieved that Skye was okay.

Her thoughts leaped ahead. *What would it be like to have nothing at all?*

"Let's think of what we can do to help Skye and her family," said Mr. Johnson.

For a moment everyone was quiet. In the stillness Heather seemed to be playing softball again. All her feelings of helplessness returned. *What can I do? It seems I can't do anything right.*

Then Lindsey waved her hand. "I'm the same size as Skye," she blurted out. "I'll bring some of my clothes."

Aaron chimed in. "I have little brothers the same age as Skye's brothers. I'll ask my mom for some of their things."

"We can bring cans of food," another girl said. "Do they have a place to stay?"

Heather was still thinking. Her mind seemed frozen by yesterday and how stupid she felt. Again she wondered, *Is there really any way I can help?*

As though hearing her question, Aaron spoke again. "Maybe we should bring money."

"Good idea," said Mr. Johnson. "They'll need to buy a lot of things."

In that instant a thought flashed through Heather's mind. *I can't play softball, but I sure know how to add money.*

Her hand went up. "If you want, I'll collect the money and turn it in to Mr. Johnson."

The teacher nodded, looking grateful.

Heather leaned back in her desk. For the first time since yesterday, she felt peaceful inside, as though she had a place. She had something to offer.

Let's Talk ... or Journal

DAY 1

Heather made a choice to help both Lindsey and Skye. Why was it especially hard for her to help Lindsey? What would you have done if you were in Heather's place?

DAY 2

Heather promised to collect the money Skye's family needed. What are some of the things that Heather gained as she helped someone else?

DAY 3

The next time the girls play softball, Lindsey could choose Heather sooner, even though Heather doesn't play well. But how could Lindsey help Heather improve her game?

DAY 4

When we aren't able to succeed at something, we can compensate, or make up for what we can't do, by achieving in other ways. In what ways did Heather start compensating for the way she felt about being clumsy in softball?

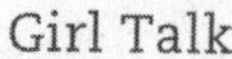

DAY 5

When Jesus was here on earth, he helped his disciples by showing them how to help others in practical ways. What did Jesus do? For clues see Matthew14:13 – 21.

DAY 6

In times when you've helped others, even though you didn't feel like it, how did you feel about yourself? What does Jesus mean when he said, "Give and it will be given to you"? (Luke 6:38)

DAY 7

I, Lois, the author of this book, can tell you from my heart that I'm grateful I can be a writer because I was so poor in math that I nearly flunked geometry. I also missed a lot of fly balls in my usual spot in right field. In what ways do you feel the need to compensate because you aren't good in doing something?

On the next two pages you'll be able to make two lists: one for ways you feel you can't succeed and one for things you know you do well.

Here's the beginning of my "can't succeed" list:

- My head fuzzes up when I do math.
- When my family moved to a different state I felt shy about trying to make friends.

Here's the beginning of my "things I do well" list:

- I can ask questions about something another girl likes to talk about. When she answers, we'll get to know each other better.
- I do my best to be a good writer.

Ways I Feel I Can't Succeed

Things I Do Well

When you look at your list on page 340, are you being honest about the things you can't do? Or are you being too hard on yourself?

When you finish your list on page 341, see if there's anything under "Things I do well" that can help you compensate for something you find hard. Draw a line from that idea over to the place needed in the list on the left.

Now look at the list on the left again and see if there's any area where you could improve if someone helped you. Think of someone you can ask to help you grow. Is there a way you can trade by helping that person?

How do you think Jesus feels about what you have learned by making these lists?

Let's Pray About It

Jesus, it bothers me when I can't do things I really want to do. If it's something you want me to learn, give me someone who will help me. Help me to take tiny little steps at succeeding until I know how to take bigger ones. And Lord, show me the things I can do well and help me grow in those ways. Thank you!

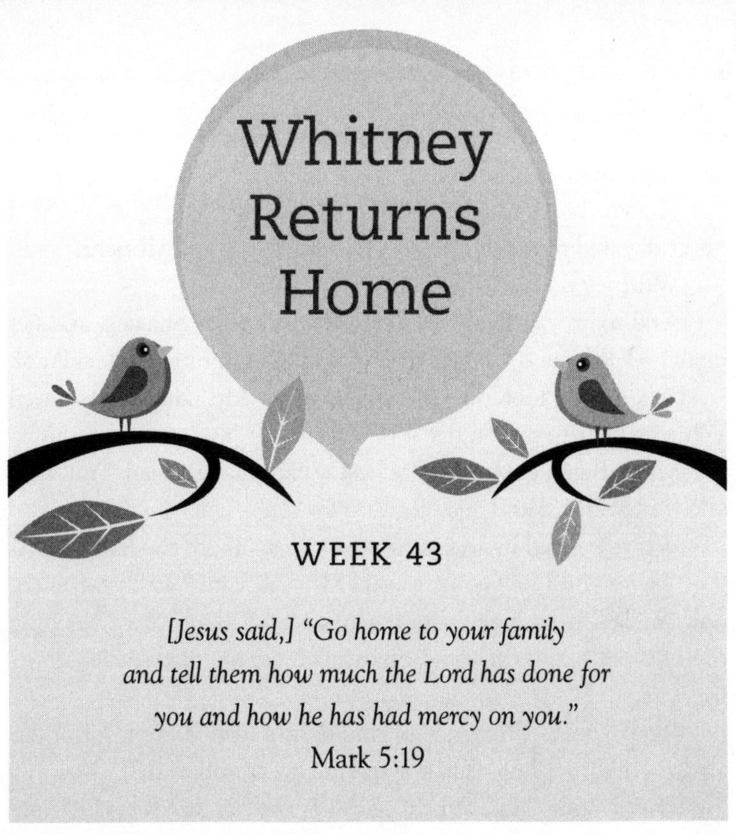

"Your family wants me to go skiing with them?" Whitney asked.

"Sure," said Shawna. "Why not?"

"I don't have skiis."

"We'll rent some."

"I've never skied before. I don't know how."

"No problem," Shawna said. "We'll teach you. It's not hard to cross-country ski. We'll take an easy trail."

Inside, Whitney felt scared. *What if I can't do it?* But she kept pushing the thought aside. Every part of her wanted to try.

Instead she asked, "You're *sure* your mom and dad want me along?"

"Yup. When we go for a weekend, they always let me take a friend. You're my first choice. Okay?"

"Okay!" But Whitney's thoughts raced off to her own family. *I can't imagine Mom and Dad wanting me along.* When they went somewhere, it was usually a bar or casino. They always left Whitney and her brother at home.

Shawna broke into her thoughts. "We'll leave right after school on Friday and rent skis for you when we get there. All right?"

Whitney nodded. "I'm good."

And so, it was all set. A week later Whitney, Shawna, and her mom and dad found an open space near the beginning of the ski trail.

"Slide your foot into place like this." Mrs. Sullivan showed Whitney how to put on her skis.

Mr. Sullivan explained the best way to move ahead. "You kick one ski backward and glide forward on the other."

Whitney tried it, and to her surprise soon got the hang of it.

"Laura and I will go first," said Mr. Sullivan. "We'll stop every now and then to make sure you're getting along okay." Jabbing their ski poles into the snow, Shawna's mom and dad started down the trail.

"You're next," Shawna said, and Whitney took her place at the top of a slight incline. "Just dig in your poles and push."

The winding trail led off through the woods. It wasn't long before Whitney felt at home on skis. She even managed the small hills without falling down very often. By the time she started getting tired, Whitney decided skiing was the most fun she'd ever had.

When she rounded a bend, she saw Shawna's parents at the side of the trail. They'd brushed snow off a picnic table, and now Mrs. Sullivan took food from her backpack. "Winter picnic!" she called.

Whitney took off her skis and dropped onto the bench. As she saw the apples and sandwiches, her stomach growled. But just as she reached out, ready to dive in, every head bowed.

Every head except Whitney's. As Shawna and her parents began praying, Whitney felt uncomfortable. Then she stared.

What a strange thing to do! Yet it seemed to mean something to them. Whitney closed her eyes so they wouldn't catch her staring. *Is that what makes them different?*

After lunch, when everyone started skiing again, Whitney asked Shawna, "How come your family has fun together?"

"What do you mean?"

"You're different."

Shawna laughed, as though she wasn't sure how to take Whitney's words. "We're different, all right."

"You are. You're nice to each other. You do things together. How come?"

Shawna's grin faded, and her eyes were serious. "We haven't always been that way."

"What happened?"

"First Mom became a Christian. Then I did. Then we prayed for Dad. We prayed a lo-o-ong time."

As they followed the ski trail, Whitney was quiet, thinking about it. *Would that work with my family? They'd probably just laugh at the whole thing.*

When twilight fell on the woods, they stopped skiing. The next morning they started skiing again. Whitney still watched Shawna and her mom and dad. *I wish my family could be like them.*

Deep inside Whitney a thought started to take shape. All day her longing grew. She wanted something more in her life. She wanted more for her family.

Off and on, Whitney asked Shawna questions. She discovered that Jesus loved her, Whitney, the way he loved the Sullivan family. On Saturday night Whitney invited Jesus to come into her life—to be her Savior and Lord.

When Shawna and her parents took her home on Sunday afternoon, Whitney knew the hard part was ahead. *I want my family to know Jesus*, she thought. Yet she felt more scared than when she faced her first time on skis.

As she sat down for supper, Whitney looked around the table. Her brother, Dustin, reached across her for a roll. Mom helped herself to potatoes, and Dad lifted a fork to his mouth.

Wondering if they could hear the pounding of her heart, Whitney bowed her head. Silently she offered the prayer she had learned from the Sullivan family.

When she looked up, Whitney saw Dustin staring at her. "What's with you?" he asked. "Did you get religion over the weekend?"

Whitney felt a warm flush reach her cheeks. "Yes, I did," she said quietly. She wondered if her heart would pound right out of her chest.

"So what are you now, a Jesus freak or something?" he asked, his voice scornful.

Then Mom jumped in. "Now, Whitney, we hope you haven't gotten yourself caught up in something that isn't good for you."

Whitney swallowed hard and wondered if she should bail out. *Should I pretend nothing happened to me? Will they ever understand?* Yet she knew she'd made a choice for something real.

Then Whitney saw the look in Dad's eyes. *He's listening,* she thought. *Maybe I'll have to pray for a long time, the way Shawna and her mom did. But Dad is listening.*

In spite of the way Dustin poked fun at her, Whitney began to explain.

Let's Talk . . . or Journal

DAY 1

What made Whitney want what Shawna's family had?

DAY 2

What do you think would happen to Whitney's family if she didn't explain how she received salvation?

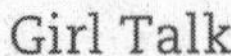

DAY 3

Whitney learned about God by watching the way the Sullivan family acted. How would you describe their Christian beliefs? What do you think Whitney told her family?

DAY 4

Jesus promised that the Holy Spirit would be our Helper. In what ways can the Holy Spirit help Whitney tell her family about Jesus?

Has there been a time when the Holy Spirit helped you talk to someone who didn't know Jesus? What happened?

DAY 5

In what other ways can the Holy Spirit help you live your life? Big clue: Look up what Jesus said about the Holy Spirit being a friend who helps and teaches you. See John 14:15 – 17, 26.

DAY 6

One of the Holy Spirit's jobs is to honor Jesus. In this story how did the Holy Spirit help the Sullivan family honor Jesus?

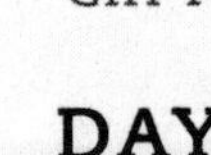

DAY 7

Whitney wondered if she could tell her family about the salvation Jesus had given her. All of us have times when we wonder if we can talk to others as Jesus wants. Not even the disciples could do it on their own. Neither can we.

The book of Acts is often called *The Acts of the Apostles*. Sometimes people also call it *The Acts of the Holy Spirit* because it shows how the power of the Holy Spirit works through people who put their faith in Jesus.

Look up the following verses to find out more about how the Holy Spirit helped the early Christians spread the good news of Jesus and his salvation.

- Before Jesus ascended into heaven, what did he tell his disciples to do? Luke 24:49

- What did Jesus promise would happen? Acts 1:8

- When was his promise fulfilled? Acts 2:1 – 6

- How did Peter change after receiving the power of the Holy Spirit? See John 18:15 – 18, 25 – 27. Then read the entire chapter of Acts 2 and especially verses 14, 21, and 41.

Let's Pray About It

Jesus, often I'm too scared to tell other people about you. Yet I believe you want me to be a Faithgirl and speak up. I know you want me to be the kind of Christian who tells other people about you. In your name I ask for all the power of your Holy Spirit to help me. Thanks, Jesus!

Throwaway Friend

WEEK 44

"God has said, 'Never will I leave you; never will I forsake you.' So we say with confidence, 'The Lord is my helper; I will not be afraid. What can man do to me?'"

Hebrews 13:6

Thanks, Dad," Heidi said as she climbed out of the car. Her best friend, Sara, said goodbye and followed Heidi.

Standing on the sidewalk, they looked up at the large SKATELAND sign. Both of them liked swooping along an outdoor path with their in-line skates, but with bad weather they needed to skate inside. All week they had looked forward to Saturday afternoon.

Minutes later Heidi and Sara tied the laces on their skates and stood up. It was still early, but the rink was filling up fast. As they moved into the flow of skaters, Heidi edged toward the middle. She wanted to practice some new turns before the rink got crowded.

She was beginning to feel good about her moves when she heard someone call her name. Looking up, she saw Annette, a girl from her school.

"Hey, this is gonna be great!" thought Heidi, waving back. Annette and her friends were the most popular kids in her class.

Last year Annette had been class president. She always managed to be in the middle of anything fun. Being Annette's friend was a sure ticket to being popular.

What can I do to have her pay attention to me? Heidi wondered, then remembered how well she skated. *Maybe Annette will notice.*

She did. When the group skating stopped, Annette came over to where Heidi and Sara waited on the sidelines.

"You're a good skater, Heidi," said Annette, not seeming to notice Sara.

Just then a special skate was called. "Triples," said Annette to Heidi. "Why don't we ask Dan?"

Heidi felt like she'd received an extra bonus. She'd had a secret crush on Dan for two years. *Skate with him?* she thought. *I'll jump at the chance!*

Before long, the afternoon seemed like a once-in-a-lifetime dream. Annette or one of her friends got Heidi into each of the special skates. She barely noticed how often Sara sat on the sidelines.

When the manager announced, "Boy's choice," Dan skated up to Heidi. *Wow!* she thought. *He's really asking me!*

As they skated away, Heidi saw Sara's face. She seemed to have put on a mask, but for a moment when she thought Heidi wasn't looking the mask slipped. Sara's eyes looked hurt.

With a jolt, Heidi realized she'd been so busy with the other kids, she'd forgotten Sara. In fact, she hadn't brought her into a single special skate.

As she and Dan moved away, Heidi once again forgot Sara. Dan was a good skater, and it was easy to keep in step. Soon they were laughing together. *He's as much fun as Sara*, thought Heidi.

In that moment a twinge of uneasiness shot through her. There it was again—

Sara. Rounding a corner, Heidi saw her sitting on the bench by herself.

When the music ended, Heidi skated up to Sara. "Would you like an ice cream?" she asked.

Acting as if nothing had come between them, her friend jumped up. And somehow Heidi found it a relief to be with Sara. *I don't have to impress her,* thought Heidi. *She's just what she's always has been—my friend.*

When they finished their ice cream, Heidi and Sara returned to the skating area. Again Heidi headed for the middle and started skating backward.

Annette found her there. "The kids are coming over to my house for supper," she said. "Want to come along?"

Do I! Heidi thought. *That isn't hard to decide.* She started to say yes, then remembered Sara.

"Sara and I came together. Can she come, too?"

A strange look crossed Annette's face. "Well, uh—"

For a moment she stood there, and Heidi guessed. Annette didn't want to say no, but she didn't want to say yes, either.

"Who's picking you up?" Annette asked.

"My dad," said Heidi.

"Why don't you take Sara home, then have your dad drop you off at my place?"

Heidi was tempted. More than anything she wanted to go to Annette's. More than anything she wanted to be part of their fun. But Heidi felt uneasy again. In that moment she knew what was wrong. *Am I throwing Sara away the minute someone else comes along?*

Heidi knew what her answer should be, but the world seemed to crash around her. *Will Annette ever invite me again?* She wished Annette hadn't forced her to make a choice.

But when Heidi spoke, she said, "I'm sorry. I'd like to come, but Sara's my friend. I don't want to deceive her."

Annette shrugged her shoulders and skated away. Heidi watched her go.

Let's Talk . . . or Journal

DAY 1

How would Sara feel if she found out that Heidi took her home, then went to Annette's? How would Heidi feel about herself if she did that to Sara?

What does it mean to be loyal to someone? What does it mean to deceive someone? Why is it cruel to deceive someone? Explain how it feels when someone has been cruel to you.

DAY 2

As you grow up, your friends may change over time because you have different interests. How is that different from what happened between Heidi and Sara at the rink?

DAY 3

In what ways would it seem good for Heidi to become friends with Annette? In what ways could it hurt Heidi to become friends with Annette? Give reasons for your answers.

DAY 4

We live in a world of throwaways — soda cans, paper plates, plastic forks and spoons. What does it mean to have throwaway friends? What would happen to Heidi if she always chose her friends based on who seemed popular at the moment?

DAY 5

In 1 Samuel 20 we read about the friendship between David and Jonathan. How was their friendship tested? In what ways did Jonathan and David stay loyal to each other?

Read I Sam 23:15 – 18: How did Jonathan help David find his strength in God?

Read 2 Sam. 9:1 – 7, 13: Why is it especially meaningful that David looked after Jonathan's son?

DAY 6

Think about your friends. Write one sentence telling about a way you have been loyal to a friend. Write another sentence telling how a friend has been loyal to you. Then write a paragraph or story about one or both of those relationships.

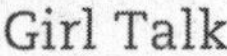

DAY 7

Hebrews 13:5 – 6 gives us a promise: "God has said, 'Never will I leave you; never will I forsake you.' So we say with confidence, 'The Lord is my helper; I will not be afraid. What can man do to me?' "

Think about the many different ways God has been loyal to you. Write about one or more of those special times. Write about a way you would like to be loyal to him.

Let's Pray About It

Jesus, you have given me some very special friends. Help me to be loyal, so I don't throw them away whenever someone who seems more popular comes around. Thanks for being my forever Friend. Most of all, I want to be loyal to you.

You Want a What?

WEEK 45

[Jesus said,] "If anyone would come after me, he must deny himself and take up his cross daily and follow me."
Luke 9:23

It all started in school that day. Kayla's friend Mary had just gotten a cool new mp3 player. And Shelly came to school with the kind of jean jacket Kayla had always wanted.

Listening to her friends talk, she wondered, *Why can't I have all the things they have?*

The rest of the day Kayla tossed it around in her mind. By the time she left for home, she had decided what to do. *I'll wait with more clothes and start with trying for a mp3 player. Maybe if I ask enough times, I'll wear Mom down and she'll give in.*

When Kayla opened the door, her mother was in the kitchen fixing supper. At her feet, two-year-old Hannah played on the floor. Around Hannah lay all the pots and pans she had taken from the cupboard.

Mom gave Kayla a hug. "Have a good day?"

Kayla nodded as though she really hadn't heard Mom's question.

At the kitchen table her little brother, Johnnie, was coloring a picture. Proudly he held it up for Kayla to see, but she barely noticed. Instead, she launched her attack.

"Mary's dad gave her a really cool mp3 player."

Mom pushed the hair out of her eyes. "Kayla, we've talked about this before."

"But I want to talk about it again. If I had a player like hers I could download all the music I like."

Instead of answering, Mom started peeling potatoes.

"I could even listen to Christian songs."

As Kayla watched, her mother's shoulders sagged slightly. *I'm getting through,* Kayla thought. *I'll wear her down, all right.*

But in that moment Mom turned from the sink. "Kayla, do you know how many people are out of jobs? And your dad and I have a lot of expenses we can't avoid. I'd like to have you think about the pressure you're putting on us."

"Aw, Mom," Kayla started. "I just want—"

Mom sighed, and the tired lines around her eyes seemed to deepen. "Kayla, have you heard yourself talk lately? 'I want, want, want.'"

"Yes, I want this," answered Kayla, her voice filled with resentment. "If you wanted to give it to me, you could. You just don't love me enough."

"The answer is no."

Kayla ran to her room and didn't come out until supper. Except for muttering "hi" to Dad, she was silent. All through supper her anger simmered. Even when little Hannah threw her plate on the floor, Kayla sat unmoved, her face stony.

As Mom cleaned up the mess, she looked as if she was going to cry. But Kayla pretended she didn't see.

Later that evening Kayla plopped down in front of the TV. Dad was watching a special on public television.

"Who is she?" Kayla asked as she saw a tiny woman wearing a long white robe-like dress.

"Mother Teresa," Dad answered. "A woman who gave her life to help the poor and dying in India."

Kayla groaned. "Can't we watch something else?"

"I want to see this," said Dad. "Your turn next—if there's something good."

Kayla waited, hoping the program would be over soon. On the screen a young woman described Mother Teresa. "Mother said she wanted to die on her feet. I think that's just what she did. She gave herself to the last drop."

Stupid way to live, Kayla thought.

But then the program showed footage of the small woman. Her white clothing was edged with a blue border, and her skin held deep lines. Something in her face caught Kayla's attention.

As Mother Teresa bowed her head in prayer, Kayla listened and remembered one sentence: "It is by forgetting self that one lives."

Suddenly Kayla had a strange feeling. She wished she could have whatever it was Mother Teresa had. In spite of her tiny size, there was something very big about her. For some reason she seemed happy inside, even though she lived among the poorest of the poor in India.

All evening Kayla tried to forget Mother Teresa's prayer. Instead, the sentence stayed in Kayla's mind. *What does it mean to forget myself so I truly live?*

Kayla tried to push the question away, but the pictures in her mind wouldn't leave. She thought about the streets of India and how she had bugged Mom for an mp3 player. She remembered the hunger and rags, and her desire for another jacket in spite of all the clothes in her closet. As much as Kayla wanted to forget the starving bodies she'd seen, she could not erase them from her mind.

Now Kayla realized it had been some time since she had thought about the choice she made when nine years old. Back then she had prayed, "Jesus, I want my life to count for you. I want to tell others about your love."

Remembering, Kayla felt ashamed. She'd avoided God for so long that it felt strange to talk with him. Yet Kayla knew she would dislike herself even more if she didn't.

Stumbling over the words, she started to pray. "Thank you, Jesus, for all the ways you have taken care of me. For all the times you have blessed me. Forgive me for being greedy—for always wanting more when I have more than enough. Forgive me for only thinking about myself. Will you help me forget myself and help others instead?"

When Kayla finished praying, it felt as if a huge sack filled with heavy stones had fallen off her back. Crawling into bed, she slipped between clean sheets and thought about the dirty streets of India. As she pulled a handmade quilt around her shoulders, she wondered how it felt to always be cold.

Then Kayla thought about where to begin. *I can't go to India. I need to finish school. I can't even leave home. But what can I do right here? Right now?*

In that moment Kayla knew where to begin. Breakfast in the short-order place down the block didn't cost as much as other meals. *Mom and Dad would like having breakfast together on Saturday morning. I'll offer to baby-sit Hannah and Johnnie.*

As she drifted off to sleep, Kayla felt she might even like herself again.

Let's Talk . . . or Journal

DAY 1

How do you think Kayla felt about herself when she kept asking for things? How does selfishness destroy self-respect?

When did Kayla's selfish feelings change? Why?

DAY 2

How would you define greed? What does it mean to be greedy? Look up the word greed in a dictionary, then think of examples.

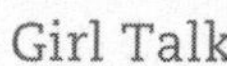

DAY 3

Kayla changed because she chose to put aside her greed for things she did not need. Are there ways in which you've been greedy? Be honest about what you've done. Think about how you need to change.

How will your life be different if you stop wanting more and more?

A dad and mom in Germany organized an anti-greed, week-long camp for 10 – 14-year old girls. From the start the camp was an experiment because the girls faced challenges that sounded unattractive. At first both girls and their parents were skeptical of these challenges, but more girls signed up than were invited. They left mp3 players, TVs, videos, play stations, computers, cell phones, and sweets at home. Their only purchased games were three jigsaw puzzles used in a group competition. Simple team games inspired great enthusiasm, and the girls creatively invented their own. The winners of team games were allowed to serve the losers by drying the dishes.

The daily program together began early and on time at 7:30 a.m. Every morning the leaders quoted from an ancient book, the Bible, that boldly says *Greed is evil and is condemned to failure!* During the camp, the girls proved they didn't mind being led in an anti-greed direction. They found greater value in being part of a community where no one was excluded and quarreling and bad words weren't heard. At the end of the week the girls declared unanimously that the experiment had succeeded.

How might such an interesting camp help you gain new ideas about what is fun? About what you really need?

DAY 4

How did Kayla start letting God use her right away? What are some practical ways you can reach out to help other people, right now, wherever you live?

DAY 5

While Jesus was here on earth, he showed us a servant's heart. What does it mean to have a servant's heart? For clues see John 13:1 – 17.

DAY 6

The Bible tells us how the name of Jesus released the miracle-working power of God …

Through prayer: Acts 1:14; Acts 2:42
Through faith in Jesus: Acts 3:16
With ordinary people doing extraordinary things! Mark 16:17 – 18

DAY 7

In Mark 9:23 Jesus said, "Everything is possible for the one who believes." If you choose to serve others, how will it change your life? Pray, asking God what he wants you to do. Take time to brainstorm with a parent and others you trust. Then write down your ideas. Come back to this list off and on throughout your life. Use your list as a check-up to decide whether you're living as you believe God wants you to live.

Let's Pray About It

Jesus, you know that every day I have food on my plate and clothes on my back. That every night I have a roof over my head and more things than I will ever need. Forgive me for being greedy, for wanting more, more, more when I already have so much.

Jesus, help me to forget myself and follow you so I can truly live. Give me a new heart attitude—a gift of caring that sees people who need help. Then show me what to do about helping them. Thank you, Jesus!

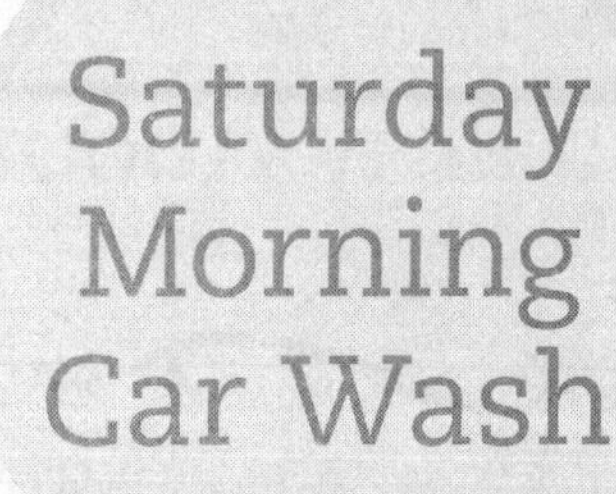

Saturday Morning Car Wash

WEEK 46

Don't pay back evil with evil. Be careful to do what everyone thinks is right.
Romans 12:17 NIrV

That afternoon McKenna and the others kids in the neighborhood started talking about how to raise money. Kelly, one of the girls living down the block, needed a kidney transplant. Her family needed money for medical bills.

McKenna took charge. She liked organizing things and asked for ideas on what to do.

"We could have a pancake supper," Chelsea suggested. "Our moms and dads would help."

"How about a carnival?" asked a boy. "We could bring things for prizes or stuff we could sell—like toys we don't use anymore."

After a lot of talk, they decided to hold a car wash on a Saturday morning two weeks away.

"My dad will let us have it in his parking lot," said McKenna's best friend. "It's on a busy corner where lots of people will see us."

"Cool!" McKenna exclaimed. "Let's make a list of what we need. First, someone for publicity. Who's good at making flyers?"

"I am," said Jessie. "And I'll take 'em to all the stores around here."

"How about a notice in the bulletin of churches in the neighborhood?"

Someone else volunteered.

"Rags and buckets?"

Three boys offered to bring those.

"Car wax?"

A fourth boy said he'd try for a discount at a nearby store.

"Well, that's just about it," said McKenna. Then as the group started to break up, she remembered one more thing. "We'll need two long hoses or three shorter ones to reach from the outside faucet into the parking lot."

"I'll bring them," Riley said. "We've got two long hoses."

"Thank you!" McKenna exclaimed. "Now, does everyone know what they're supposed to do?"

Picking up the list, she read off each person's job. "Then we're all set. Talk about the car wash wherever you are. The more customers we get, the more money we'll make for Kelly. And everyone be there at eight-forty-five, ready to work."

The Saturday of the car wash dawned warm and sunny. As the kids gathered at the parking lot, McKenna knew the girls had done a great job on publicity. Wherever she had been the last few days, people had promised they'd show up. Now, fifteen minutes before the car wash was to start, McKenna checked to be sure they had everything.

"Buckets? Rags? Wax? Yup. And plenty of kids to help." McKenna was pleased.

But the next moment she felt a jolt. "Where's Riley with the two hoses?"

No one had seen him that morning. McKenna's heart started to pound. "Uh-oh, are we in trouble?"

McKenna whipped out her cell and called Riley's house. When no one answered, she felt relieved. "He must be on the way here."

But the minutes passed and Riley didn't show up. McKenna started to panic.

"Anyone know where Riley might be?"

McKenna looked around. "Who else has long hoses? Come here. Call your mom or dad."

Just then their first customer drove in. A moment later three other cars lined up behind the first. McKenna looked at them, glad for the business. "But oh, wow! How can we keep up without a hose?"

She sent three of the boys with buckets to the faucet. But the cars were too dirty. Soon muddy brown water filled each bucket.

McKenna felt frantic. "We're gonna lose customers," she said.

She was right. The driver of the third car gave a quick beep. McKenna tried to set up a bucket brigade, then went over to explain what was wrong. The man pulled out of line and drove off.

The driver of the fourth car got out. "Hey, what's the trouble? Can I help?"

McKenna felt relieved when she recognized Mr. Wong, a man from her church.

"I've got two long hoses," he said. "I live three miles from here, but I'll see what else I can round up." He jumped back in his car and drove away.

Just then another driver pulled in. When McKenna explained, the woman said, "Sorry, I wanted to help out. But I can't wait around all day."

The man in the next car felt the same way and left.

McKenna didn't blame them, but she felt more angry every minute. Each customer they lost meant less money for Kelly. "All that publicity wasted!"

But McKenna also felt embarrassed. It hurt to plan something and not have it work. *I wonder if people think it's my fault.* She dreaded seeing another customer—someone who would think she didn't know what she was doing.

Just then Riley rode up on his bike. McKenna pounced on him. "Where are the hoses?"

"Hoses?" Riley looked blank, then remembered. "Ohhh. I forgot."

"You *forgot?*" McKenna asked. "The whole car wash depended on you, and you *forgot?*"

She couldn't remember ever being so angry. Picking up a

bucket, she dumped the muddy water over Riley's head. "You take the world's prize for messing things up!"

As Riley sputtered, McKenna picked up another bucket and stomped over to a waiting car. The moment she reached the driver, she turned on a smile, but inside she burned with anger. In her nicest voice she started to explain.

Just then Mr. Wong came back. In a minute or two he had his two hoses hooked up and ready to use.

McKenna closed her eyes, took a deep breath, and went back to work. She could hardly wait to spray down the dirtiest vehicle that drove in.

Let's Talk ... or Journal

DAY 1

Being responsible means being someone other people can count on. How did everyone except Riley take responsibility?

What does it mean to say, "A chain is only as strong as its weakest link"? Who was the weakest link? How did everyone suffer because Riley forgot his responsibility?

DAY 2

Did McKenna have a right to be angry about the hoses? How do you feel about the way she showed her anger? Give reasons for your answers.

When the car wash is over and McKenna cools down, she needs to talk more with Riley. What do you think she should say about how she feels? What could Riley do to try to make up for what he did?

DAY 3

What are some things that make you angry? Try beginning with the words, "I feel angry about ..." and finish writing the sentence.

DAY 4

Sometimes it's better to talk with an adult who will help you instead of talking with the kid who made you angry. What good steps can you take to deal with the things that make you upset?

DAY 5

When was Jesus angry about things people did? Check Mark 3:1 – 5 and John 2:13 – 17 for big clues.

DAY 6

What's the difference between being angry about something with good reason and holding a grudge? Does McKenna have a right to hold a grudge toward Riley? Why or why not?

DAY 7

When Peter denied his relationship with him, Jesus could have held a grudge and stayed hurt and angry. Check out John 18:17, 25 – 27. How did Jesus make sure that Peter knew things were okay between them? See John 21:15 – 17. What words did Jesus use?

Let's Pray About It

Jesus, when I feel upset, help me handle my anger in the right way. Help me talk to the right person about my problem. Help us work together to figure out what to do and put the problem behind us. And Jesus, help me to take responsibility and do my job whenever needed.

Anya's workout time that morning had been shot through with glory. Though there were no windows, it seemed that sunlight washed the gym. When she came down off the uneven parallel bars, her gymnastics coach cheered her on. "You've got it, Anya!"

Now she was back after school, making sure of every part of her routine. She wanted nothing to distract her from the perfection she'd like to achieve.

With a flying run Anya grabbed hold of the lower bar. Up, over, beat, twist. As she worked out, she sensed rather than saw that people had stopped and turned to watch. Yet she kept on, sure in her timing, holding her concentration. If she won at the meet tomorrow, who knew how far she could go?

With a final twist, Anya was on the mat, arms stretched high above her head, her spirit soaring.

The applause came. "Perfect, Anya! Absolutely perfect!"

called her coach. "Now take a break. Go home and get a good night's sleep. You're ready for the meet."

She knew he was right. She was tired, but wanted to do her routine again.

"Just one more time," she answered.

Taking her first position, Anya poised her body, letting the routine go through her mind. Then she took a deep breath.

The run came easy. She reached out, grabbed the bar, swung up into a handstand. Down, under, swing, reach.

Not quite right, Anya told herself. Somehow her timing was off, and she fought to recover. Up, over, beat, reach.

The next moment Anya felt the floor coming up. Instinctively she reached out, and her left hand took the fall. Pain shot through her arm, sucked down like a giant wave, and washed over her body. Then her world went black.

Several hours later, Anya looked up from a hospital bed. She seemed surrounded by bright light. Her mom stood at the side of the bed, her coach nearby.

Have they been crying? Anya wondered. *Coach Sanders wouldn't. He'd never cry.* She drifted off again, then came back.

I don't like the look on their faces, she thought. But her eyes felt weighted. She couldn't seem to keep a thought in her mind. Again she drifted off, then opened her eyes.

Have I been crying? she wondered this time. *What's wrong?*

Then Anya felt the cast on her hand and arm, and the shock went through her. *I don't want to ask,* she thought. *If I don't ask, maybe it won't be true.* She pushed the question to the back of her mind, trying to avoid it.

But she couldn't avoid her mother's eyes. Mom reached out and pushed the hair back from Anya's forehead. "Take it easy, Annie. I love you," she said.

Annie! Anya felt sick all through. *Mom hasn't called me Annie since I was a little kid. That's what she called me when she put me on her lap, washed my scraped knees, and kissed the bandages.*

No longer could Anya escape the question. "What happened?" she asked aloud.

Coach Sanders took her good hand. "Sorry, Anya. I saw you going, and I couldn't reach you in time—"

It's bad, Anya thought. *Really bad.* But she couldn't quite take it in yet. Her eyes felt too heavy.

Anya drifted off to sleep, but a few hours later, she came wide awake. This time she had no choice but to face what had happened. A broken wrist. Not just one bone, but two had been shattered and crushed. Yes, a specialist had operated on it. Yes, he had done all he could. But—

Like a little child she whimpered. Tears streamed down her cheeks. With every waking moment, Anya felt questions gnaw inside her. *Will I ever be able to work on the uneven bars? Will my wrist be strong enough for handstands? Will I ever compete again?*

In the dark of night the questions haunted her, questions she was afraid to ask. The next day she knew she must.

Her doctor shook his head. "I don't know, Anya. I wish I could tell you something different. Yet it would be worse if I said everything is going to be okay. Down the road you might find out I lied to you. I have to be honest in telling you it's the worst break I've seen, and I've seen a lot."

He didn't have to say more. Anya remembered her mom's expression when she first woke up. She remembered how Coach Sanders had looked. She couldn't escape what she had seen in their eyes.

It can't be true, God, *can it? You wouldn't let this happen!*

It had been a long time since Anya talked with God, but now she had plenty to tell him. *You're supposed to be a God of love. How can you do this to me?* She wanted to shake her fist at him.

When she left the hospital, Anya returned to the apartment where she lived with her mother. One day when her mom was gone, Anya shouted her rage. "God, I wanted to be a champion gymnast! How can you wreck my life this way?"

The sound of her words seemed to bounce back at her. The apartment walls closed in around her, but the questions would not stop. "Why, God, why? Why *me?*"

In the silence that came, there were no answers. Instead, the silence seemed to bleed with Anya's pain.

The next morning she got up early, the way she used to. Every day she went into the gym and watched the others work out. More than once her coach tried to get her off the bench.

"C'mon, Anya," he said. "Come over here and give tips to the others. Tell them how to improve."

Each time Anya shook her head, telling herself, *He's just trying to make me feel better. I'm not really needed.* Then a deeper thought plagued her. *If I can't be a gymnast anymore, why should I help someone else?*

As the days went on, Anya's anger and discouragement grew. Then one morning her coach found her outside the gym, trying to hide her tears. This time he made no request for help. His voice was soft, but there was steel running through it.

"Anya, I taught you to be a champion. You're not acting like one." Whirling around, he returned to the gym.

Afraid to face her own feelings, Anya fled. *I don't have to go back*, she told herself. *I'll just stay away.*

But that night she had a dream. Anya saw herself poised, standing ready for her routine. As she started to run, her feet bit into the floor. Faster, faster. Grab the bar. Up, over, under, twist. Reach out, up to a perfect handstand. Down, under, up. Another flip. Then her feet hit the mat. Standing with up-stretched arms, she waited for the applause. It thundered around her.

Anya woke up crying. She pulled the blanket over her head. Cushioning her left wrist with her pillow, she cried until her body shook. *It's in me, isn't it, God? Will I always want to be a gymnast?*

Anya didn't know the answer, but suddenly she felt a stillness within. Something inside had changed.

Pushing back the blankets, Anya dressed, said good-bye to Mom, and started for the gym. As she opened the door, she made her decision. *Okay, God. If I can't be a champion gymnast, I'll be the best coach there ever was.*

With her head high, Anya walked over and stood near the uneven parallel bars. She was ready to help someone else. When Anya decided something, she meant it.

Let's Talk ... or Journal

DAY 1

Why was Anya afraid to face the fact that her wrist was broken? After something difficult happens, people often feel angry with God. What reason does Anya give for feeling angry with him?

What happened when Anya went beyond being angry *at* God and started talking *with* him about her feelings? How did Anya choose between feeling sorry for herself and going on with her life?

DAY 2

When it becomes impossible to reach a goal, it sometimes helps to substitute something similar. As Anya works toward a new goal, what achievements might make her happy?

DAY 3

It's good to have dreams about accomplishing something worthwhile if you keep those dreams in balance and don't let them control you. Do you feel Anya's dream of being a gymnast had started to control her? Why or why not?

DAY 4

When Jesus was twelve years old, he knew what his heavenly Father wanted him to do. What did Jesus tell his earthly parents? For a big clue see Luke 2:49.

DAY 5

God wants to help you know what he wants you to be. Sometimes people think that if God calls them to be something it will be exactly what they don't want. Instead, if God calls you to do something, he will give you the desire to do it. Is there some way God is calling you to do something special with your life?

Having a vision means that you know the way that God wants to use your life. For instance, when I was nine years old, I, Lois, knew God wanted me to write books to tell others about him. If you know what your vision is, do your best to put it in one sentence. Write it down here.

DAY 6

If you don't know what God wants you to do, ask him to show you. As you read your Bible, write down the verses that the Holy Spirit makes real to you. Those verses might seem to "jump out" or have a holy spotlight because they fit what you're wondering about. As you talk with people or watch what they do in their work, write down what you notice. See if the ideas you receive fall into a pattern. Notice the areas in which you have special interest and ability. It's fun doing the things God has equipped us to do!

DAY 7

When God gives you a vision for your life's work, you will probably need to develop certain skills or knowledge. If you follow the steps God puts in front of you, he will help you be ready for what you need to know. For instance, you may need to get special training or experience in something. What is a goal you're trying to reach?

Remember something important: If God calls you to do something, he gives you the desire to do it. Is there something that he is giving you the desire to do? In whatever kind of work you enter how can you honor him?

Let's Pray About It

It's hard to be happy and content, Lord, if things aren't going my way. Help me to turn from feeling sorry for myself and be what you want me to be. Give me a big vision for how you want to use my life. Then show me how to take the steps you want me to take. Thank you, Jesus! I look forward to seeing how you lead me.

WEEK 48

Don't you know that your bodies are temples of the Holy Spirit? The Spirit is in you. You have received him from God. You do not belong to yourselves. Christ has paid the price for you. So use your bodies in a way that honors God.

I Corinthians 6:19 – 20 NIrV

Without making a sound, Darcy closed the back door behind her. Like a shadow, she crept down the steps, then through the yard. A moment later she knocked on her neighbor's back door.

To her relief Shannon was the one who answered. "Hi, there! C'mon in. Haven't seen you for a while."

"Hi, yourself," Darcy said, and then felt shy. But Shannon made her feel welcome.

"I've missed you. Remember how we used to talk about stuff?"

Feeling miserable inside, Darcy nodded. Now that she was here, she didn't know where to begin. Again Shannon filled in the gaps.

"I just made some of your favorite cookies."

As Darcy sat down at the kitchen table, it seemed like old times. Shannon was eighteen and had always seemed like an older sister to Darcy. Whenever things got too tough at home, Darcy escaped and came here.

Shannon knew that. "What's the matter?" she asked after the third cookie.

"I just—" Darcy felt too old to cry, but tears spilled down her cheeks.

"Your mom and dad fighting again?"

Darcy nodded.

"How are you feeling about it?"

Darcy thought for a moment. "I'm not scared the way I was when I was a little kid. Then I wondered if one of them would hurt me. Beat me up, I mean. They never have, but—"

Darcy stopped talking and tried to think it through. "Now I get scared in other ways. Boys at school notice me, and sometimes I like them."

Shannon waited, so Darcy had to go on. "But what if—?"

"What if what?"

Darcy didn't smile. "What if they treat me the way my dad treats my mom?"

"That's a good question."

Darcy leaned forward. "Shannon, when I see your mom and dad together, they have a good time. They act like they love each other."

"They do," Shannon said. "Every now and then they disagree about something, but they talk it out. They *do* love each other."

"And when I come over here, it's different from at home." Darcy looked down at the kitchen floor. She was afraid to tell Shannon how upset she really felt.

Just the same, Shannon guessed. "Darcy, are you wondering about this because when you grow up, you want to be happy like my mom and dad?"

"Sounds kind of dumb, huh? Thinking about it now?"

"Sounds kind of smart to me."

"For you it's easy," Darcy said. "You've watched your mom and dad all your life. You can try to be like them. But what about me?"

"You're right." Shannon's green eyes were deep and serious.

"It probably *will* be easier for me. I *have* learned a lot of good ideas from my mom and dad. But you can learn from them too. Pick out what you like about the way they live. They aren't perfect any more than anyone else. But try to remember what you like."

"But—" Darcy didn't know how to say it. She tried again. "Why do your mom and dad have it so good, and my mom and dad have it so awful?"

Shannon thought for a moment. "Well, the most important thing is that my mom and dad are Christians. That doesn't always mean a marriage is good, but it helps. Mom and Dad pray together, and when they disagree about something, they ask Jesus to help them know what to do."

"How did they find each other?"

Shannon grinned. "When I was a little kid, I thought this was so romantic. But now I think it's something really important. When my mom was still a young girl, her mom—my grandma—taught her to pray about who she'd marry. And my dad's dad—my grandpa—taught him to pray about who *he'd* marry!"

"How did they know what to look for?"

Again Shannon grinned. "Well, I can tell you *that.* Or I'll tell you what *I'm* looking for! Mom says the kind of marriage I'll have depends a lot on the kind of choices I make. It's important to know what we want *before* we start dating someone. That's why we need to spend time with kids in groups—to figure out what boys are really like."

Shannon stood up, poured Darcy some milk, and sat down again. "First of all, I want to marry a Christian. Someone who feels as strongly about being a Christian as I do. Some girls marry a guy who goes to church, but if he doesn't really love and honor the Lord, they still wind up having a problem."

For a moment Shannon was quiet. "And I want someone who respects me."

"Like your dad respects your mom?" Darcy asked.

Shannon nodded. "But you need to figure that out long before you start dating someone. If someone really loves you, he cares about what happens to you. He wouldn't purposely do something to hurt you."

Shannon leaned forward. "Darcy, it's important to be able to do the things you want to do with your life. Like graduating from high school. Getting trained for a job or going to college. You want to wait for a husband you *really* love. If a guy doesn't respect you, he'll make you lose respect for yourself. And self-respect is one of the most important things you have."

For a moment the kitchen was quiet. Then Darcy thought of another question. "How will I know if I really love someone?"

"He'll be someone you think a lot of." Shannon's ideas tumbled out. "You'll respect him and like the way he acts. You should be able to talk with him, even about hard things. You have fun together, even if it's just taking a walk. You don't have to spend big money to enjoy being together. You miss him when he's gone, and you like doing nice things for him."

"And he's good-lookin'—"

Shannon grinned. "Of course!" Then her eyes turned serious. "But Mom says that when you love someone, no matter how that person looks, he seems good-looking."

"What about love at first sight?"

Shannon laughed. "You've really been thinking about this. Well, from what my mom says—"

A voice interrupted. "And what does your mom say?"

Darcy looked up, glad to see Shannon's mom, but wishing she hadn't come now.

"My mom-m-m says," Shannon drawled, "there's a difference between being attracted to a boy and really loving him. You can like the way a boy looks at first sight. But love is more."

Shannon and her mom said together, "Love grows."

"You need to give a relationship time so you know for sure," said Shannon's mom. "And if God doesn't put that sureness—that peace—in your heart, it's much better to *not* get married than to marry someone who isn't the right person for you."

Listening to Shannon's mom, Darcy couldn't hold back the rest of her questions. "If I ask him, will God *really* show me the path to take? Will he show me if I should get married or not? And if I should get married, will he show me *exactly* who it should be?"

"Yes! Yes! Yes!" Shannon and her mom spoke in unison.

Feeling as if a weight had rolled off her back, Darcy grinned. "Yes! Yes! Yes! to both of you also!"

She stood up. "Gotta go now. Thanks for the cookies."

Shannon went to the door with Darcy and gave her a hug. "Come over again soon, okay?"

Darcy nodded, knowing she'd be back. "Thanks, Shannon," she said softly. Then she bounded across the yard and slipped through the back door. As she tiptoed up the stairs to her room, the house was quiet. Mom and Dad had stopped fighting. Until the next time.

As Darcy crawled into bed, she prayed for them. Then, for the first time, she prayed about whom she might someday marry.

Just before she fell asleep Darcy smiled to herself. By starting now she could pray for a long time. It was going to be fun to see how God helped her with one of the most important choices she'd ever make.

Let's Talk . . . or Journal

DAY 1

Why is it important to spend a lot of time in groups of kids before you start dating one person?

What are some of the character qualities you want to find in the people you choose for your closest friends? How can you learn to recognize those qualities in both boys and girls when you're with other families or with groups of kids your age?

DAY 2

Proverbs 4:23 says "Above all else, guard your heart, for it is the wellspring of life." What does it mean to guard your heart? Why is it important to know how you want to handle yourself before you start a serious relationship with one person?

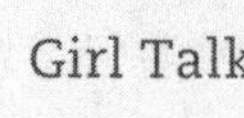

DAY 3

Both boys and girls need to be responsible in the way they act. In what ways do you want a boy to respect you and be thoughtful about what's best for you?

How can you as a girl be thoughtful and responsible in the way you treat a boy?

DAY 4

Go back to the beginning of this week's story and read 1 Corinthians 6:19 – 20 again. What does it mean to be a temple of the Holy Spirit? What does it mean to honor God with your body?

DAY 5

If you are old enough and have the blessing of your family, growing in a relationship with a person you love and plan to marry can be exciting and fun. But some relationships offer only misery. What makes the difference?

DAY 6

What are some ways to know if love is real? Some clues are in the story. For more ideas take a look at 1 Corinthians 13.

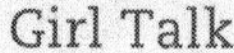

DAY 7

As a girl, it's important that you dream big about your future. What character qualities would you like to see in the young man you someday marry? You can make a lo-o-n-n-ng list!

What kind of husband do you want to have — one who wants to work and pray with you to have a Christian home? Or one who doesn't care? If you want a Christian home ask God for a godly husband who will love and cherish you and walk in God's way. Prayer in the name of Jesus works! But be sure to wait for God's timing.

Let's Pray About It

Thank you, Jesus, that I can learn a lot about other kids by having fun in a group. Help me to recognize the character qualities that are important in my special friends. If you want me to get married someday, I ask in your name, Jesus, for someone with the good qualities that are important both to you and to me. Lord, I want to marry the Christian who is your best choice for me.

The Day of the Storm

WEEK 49

Love is patient. Love is kind. It does not want what belongs to others. It does not brag. It is not proud. It is not rude. It does not look out for its own interests. It does not easily become angry. It does not keep track of other people's wrong.
I Corinthians 13:4–5 NIrV

As Peter sat at the supper table, he stretched out his leg. Suddenly he kicked his sister, Pam.

"Stop it!" Pam glared at her twin.

Pete's leg was already back under his chair. He looked as innocent as a newborn baby.

Mom sighed. "What's the matter with you two? All day long—fight, fight, fight."

Dad put down his fork and looked up. "Leave your sister alone, Pete. As long as you're done eating, you can start the dishes."

"Dishes? That's girl's work!"

"Girl's work?" asked Dad.

"Yeah, girl's work! You don't really expect me to do the dishes, do you?"

"Yes, I do. That's why I asked."

"But only girls do dishes. That's Pamela's job."

"You just don't wanna do 'em," she growled.

Mom looked at Pam, then at Pete. "I think she's right, Pete."

Groaning, he stood up. With every dish he carried to the sink, he had a new complaint. Finally Dad said, "No more comments, Pete, okay?"

"Yeah, Peterrrr!" Pam drawled.

Mom looked at Dad and rolled her eyes. Clearly she was tired of their arguments.

Dad looked thoughtful. "Pam, I'd like to have you mow the lawn."

"Dad! You've gotta be kidding. *Me* mow the lawn?"

"Yes, for a change I want you to mow the lawn," answered Dad. "It's going to rain soon, so get started right away."

"But what if someone sees me? I'd be so embarrassed doing my brother's work!"

Dad grinned. "Oh? *His* work? You're sure?"

"I'm sure! I don't wanna get all hot and sweaty!"

"Hey, I'll trade with you, Pam," Pete said quickly.

Dad winked at Mom. "Nope, no trades. Not tonight. I think we should do a bit of thinking about male and female roles around here."

"Oh, Da-a-a-d!" the twins groaned, complaining together for a change.

"I mean it!" Dad said. "Is there such a thing as boy's work and girl's work? Or can we all just pitch in when something needs to be done?"

Mom smiled, but neither Pam nor Pete seemed to like Dad's idea.

"I haven't thought much about it before," he said. "But maybe your mom and I have taught you to fill certain roles just by the way we treat you. Is that good or bad or somewhere in between?"

Pete jumped on it. "That's good! Look at the name you gave me. I'm a rock!" He flexed the muscles in his arms. "Strength, power, everything you want!"

Then Pete had an idea. As he picked up another plate, he

let his voice sound only half interested. "What does Pam's name mean, anyway?"

"Loving, kind," answered Mom, falling into the trap. "All honey."

"All honey!" Pete hooted. "She's all honey, all right!"

Pam's eyes glistened with anger. "I don't know why I have to have you for a brother! And a *twin* brother at that!"

Dad's grin faded. "Okay, that's enough. Both of you get to work." He stood up. For a moment he peered toward the trees in the backyard. "Seems like it's getting dark faster than usual. Get the mowing done right away, Pam." Dad picked up his paper and went into the living room.

As Pete washed the dishes, he stared out the kitchen window. Before long he noticed dark clouds moving in. Through the open window he sensed the stillness. Not a leaf on the nearby maple moved.

Soon the clouds were directly overhead. Watching Pam take slow turns around the yard, Pete felt uneasy. He was still scrubbing pans when the sky changed to an eerie green.

Pam had only half of the lawn mowed when the wind came up, whipping through the trees. Pete left the dishes and headed for the backyard. "Hey, Pam! Run for it!"

Grabbing the handle of the mower, he raced for the garage. The moment he pushed the mower inside, he slammed down the door and followed Pam.

Near the house, the rising wind pushed him against the wall. A strong gust ripped through a nearby maple, and Pete heard a crack. A large limb landed on the lawn.

Dad met him at the door. "Head for the basement!"

With a bound Pete reached the steps and took them two at a time. Partway down, he twisted his ankle and tumbled the rest of the way.

When he landed at the bottom of the steps, Pete moaned. Clutching his ankle, he rolled on the floor. "Ow, ow, ow!"

Mom, Dad, and Pam followed him down the stairs and knelt around him.

"Did you hit your head?" Mom asked.

"Oh, Pete, I'm sorry," Pam said. "It's 'cause you were helping me."

"It's 'cause I was doing girl's work," Pete growled. "If I'd been mowing the lawn, I'd have been done!"

As he tried to sit up, he moved his leg and winced. "Owww!" Lying back down again, Pete groaned.

"Just lie still for a minute," Dad said.

"Did you feel anything snap?" asked Mom.

"I landed so fast I'm not sure."

"Can you move your foot?" Dad asked.

As Pete tried to move his foot, he winced. The pain brought tears to his eyes.

"Boys aren't supposed to cry," Pam said sweetly, sounding like her old self.

Suddenly Dad and Mom laughed.

"I don't see what's funny," Pete grumbled. "I'm lying here dying, and you're all laughing."

Just then the lights flickered and went out. In the darkness Pete heard Mom laugh again, but this time there was a nervous sound in her voice.

"Take it easy, honey," Dad told her. "Where's the flashlight that's supposed to be down here?"

"On the shelf," Pam said. "Just a sec. I'll get it."

In a minute she turned on the flashlight. Then she lit the candles they kept in the basement.

Dad turned on the battery-operated radio they stored nearby. "Straight-line winds have left a path of destruction through the center part of the state—"

Mom was still on the floor next to Pete. "I think it's a sprain."

Dad slid a pillow under Pete's head and slipped off his shoe. Gathering around Pete, the family waited in the basement until sounds of the storm moved farther away. At last the thunder rumbled off in the distance.

"The brunt of the storm has now left the metro area," the newscaster told them. "Cleanup crews are clearing the main roads.

Go out only if necessary. Remember that any electric lines that are down may be live."

"We better take you to urgent care," Dad told Pete.

He and Mom helped Pete up the steps and into the car. As soon as Pam jumped in, Dad backed out of the driveway. He drove slowly, weaving around the branches in the road. "Good thing we have only six blocks to go."

But for Pete it seemed like sixty miles. Staring out the window, he tried not to move his ankle. It hurt more every minute.

Around them, chain saws roared as crews tried to clear fallen branches. An electric company van blocked one street where three people worked on a power line.

When Dad stopped the car, Pam pointed up at a post. "See that woman? She's working with the men!"

"Hush!" Mom said. "Leave Pete alone!"

Dad turned the car, but two blocks away they ran into trouble again. The signal lights were off, and the few cars that were out moved slowly. Someone in a yellow rain coat waved them around another fallen tree. Pete didn't need Pam's help to see that the police officer was a woman.

At the hospital, Pam stayed in the waiting room, and Mom and Dad helped Pete into the emergency room. Before long, a man dressed in a white shirt and pants appeared. As the man started asking questions, Pete had a question for him. "Are you the doctor?"

"Nope, I'm a nurse. Let's see what you've got here." Gently he pulled down Pete's sock. "Now, this is going to be a bit uncomfortable, but I'm going to cut off your sock before there's any more swelling."

When Pete left the hospital, Mom was on one side, Dad on the other. Pam trailed behind. The doctor said it was a bad sprain. Pete would have to use crutches and stay off his ankle for a while.

In the days that followed, Pete took full advantage of the doctor's orders. Whenever he could, he ordered Pam around. But often he thought about all that had happened the day of the storm. He started watching how Dad handled certain things.

"Here, let me get that," Dad told Mom one day when she brought home heavy bags of salt for the softener.

Another time when Mom was praying Dad said, "Praying isn't a sign of weakness. It's not just woman's work." After that, Pete noticed how often Dad prayed, when it seemed he was just sitting in his chair.

On a night when Mom was really tired, Pete caught Dad doing the dishes. At one time Pete would have said, "That's sissy stuff!" Instead, he asked Dad, "You're making things easier for Mom, aren't you?" It wasn't really a question. Pete knew the answer.

Dad smiled. "When you were a baby, your mom worked extra long hours because I couldn't get a job. I changed your diapers. I did the dishes. I did all the things your mom would have done if she had been home. I love and respect your mother and want to help her."

As Dad let the water out of the sink, he winked. "And remember? Sometimes in the middle of winter, she helps me shovel snow."

Lying in bed that night, Pete remembered Dad's words. "I'm glad I'm a boy," he told himself. "I *like* being what I am."

He would never ask Pam how she felt about being a girl. Pete thought he knew exactly what she'd say.

Then to his own surprise, Pete had another thought. *I wonder how God wants me to serve him? And how will Pam use all her abilities?*

Maybe he should be a bit nicer to Pam tomorrow. But of course he wouldn't want her to die of shock.

Let's Talk . . . or Journal

DAY 1

When Pete said that doing dishes is girl's work what do you think he was really saying? What happened as long as Pam and Pete kept teasing each other? Did either of them seem happy? Give reasons for your answer.

DAY 2

Pam said, "Boys aren't supposed to cry." What do you think she was really saying? Can you remember a time when Jesus cried? For a big clue see John 11:35, the shortest verse in the Bible.

Why is it important that both girls and boys feel free to cry? Explain your reasons for thinking that way.

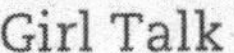

DAY 3

As a man and a woman, the mom and dad in this story have God-given differences. Yet that doesn't divide them. How did they use their differences in the way they worked together?

The twins' parents seem happy in their male and female roles. What qualities make their dad a special person? What qualities make their mom a special person?

DAY 4

When we care about others, we want the best for them, the way Jesus does. In a home what's really important about how the work is done?

DAY 5

God has created you to be a very special young woman. Give examples telling why you like being a girl.

DAY 6

A role model is someone who helps you know what kind of person you want to be. A role model acts in a way you'd like to act, or does things you'd like to do. What women in the Bible would you like to be like? Why?

DAY 7

Who is the very best role model any of us can have? When you know that, you have caught onto an important reason for living. Explain why.

Let's Pray About It

Father God, thank you for the way you created me. I like being who I am. Thank you that I live at a time when I'm free to try many different kinds of work. I could even become the president! Help me to appreciate boys and men who live the way you want them to live. But thank you for the awesome things I value about being a girl. And Jesus, whatever kind of work I do, help me to use my life in serving you. Thank you!

Greener on this Side

WEEK 50

Turn my eyes away from worthless things;
renew my life according to your word.
Psalm 119:37

Through the school bus window, Annie gazed at the farms they passed. White houses shone in the autumn sun. Silos stood tall. Now and then a long-legged horse took off, running across a field.

Annie felt as if she were seeing it all for the first time. Sneaking a look at Vanessa, Annie wondered how her friend from school would like her house and family.

I was crazy to invite her home, Annie thought as nervous jiggles bounced around her insides. *What made me do it?*

As though she could hear Annie's thoughts, Vanessa spoke. "I've always wanted to visit your house."

Then Annie remembered how this had come about. Vanessa had practically invited herself! Would she be disappointed in what she saw? Would she like Annie's older brother and sister, Josh and Sue? Even now they sat at the back of the bus with the junior high kids. And what would Vanessa think of the room Annie shared with her four-year-old sister Dawn?

Around Annie, kids talked about what had happened at school that day. But Annie was quiet, thinking back to her visit to Vanessa's. What a room she had! A canopy bed with a flouncy spread. Her own mp3 player and computer. Special mementos from all the places she had visited. And a beautiful, big, quiet house. As an only child, Vanessa had no brothers or sisters to fight with or mess things up!

Brakes squealed, and the bus ground to a halt. Silently Annie began to pray. *I'm scared, Jesus. I don't know if I can handle it if Vanessa doesn't like our place. What if she even tells me so, the way she does when she doesn't like something at school? You take care of it, Jesus, will you?*

Out of long habit, Annie stood up, clutched her backpack, and followed Sue and Josh down the steps. Vanessa trailed behind.

At least our driveway isn't muddy right now, Annie thought.

As always, her little sister, Dawn, stood at the door, waiting for Annie, Josh, and Sue to come home. Annie knelt down to give Dawn a hug. "Hi, sweetie. This is my friend Vanessa."

Vanessa also knelt down, looking into the little girl's face. "How old are you?" she asked.

Dawn held up four fingers. "Next year I go to kindergarten!"

When Vanessa smiled, Dawn tucked her hand into Vanessa's. "I made cookies for you today."

Annie grinned, knowing Dawn must have had quite a bit of help from Mom. The aroma of freshly baked cookies still lingered in the air. Annie walked into the kitchen and introduced Vanessa just as Mom poured large glasses of milk.

Mom's smile was as warm as the kitchen. *So far, so good,* Annie thought as she and Vanessa joined Sue and Josh at the table. But five minutes later, as the conversation turned toward another boy from school, Josh rolled his eyeballs toward heaven and smirked at Sue.

"Stop it!" she cried, beginning to blush.

He grinned as he poured himself another glass of milk. "You do too like him! Say that you do!"

"Joshua." Mom's voice held a warning.

Sue's face was completely red and her eyes bright. "Be quiet, Josh!" she muttered. "We have company!"

"I saw you looking at him. I saw you passing notes on the bus!"

"He sent the note to me first!" Sue stood up. "And what about Adrienne? You seemed *very* interested in helping her with her homework during study hall today!"

Annie wanted to crawl under her chair. Again she sneaked a look at her friend. Vanessa had a quiet smile on her face. She seemed just plain interested. How could anyone be interested in watching a brother and sister tease each other?

Now Vanessa leaned forward with her elbow on the table. Resting her chin on her thumb, she hid her mouth behind her fingers. What was Vanessa doing? Laughing at Josh and Sue?

Mortified to tears, Annie pushed back her chair. *Well, I guess I'd better get it over with. I wonder how Vanessa will like my room.*

Moments later Vanessa stood at the door. As she looked around, Annie watched her. Vanessa's gaze stopped on the second bed.

"Dawn sleeps here, too?" she asked. "You get to talk at night whenever you want?"

Annie nodded. *What is Vanessa thinking?* she wondered.

Then suddenly Annie knew. The surprise of it filled her heart with warmth. Through Vanessa's eyes, Annie saw her brother and sisters—even her home—in a new way.

"You like our family, don't you?" Annie asked. "I never thought you would."

Let's Talk ... or Journal

DAY 1

Why was Annie surprised by Vanessa's reaction? What clues tell you how Vanessa felt about what she was seeing?

DAY 2

What if Vanessa hadn't liked Annie's room and family? What would Annie need to decide?

DAY 3

Farm animals often stick their heads between barbed wire to munch the grass on the other side. They think it's better than the grass on their own side. Why did Annie think the grass was greener on Vanessa's side of the fence?

DAY 4

What matters most — the material things in a home or the love and support that family members give to each other? Why?

DAY 5

Loyalty in a family means sticking together, building each other up, and telling other people good things about your family. (That kind of loyalty is not the same as needing to talk with an adult you trust if a family member is hurting you in some way.) Why is it important to be loyal to your family?

What are some ways you can show loyalty to your family? Give examples of ways your family has shown loyalty and support to you. Write two or three sentences or a story telling about those times.

DAY 6

God wants families to offer love and caring for each other. In addition to loyalty, what other qualities make us feel that a home is a good place to be? What are the good things you especially like about your home and family?

DAY 7

How can you pray for your family? What are some things you'd like to ask God to do? Begin a list of what you'd like to pray for your family. Come back to this page and add to your list every now and then. When you know God has answered a prayer, write, "Thank you, Lord!" next to it.

Let's Pray About It

Jesus, when I compare what other kids have to what I don't have, that's paying attention to worthless things, isn't it? Even though I'm not perfect and my family isn't perfect, thank you for giving us to each other. Thank you that this is where I belong. Give each of us your big love for one another.

Gift from a Grandma

WEEK 51

"I will look with favor upon the faithful people in the land. They will live with me. Those whose lives are without blame will serve me."
Psalm 101:6 NIrV

Skates flashed in the afternoon sun. Her long blond ponytail flying out, Siri spun like a swiftly moving top. As she twirled to a stop, her friends clapped.

Connor's eyes shone in admiration. "You did it, Siri! Way to go!"

"You didn't even wobble," said her best friend Amy.

Siri felt the warm flush of being praised spread across her cheeks. It felt good to do something well, and the crisp afternoon air gave the day a special brightness. Around her, the pond was filled with skaters, some sure of themselves, others still wobbly. Siri wished the day could last forever.

"Hey, you know what would be fun?" asked Amy. "Let's have a skating party tomorrow night."

"Sounds great!" Connor said. "It's the only night this week when they'll have the lights on."

Happiness welled up inside Siri. "That's a good idea, Amy. You and I can ask the girls, and, Connor, why don't you ask the boys, and—Oh no!"

"What's the matter?" Connor asked.

"The kids at church are going to a nursing home tomorrow night. We're supposed to sing Christmas carols and talk to people."

"Oh, Siri!" Amy made a face. "Can't you skip it? It would be so much more fun to be here."

"I know." Siri thought about being cooped up inside stuffy halls. Then she thought about how much she liked to skate. Besides, Connor would be here, and of all the boys in their homeschool group, he was the very nicest.

"No one will ever know if you skip the singing," said Amy.

"Maybe you're right," Siri answered. "But what if everyone thinks the same thing? What if no one shows up?"

She looked at Connor, hoping that he, too, would tell her not to go, but he didn't. Instead, he asked, "Can you do both? Come here after the nursing home?"

Siri shook her head. "It's way downtown." But her thoughts raced on. *If I could figure out a way to get out of singing—*

Suddenly Siri made a quick turn on the ice. *I promised I'd be there. The church kids set the time for when I could come.*

As she scraped to a halt. Siri knew she was only trying to fool herself. "You have the party anyway," she told the others. Siri knew her words were right, but inside she felt awful.

The next evening Siri still felt disappointed about not being with her friends. Going up the steps of the nursing home, she couldn't help but think of the skating party. Yet she looked around the small caroling group and knew she was needed.

Warm air greeted them as they started down the hall. "Joy to the world! The Lord is come!" Siri had a strong voice and sang as loud as she could but wondered what Amy and Connor and the others were doing.

A heavily decorated tree stood in the middle of the large room they entered. Its soft lights cast a glow on the elderly people gathered around. "Away in a manger, no crib for his bed, the little Lord Jesus lay down his sweet head— "

In that moment all thoughts of the skating party vanished, for Siri caught sight of a little white-haired lady sitting in a wheelchair. Dressed in her Sunday best, she sat with her hands folded in her lap. Her gaze clung to the faces of the singers. Quietly, as though the woman didn't know what was happening, a tear started down her cheek.

When they finished singing, Siri went to her. "I'm Siri," she said. "You remind me of my great-grandma Lydia, who died last year."

"And you look like my granddaughter who lives far away," said the little lady. "Call me Grandma Dee if you like." Her smile was like the sun coming out from beneath a cloud.

After talking for awhile, it was time for Siri to go. Grandma Dee reached forward to tuck something into her hand. "Thank you," she said. "You brought Christmas to me."

Looking down, Siri saw a white handkerchief with beautiful lace around the edge. She knew the little woman had used it to dry her tears.

Grandma Dee smiled again. "I love you," she said.

Now it was Siri's turn to blink away tears. "I love *you*," she answered, as if she were talking to her great-grandma. Leaning forward, she put her arms around the little woman.

As Siri gave her a quick hug, she felt surprised at how much her new friend meant to her. Then she turned and hurried with the others to the van.

For the first time since entering the building, Siri remembered the kids skating. Yet she didn't feel sorry. Siri knew she had made the right choice. And maybe they could find another time soon when she could go skating.

Quietly Siri started humming a Christmas carol. *Should I go back to see Grandma Dee again?* she asked herself. Deep inside she knew the answer was *yes*.

Let's Talk . . . or Journal

DAY 1

Why was Siri's choice especially hard to make? If Connor is as nice as Siri thinks, how do you suppose he felt about Siri's choice to go to the nursing home?

DAY 2

Why was it important that Siri kept her promise? Why do visitors mean so much to people in a nursing home? What did Siri receive that was better than a handkerchief?

DAY 3

Once in a while, a person may promise to do something with you and then not be able to do it because of illness or another good reason. If that happens, how can you help the person who really wanted to keep the promise? Give examples for what you can do.

DAY 4

A person who keeps promises is someone other people can trust. Would you like to be known as someone who keeps promises? Why? What are some ways in which you've needed to make hard choices? What are some important promises you've made and kept?

DAY 5

In the Bible the word *talent* was first used to refer to a unit of weight, then a unit of coinage (money). Our present-day use of the word talent comes from the parable starting in Matthew 25:14. Now we usually use the word to mean something in which we are especially gifted. What talents has God given you? How do you like to use your talents?

DAY 6

Can you create a story where a girl does something helpful that she didn't want to do? Like Siri, she could be surprised by how it came out. But think of a new character (maybe yourself!), an entirely different sacrifice, and a different kind of ending.

DAY 7

What does God call a person who does something faithfully and well? For clues see Matthew 25, verses 21 and 23.

Was there any difference in the reward received by the five talent person and the two talent person? Explain.

If you are reading this story at Christmas time you will soon be entering a New Year. Think about how you want to honor the Lord in your New Year. What commitment do you want to make to him?

Let's Pray About It

Show me, Lord, how you want me to give to others. Help me plan my time so I can have fun with my friends but also keep the promises I make. Give me your love for the people you want me to help. Thank you for the way you love me all the time—every day and every minute. And thank you that your love is forever.

And Lord, as I make new beginnings in my life show me how you want me to live for you. I commit myself fully to you and ask you to help me in every way needed. Thank you, Lord and Friend, Savior and King!

Run to Win

WEEK 52

"I have fought the good fight, I have finished the race, I have kept the faith."
2 Timothy 4:7

Jennifer bent down, checked her shoelaces, and made sure they were tied well. As she went through her warm-ups, the spring sunshine lit her face.

Jen the runner. Jen the track star. Jen the cheerleader, quick and light. Jen, wanting with all her heart to be a champion athlete.

But that was then. Her old school. The one where she knew everyone, and everyone knew her. Once she would have been out there, along the sidelines, cheering everyone else on. Once her friends would have come alongside, giving high fives, cheering *her* on. Yes, that was then.

Now, deep inside, Jen felt lonely. *Can I run like I did when I had friends surrounding me? It's hard being the new kid in town.*

Looking around the field, Jen saw the long white lines someone had sprayed on the grass that morning. Everything was ready for the school field day. Yet her thoughts weren't on the hundred-meter dash. Instead, she noticed Mona, a classmate who would run against her. *I wish I could laugh and feel sure of myself the way she seems to do.*

Two months before, after Jen's family spent a lot of time praying about it, her dad bought a restaurant in town. He believed God wanted them here. Jen had to admit that she thought so, too. It wasn't always fun working together in the restaurant, but she liked the way Dad chose background music with Christian melodies.

Still, it hadn't been easy for her to change schools in February. Since moving to town, she had needed to make some hard choices. Last week when Jen said she didn't want to go to a party with older kids and no parents, Mona was one of those who laughed at her.

Now, Mona's friends gathered around her, and Jen remembered their cruel words. They still felt like sharp needles, pricking her skin and bringing hurt.

Even worse, there were times when it was hard not to envy Mona. Again Jen thought, *I wish I could feel sure of myself like Mona does.*

Then Jen remembered one of the melodies Dad played the night before. Though the CDs didn't have words, Jen knew them. Trying to work up her courage, she hummed softly to herself. *In my life, Lord, be glorified. Be glorified.*

Lifting her head, Jen smiled. A minute later she heard a voice behind her. "You'll do great, Jen!"

It was just the encouragement she needed. Jen turned. "Thanks, Devin. You'll do great too!"

Soon he was ready to start, and Jen cheered from the sideline. Surging forward, Devin settled into his stride, and soon crossed the finish line. A roar went up in the bleachers.

Now it was Jen's turn. Waiting at the starting line with Mona, Jen prayed. *Help me win, Lord. Help me feel I'm a part of this town.*

Then, as Jen dug in for the start, she remembered the athlete Eric Liddell. When he stood for what he believed, he gave up the opportunity to win in his best event. Yet he qualified for the 400 meters—an event Eric wouldn't have dreamed of trying at the Olympics. And he discovered that the 400 meters was the race that fit him best.

Even now, thinking about it surprised Jen. Because of his choice to honor the Lord, Eric ran the race he was created to win.

By comparison, Jen's school field day didn't seem important, not even to her. No gold medal waited at the end. No finish line with a great crowd of cheering onlookers. But in that instant there was something she knew. *I don't have to be sure of myself. I'm sure of God.*

Suddenly Jen's prayer changed. *Whether I win or lose I want to honor you, Lord.*

"On your mark!" shouted the starter. "Set! Go!"

With a push Jen was off like a greyhound. Faster. Faster. Mona edged up. Out of the corner of her eye, Jen saw her and put on more speed. Feeling as if her lungs would burst, she crossed the finish line.

"*Yaaaaaay, Jen!*" came the cry. "*Yaaaaaay, Jen!*" But it was a halfhearted cheer, and she knew it.

Thanks, Lord, she prayed as she walked back for her sweatshirt. *Thanks for helping me win.* But when Jen reached the bench she stood there, wondering what to do. The excitement she had felt in crossing the line already sagged, like air leaking out of a balloon.

Slowly Jen picked up her sweatshirt. As she turned, she almost bumped into a few girls.

"Congrats, Jen," they said.

"Thanks!" Jen tried to put warmth into her words. But it wasn't hard to guess their thoughts. They had wanted Mona to win.

Almost at once the girls walked away. When they headed for the group around Mona, Jen watched them. All their lives they had been together. *Kindergarten. Birthday parties. The party with older kids and no parents.*

As Jen pulled on her sweatshirt, she brushed a hand across her eyes. Not for anything would she let them know how she felt. Instead, she looked around.

Where's Devin? Where are the girls who have been nice to me? Not seeing them, Jen's balloon of hope gave its final sputter of life.

As she left the track and started toward school, Jen had all she could do to not let her shoulders slump. In every way her win seemed empty.

Not seemed, she decided. *It* is *empty.* Again she wished her long-time friends were there.

Jen was part way across the field when she heard a girl call her name. Kate with her friend Misty. Pretending she didn't hear, Jen kept going.

Then from another direction she saw two boys head her way. Devin and his friend Nick. But by now Jen was afraid she'd cry if she talked with any of them.

Walking fast, she picked up speed. Just the same, the girls caught up. When Jen ground to a halt, Misty glanced around, as though making sure no one was close enough to hear. But Kate exclaimed, "Hey, Jen, you did good!"

Then she lowered her voice. "We went to the party where you didn't go. The neighbors didn't call the cops, but they should have."

Moments later, Devin and Nick reached them. The four gathered around Jen.

What's this? Jen wondered. *They're surrounding me?*

As Jen glanced from one face to the next, she saw the look in their eyes. The look that said they were proud of her. The look that said they cared.

In that moment Jen felt welcomed to her new town. *They're holding me up. They want to be friends.*

"Nick and I didn't go to the party," Devin told her. "But we heard everyone talking about you. All the awful things they said."

Sure. Jen could imagine.

Devin grinned, looked her straight in the eye. "Jen, you're the first girl in a long time who's said no to everyone else. You not only said no, you told them why. You had the courage to do it."

Jen stared at him, then at Nick, Kate, and Misty.

"What helped you?" Misty asked.

As Jen straightened, it was no longer hard to stand tall. Once again she could run to win. Once again she could cheer someone else on. "You mean *Who* helped me? I'd like to tell you."

Let's Talk . . . or Journal

DAY 1

Why did being new in town make it especially hard for Jen to stand up for what she believed? How can our wanting to be liked get in the way of being true to Jesus? Give examples.

DAY 2

What did Jennifer mean when she thought, *I don't have to be sure of myself. I'm sure of God*? Have you ever felt that way? Explain why.

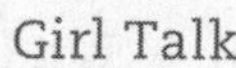

DAY 3

There are at least three and possibly five ways in which you might feel Jennifer won in this story. What are they?

DAY 4

If we ask Jesus to help us in a sports event does that mean we will always win? Why or why not?

In what ways do you think God honors someone who honors him? Are God's people always honored in an outward way? Give reasons for your yes or no answer.

DAY 5

In the Bible we read about a great number of people who paid a high cost to be faithful to the Lord. The eleventh chapter of Hebrews lists a few of them, including Noah, Abraham, Moses, Rahab, Gideon, Samuel, and many others. Through the centuries the list of people who have been faithful to God has grown longer than any sports Hall of Fame could possibly number. God doesn't expect us to always win first place, but he does ask us to always be faithful to him. What does it mean to be faithful to the Lord?

Tell about people you know personally or people you have read about in the Bible who have been faithful to the Lord.

DAY 6

In Hebrews 12:1 Paul refers back to Hebrews 11 and writes, "A huge cloud of witnesses is all around us. So let us throw off everything that stands in our way. Let us throw off any sin that holds on to us so tightly. Let us keep on running the race marked out for us." (NIrV)

Think about an athletic event and the huge crowd often in the stands. Paul says that in heaven we have a similar crowd caring about what happens to us and cheering us on. Then Paul tells us how to run the race marked out for us:

"Let us keep looking to Jesus. He is the author of our faith."

"Let us fix our eyes on Jesus, the author and perfecter of our faith, who for the joy set before him endured the cross, scorning its shame and sat down at the right hand of the throne of God."

How can the Holy Spirit help you be faithful? Can you think of a time when he helped you or someone you know to honor Jesus? If so, describe what happened.

DAY 7

In the movie *Chariots of Fire*, Eric Liddell says, "When I run I sense his pleasure." What do you believe it means to sense God's pleasure? How do you think God feels about your playing in sports you enjoy? How do you think he feels about other activities you love such as writing, singing, playing an instrument, painting, or being in drama? Give reasons for your answer.

Go back to 2 Timothy 4:7, the verse at the beginning of this story. What do you want to do to fight the good fight, finish the race, and keep the faith?

Let's Pray About It

Jesus, it's hard when I need to stand alone, but I know you did it for me. Thank you that when kids make me feel lonely, you are still my best friend. With all my heart I commit my entire life to you. I choose to be faithful, to run close to you. In your name I ask for all the power of the Holy Spirit and the courage I need. Thank you that no matter what happens in my life, you will always be with me. I give you praise!

A Final Promise

Well, how are you doing? Have you been making some real-life choices? Have you discovered the secrets you unlock with every good choice? If so, you might like to know something more.

When you make the choice you believe Jesus wants, you may struggle afterward. You might ask yourself, *Did I do the right thing?* Or, if kids give you a hard time, you could think, *Well, I made the best choice. But nobody cares about me.* You feel miserable because you keep telling yourself you're worthless. Your feelings about yourself depend on whether others approve of you.

It's important to have approval from wise people who love God. A parent or grandparent, your pastor, Christian teachers and friends. It's not worth having approval from people who would force you to make wrong choices. Or from kids who would make you feel sorry about good choices.

If you keep knocking yourself down, that can be harder to deal with than what other people think and say. God does just the opposite. When you make the choice you believe Jesus wants, the Holy Spirit will support you—if you let him. He works in your good choices to help them become good habits.

And there's something else. Paul writes, "Consider him [Jesus] who endured such opposition from sinful men, so that you will not grow weary and lose heart." If you need to say no to a temptation, you might wonder, "Is it worth it?" But when you *do* say no, you can look back later and think, "Whew! I'm glad I made that choice!"

When you think about places where you could have fallen into deep, squishy mud, you'll be able to say, "Thank you, Jesus! You helped me escape that and stay with you! You showed me how to walk on firm ground!"

Every time you make a good choice, you make a footprint in the direction you want to go for your life. The Holy Spirit gives you peace about the wise choices you made—unless you keep going back and wondering if you did the right thing. Our heavenly Father also has special ways of showing that you are of value to him.

Sometimes you know that right away because you sense his love for you. Other times it takes a while. It may even be hard to see. When God honors you for being faithful to him, it might not come in the way you think. It may not come in an outward way or at the time you want. But it *will* come in God's best way!

The Bible gives God's word for it—the promise that encouraged Olympic hero Eric Liddell. You, too, can claim that promise at a moment of choice. "Those who honor me I will honor" (1 Samuel 2:30).

So keep on reaching up. Be a Faithgirl. Run close to the Person who is always ready to help you. His name is *Jesus*.

Big-time thanks
to
Elise Johnson
for the use of her story,
"The Hidden Puzzle Piece"

and to all who have
helped me make good choices
My husband, Roy
Jeff and Cynthia
Daniel, Justin, Jennifer
Kevin and Lyn
Nate and Karin
Marilyn Anderson
LeAnne Chisolm
Dean Olson
Chuck and Lori Peterson
Lee Roddy
Beverly Kline
Lee Hough
The friends who faithfully prayed.

My deep appreciation for the insights
of my editor, Kathleen Kerr,
and the help of
Bruce Nuffer
Barbara Scott
Annette Bourland
and
the entire Zonderkidz team.
Most of all, my gratitude
to my Lord, Jesus Christ,
for helping me run close to him.

Cool Guide to Finding Your Way

Lois Walfrid Johnson is a trusted friend of families who wants to make reading fun. All four of the books that inspired *Girl Talk* received the Gold Medallion Book Award from the Evangelical Christian Publishers Association and the C. S. Lewis Medal for Best Series in the year it was published.

Lois' bestselling Adventures of the Northwoods novels have also warmed the hearts of people throughout the world and received numerous awards, including four Silver Angels from Excellence in Media and the Wisconsin State Historical Society Award for Distinguished Service to History. Readers from over 40 countries have written to say "I love your books. I can't put them down." Even better, "God used your book to change my life."

The author of 38 books and 14 updated editions, Lois has also written the Riverboat Adventures Series (steamboat, Underground Railroad, and immigrant history). Her Viking Quest series offers a world view in which her characters start in Ireland, travel to Norway, Iceland, Greenland, and then sail with Leif Erickson to the New World. A speaker, teacher, and former instructor for *Writer's Digest* School, Lois teaches writing in schools, home-schooling groups, colleges, universities, and writer's conferences.

Lois and her husband Roy especially enjoy time with family and friends and talking with young people like you.

See www.loiswalfridjohnson.com.